Biography of a Small Town

Biography of a Small Town

Elvin Hatch

Columbia University Press : New York : 1979

The Andrew W. Mellon Foundation, through a special grant, has
assisted the Press in publishing this volume.

Library of Congress Cataloging in Publication Data

Hatch, Elvin J
  Biography of a small town.

  Bibliography: p.
  Includes index.
  1. Cities and towns—California—Case studies.
2. California—Rural conditions. 3. Community life—
Case studies. I. Title.
HT123.5.C2H37   309.1′ 794   79-313
ISBN O-231-04694-4

Columbia University Press
New York   Guildford, Surrey

To Kristen and Catherine

Contents

Acknowledgments

DEANNA HATCH CONTRIBUTED substantially to the research behind this book, and her suggestions about the manuscript were most useful. I also thank both Jim Williams of Gavilan College, who brought to bear his considerable knowledge about the history of small towns in America in commenting on the manuscript, and Charlotte Symons for her literary advice.

A very different version of this work was written over a decade ago as my Ph.D. thesis in anthropology at UCLA. This book has benefited a great deal from the advice of my thesis advisers, who not only helped focus the research but also helped shape the thesis and thus, to some extent, the book. They include Herman Bleibtreu, Eugene F. Brigham, Pedro Carrasco, John Horton, Hilda Kuper, William A. Lessa, and M. G. Smith.

The field research was supported by a Public Health Service fellowship (5 F1 MH-29, 955-02 [BEH]) from the National Institute of Mental Health. Typing of the manuscript was assisted by a general research grant from the Academic Senate of the University of California. Finally, publication costs have been borne in part by funds from the Mellon Foundation. I am grateful to all of these sources of support.

Introduction

AT ONE TIME the small country town was prominent in the daily life of the U.S. citizen, for until early in this century the rural community was "the basic form of social organization experienced by the vast majority of Americans" (Smith 1966:vii). This form of local organization also enjoyed a special place in the American self-image, for it was often felt that one of the strengths of the United States—its individualistic, freedom-loving character—was rooted in the rural, small-town background of its inhabitants.

Yet today the rural hamlet is something of an oddity. The center of gravity in America has shifted so far toward the urban pole that the country town has become almost legendary, and the rural community is now experienced by most Americans at second hand, through newspaper articles and television news features.

At the same time that this came about, fundamental changes were under way in the small towns that remained. One of these changes was a considerable decline in local cohesion and vitality. Early in the century the social organization of the countryside was based on the principle of locality, but this is much less true today, for the typical farm village is undergoing a process of social deterioration.[1]

The gradual slippage of the country town from its former high position has been accompanied by far-reaching changes in values and world view. The nation as a whole has moved from a condition in which agrarian philosophy and values were paramount to one in which urban sophistication and the values of the business world hold sway.[2] This shift is symbolized by the replacement of the corner grocery store with the supermarket. More abstractly, it is signified by the declining importance of rural individualism in American values and by a growing emphasis on the virtues of efficiency and productivity in big business. What is occurring is a shift "from a rural–agrarian nation to an urban–industrial one" (Shideler 1973:284).

The urban–industrial patterns of the larger society have penetrated to the countryside and have altered the small communities that have survived, especially through changes in farm operations themselves. During this century farming has changed from a way of life emphasizing the rural virtues of neighborliness and family solidarity, to a business. The farmer today is a sophisticated businessman with one eye on his margin of profit and the other on the efficiency of his operation.

The social deterioration of the country town and the growth of urban–industrial values are closely interrelated, for a well-developed business ethic works against local values. As the farmer focuses increasingly on business and career, community participation and cohesion lose their hold and no longer confer the prestige they once did on those who devoted time and energy to community affairs.

This book is about the social history of one very small town in California. The focus is on a particular feature of local life—the feature that enables a person to say that this is a community, that it is something other than a mere aggregate of households—and on how this feature of community had changed from the time of the town's founding in the late nineteenth century to the time of my field research there in mid-1960s.

An obvious element that made this locality a community rather than merely an aggregate of households was a body of common affairs—local undertakings, events, controversies, and the like. A substantial number of the local people were engaged in a distinctive community life. But it is not adequate to say that local affairs alone made this town a community. I will suggest that to understand the local life it is necessary to understand a set of cultural ideas that underlie it: ideas about what a respectable community should be like and what it should achieve, about how this particular locality lived up to those standards, about how the community was organized and run, and about how it was set apart from its neighbors. This may be called the ideological dimension of community, and it is crucial. It consisted of the set of images on which people acted in engaging in local affairs, and indeed it defined what those local affairs were and helped give them shape. Awareness of the ideological dimension of community is essential to understanding the small town in America.

The book is divided into two parts. The first is an account of the locality as it was before about 1940. I discuss the nature of the community hub and its role in the local social system, the agricultural patterns and system of social stratification, the community life and factional divisions, as well as the patterns of leadership—and I do so always with an eye toward conveying the underlying cultural ideas. In short, I present a community study of the locality as it was before World War II. The second section of the book is in a sense a separate community study, for after the war the locality underwent a transforma-tion. Changes had been under way for decades before the war, but they were stimulated and intensified enormously once the United States entered the conflict.

The community I studied, Starkey (a pseudonym), was originally settled by homesteaders in the 1880s and 1890s, and the locality was fully established as a small but cohesive village by the turn of the century. Even today it maintains a sense of distinctiveness and cohe-sion, and by all accounts it has not changed drastically in size since about 1900. It is located in a part of California that is overwhelmingly rural in appearance and outlook,[3] with the result that in many respects the community is still a country town.

And yet the community has not been left behind by the changes taking place in the larger society, for although the region is predomi-nantly rural it has shared fully in the industrial and technological developments of this century. The farmers and ranchers have adopted modern standards of efficiency and cost accounting, employ expensive and sophisticated machinery, and constantly experiment with new seed strains, agricultural methods, and the like. Similarly, the families of the community enjoy most of the material advantages—such as television and the automobile—that are available in the city.

Starkey is located in the Central Coast region of California, an area that is devoted largely to agriculture. This region lies between the state's two major urban concentrations—the Bay area, dominated by San Francisco, and Southern California. Starkey itself seems little touched by these conurbations, for it gives the impression of a sleepy and somewhat dilapidated farm town surrounded by open, rolling hills and occasional farmhouses. The population of the community suggests just how rural it is, for it consists of fewer than 200 hoseholds.

Several similar communities are located some fifteen minutes or so by car from Starkey. Each of these is little more than a cluster of houses, from 20 to 100 at most; the community's other members live on the farmland beyond. Typically these villages include a post office, a school, and a store or bar, and some contain a community hall as well. None has a bank, a newspaper, or even a barbershop. All of these hamlets are aware that they have much in common, for they were founded by homesteaders at about the same time, are today engaged chiefly in dry-land grain farming and cattle ranching, have undergone similar social and economic changes, and are linked together in an intricate network of kinship and friendship.

These communities are also alike in their dependence on a somewhat larger town, Oak Flat,[4] a community of fewer than 10,000 people about twenty-five minutes by car from Starkey. Oak Flat plays a significant role in the daily lives of Starkey residents, for it is where most of the Starkey men and women buy their clothes and appliances, do their banking, attend movies, and the like. Most Starkey households have some contact with Oak Flat several times a week, and to a certain extent the members of the smaller community identify with the larger one. In particular, Starkey residents view themselves as part of the general hinterland of Oak Flat and exhibit a distinct interest in scandals, changes in ownership of local firms, and other matters taking place there. Starkey is by no means dominated by the larger community, however, partly because of the distance between them.

A second larger community to which Starkey looks for consumer services, and with which it identifies, is the county seat, Saint Thomas, which is about an hour's drive away and has a population of under 30,000. Most Starkey families have occasion to drive to Saint Thomas at least once or twice a month to shop, and some go there several times a week. A greater range of merchandise and a greater variety of specialized services are available in Saint Thomas than in Oak Flat. Saint Thomas is conceived of as the political and administrative hub of the region, since this is where the county offices are located and where the county supervisors meet each month.

Starkey residents tend to identify with Saint Thomas almost as strongly as they do with Oak Flat, although the nature of that identification is different. Oak Flat is viewed with a mixture of attachment, jealousy, and disdain, the latter reflecting the fact that Oak Flat is no more than a rural community serving the local farm population. It is hardly conceived of as a place to boast about. On the other hand, the attachment that is felt toward Saint Thomas is combined with both pride and distrust. The pride reflects a feeling that Saint Thomas is a small but sophisticated city that supplies the county with such modern facilities as art galleries, a college, and cut-rate drugstores, whereas the distrust is due to Saint Thomas' size and its commanding influence in the county. This distrust is fostered as well by the feeling in Starkey that the residents of the larger community view the farm population in the outlying areas as countrified and unsophisticated.

Starkey's appearance gives impressions of rural parochialism and decay. The town itself is small and seems to be in poor repair; on most days the short, unmarked streets are empty, as if the town had recently been deserted.

The several side streets are lined by rows of small, wood frame houses, fewer than 100 in all, separated by occasional unkempt vacant lots. Most of the houses were built before World War II; a few are examples of late-nineteenth- and early-twentieth-century handicraft. Most of them are shaded by large old trees, giving the town an oasis-like quality. The streets lack curbs and sidewalks, so the edge of the black-top dissolves into a narrow strip of compacted earth separating roadway from yard. There is seldom a sign of human or animal life in these yards, all of which are small; some are well kept, others hardly distinguishable from the strip of dirt bordering the roadway.

The main street of the town was once a busy two-lane highway, but in the early 1960s the latter was rerouted by the state highway department, and now it runs along the river bank opposite Starkey and bypasses the town altogether. Today the tranquility of the main street is upset chiefly by an occasional car or pickup truck being driven into town for groceries or mail.

The main street is short, stretching only about four blocks. At either end it turns abruptly into a well-maintained country road. Like the side streets, the main thoroughfare has no curbs or sidewalks, the roadway being bordered on either side by a strip of dirt that gives an unmistakably rural appearance to the small town center. An impression of decay is also created by the occasional vacant lots scattered along the main street, together with the empty shells of two service stations and a garage—abandoned relics of a time when highway traffic was a significant element in the life of the town. This sense of decay is also fostered by the exteriors of the local restaurant, bar, and motel, as well as one of the two grocery stores, which are old and decrepit and lack any landscaping to soften their stark contours, which rise directly from the narrow margins of bare earth separating them from the street. Along one of the side streets can also be found the Community Hall, which occupies a small, weed-choked lot. The Community Hall needs paint and repair and looks unused.

Yet some of the property along the main street is very well kept. The second grocery store is a modern structure with metal siding and plate glass windows. The small post office next door is equally new and well cared for, and between it and the grocery store is a shady, tidy strip of grass. Nearby is the Starkey Methodist church, a turn-of-the-century wood frame building that is kept freshly painted and is nearly surrounded by lawn. Beyond the church is the high school, constructed of brick in the 1920s. The main building is small, containing a handful of classrooms that accommodate only about 100 students. The high school fronts on the main street, from which it appears to be set in a quiet, grass-carpeted grove. Behind the high school, along a side street, is the grammar school, similarly well kept but much newer and more modern in design. Across the main street from the high school is the community park, several acres of lawn and trees. In one corner of the park is the Women's Clubhouse, which is in near-perfect condition, as are the swimming pool and tennis courts adjacent to it. Close by is the state road crew facility, encircled by a stand of splendid old trees that give the appearance of yet another park. Beyond the road crew facility is the fire station manned by the California State Division of Forestry; the newly built concrete block building is so spotless that it appears unused, and the acre or so of grounds surrounding it is well groomed.

Even the portions of town that are well maintained appear deserted, because in spite of the attention devoted to them they seem to be all but empty during most of the day. The high school itself appears nearly lifeless to anyone passing by on the street, since most school activities take place either inside the building or in the court behind it.

The impression of abandonment is also experienced by the stranger who stops to enter the commercial establishments in town. Stepping inside the cafe, he may see one or two people at the counter drinking coffee and talking with the waitress. Conversation stops while they glance at him as he takes a seat, and does not begin again for several moments. The waitress is tall and gray-haired and wears a white, wrinkle-free dress and a striped apron. She is not unpleasant to the stranger, but she makes no attempt to engage him in conversation and shows a trace of impatience that he is there at all. She gazes absently into the distance while waiting for his order; when he finally leaves she manages to say good-bye, but without looking directly at him. Even the people seem lifeless and remote.

At the store the experience is somewhat different. The building is deserted except for two clerks and the stranger himself. Both clerks are stocking shelves as he enters, and one of them, a plump, middle-aged woman, greets him with a smile. She is friendly, and if asked she is happy to talk about the town—how it got its name, when the church was built. But she seems relieved to go back to work as the stranger turns to leave.

The small post office next door is also empty except for the postmaster himself, a competent, impersonal man who is pleasant in spite of his briskness. He is sorting mail into a wall of post office boxes and avoids conversation.

The bar across the street is characteristically dark, with rows of glasses set upside down on white shelf paper, plastic rotating beer advertisements lit from within, and antlers hung at various heights on the wall. The two or three customers are farmers or cowboys in work clothes; they talk in low tones and look at the stranger with guarded curiosity. The bartender asks what he will have but otherwise shows little interest in him. The languor of the cafe is repeated here.

Several times during the day the quiet of the town is broken by short bursts of activity. At about 7:00 in the morning a wave of customers arrives at the cafe, mostly men stopping for coffee and conversation before work. Most of them are gone before 8:00, leaving behind a handful of the less hurried, who may linger an hour longer, maybe two. Midmorning is the time of peak activity. Mail is not delivered to Starkey residents, so most of the families visit the post office before noon to check their boxes; some also buy groceries. As many as eight to twelve cars or pickup trucks at a time are parked along the main street, having been driven to town by farmhands, ranchers, or their wives. A few of the people living in town leave their small houses on foot at this time to pick up the mail. This rush of activity lasts forty-five minutes or an hour at most.

Another busy time of day—shorter but more intense—is the noon hour, when groups of high-school students stroll down the main road to buy something to eat or to check their family mailboxes. A flurry of automobile traffic also appears just before and after school, but it is short-lived and centers mostly on the school itself.

A liveliness of a different order appears chiefly in the evenings. It passes virtally unseen by the visiting stranger, who would surely begin to doubt his impression of Starkey as a deserted town if he were aware of it. This is the organizational life of the community. Regular weekly or monthly meetings of organizations are held nearly every night of the week: Lions Club meetings, gatherings of the Square Dance Club, official meetings of the Starkey Unified School Board and of the Board of Trustees of the local Methodist church, among others. Regular events of this kind attract from seven or eight people to several dozen. Community affairs of much larger scope occur sporadically throughout the year. The Starkey Barbecue is given in the park in the spring and is attended by about 1,000 people. High school basketball games, Baccalaureate services, and the Community Christmas Program attract several hundred. A few other affairs draw smaller but still substantial crowds; one example is an annual dinner sponsored by the church, normally attended by over 100 residents.

The sense of desolation felt by the passer-by is not shared by those who live in the community. Residents are quick to mention that the town is less lively today than in the past, but the idea that it could appear God-forsaken and uninviting strikes them as odd.

This is partly because the town is familiar to their eyes, so what seems lifeless and forbidding to the stranger is perceived quite differently by them. The occasional visitor sees a forsaken park, but the resident sees the site of the annual Starkey Barbecue and of occasional potluck suppers. He or his father may have helped stake out the grounds for the park and plant its lawn and trees. Besides, the park is not truly forsaken, inasmuch as it is looked after by the caretaker, Edgar

Smith, who has lived in the community since the Great Depression and can almost always be found working somewhere on the park grounds. If he is not there he is usually at home around the corner or at the church a block away.

The instance of the park caretaker is suggestive, for much of the feeling that the local residents have for their town—and that forestalls any sense of desolation in their minds—derives from their knowing about the other people living there. No one in Starkey knows everyone else—newcomers are constantly appearing—but few people live there whom a given individual has not at least heard of. Consequently, the houses that seem empty and forlorn to the passing stranger have a different appearance to the local resident. They are occupied by living people with reputations to uphold or live down, people whose past is common knowledge and whose personal worth and idiosyncrasies are much discussed. Where the passing stranger sees vacant yards and closed doors, the resident sees the widowed Martha Newman's house, the place where Fred Baker's hired man lives, or the old manse where John Holden and his family now reside. The coldness that the stranger feels as he enters the cafe is less remarkable to the resident, who is accustomed to the waitress' manner and who not only knows the customers by name but may also be related to one or more of them. In short, where the passer-by sees a depressing emptiness and aloofness, the community member sees people and places to which human stories are attached.

To the local resident Starkey is unusual for a small town. According to local opinion, the community's luster may be fading but there persist an independence and a community spirit that have always set this locality apart from its neighbors.

This local pride perhaps helps explain the ready acceptance of my research in Starkey. I lived there with my family for two years, from the summer of 1965 to the summer of 1967, and I never felt excluded from local affairs and never found it impossible or even difficult to obtain information—although I systematically avoided asking personal questions about money matters.[5] Most Starkey residents regarded it as both appropriate and gratifying that I had come to study the community, for local history was of immediate interest to them. This was also a reasonably sophisticated group of people, and most of them had a layman's grasp of what anthropological and historical research is about. Once my presence was known I was frequently invited to family gatherings, brandings, and the like, and was often sought out to be given information—often highly personal—that was deemed important for my research.

Starkey is representative of other towns throughout America. Boosterism, the growing tendency for community organizations to resemble special-interest groups, the increasing size of farms and ranches, and the growing capitalization of the farm enterprise are fundamental to rural communities in nearly all parts of the United States.

Yet Starkey has always been a particularly small community, and it is important to explain the advantages of choosing a small town for study. One is that in such a locality an investigator can grasp the local social system—with its animosities, friendships, kinship loyalties, and the like—in considerable detail. It is therefore possible to "see" local events in full context.

A second advantage of studying such a small town is that it makes it possible to isolate the ideological dimension of community. In larger towns, and especially county seats, significant political decisions have to be made about such matters as changes in zoning regulations and the allocation of public funds. Starkey, however, was never an incorporated town with the power to levy taxes; it had no town budget to spend, no mayor or councilmen to influence—although it was a school district with an elected school board, which is hardly comparable. As a result, local affairs in Starkey were strikingly devoid of manipulation of political power or competition among factions motivated by different economic interests. Rather, local affairs were manifestations of such features as the local desire to make the town a meritorious place and the individual's desire to acquire a reputation as a community-minded and upstanding citizen. In short, in the study of a town the size of Starkey it is possible to view the way the ideological dimension of community works "uncontaminated" by ulterior motives of an economic or political nature. The ideological dimension of community is a factor in larger towns as well, but it tends to become blurred and therefore difficult to define in such localities because of these other motives.

Setting aside the question of size, Starkey is representative of the type of American community that Page Smith (1966) refers to as the cumulative town. This is a locality that typically began in the context of the frontier by the opening of government land to settlers and grew by the accumulation of individuals seeking their personal fortunes—or at least a living—as farmers, merchants, and the like. One of the features distinguishing the cumulative town is that it was not a community at the beginning; rather, it was an agglomeration of individuals who had little in common. Yet a community soon emerged, and Starkey can serve as a case study of the process of community formation in cumulative towns.

From the nineteenth century to the present, although to a decreasing extent, community activities all over the country have exhibited a pattern of boosterism, for local affairs have centered on improving the hometown and stimulating its growth. Starkey is representative in that programs of local improvement have been a focal point of the community. Boosterism springs from several sources, one of which is economic: by boosting the hometown the community member stands to profit from higher real estate values and increased trade. On this point Starkey is somewhat atypical, for economic interests seem to have played very little part in its improvement programs. In Starkey it is possible to isolate an aspect of boosterism that is "uncontaminated" by economic interests. I mean the ideological dimension of community, which involves an ideal image of what a small town should be like and what it should try to achieve.

It is surprising how little in Starkey is distinctively Calfornian; with a few exceptions it could easily pass for a community in Washington, Oregon, Idaho, Montana, the Dakotas, Nebraska, Kansas, or elsewhere. This is true in part because of Starkey's pioneer roots; its rural, grain-and-cattle character; and its distance from large cities. For years the residents of this town have looked upon themselves as country people who have more in common with the rural populations of Nevada and Oregon than with the city people in San Francisco and Los Angeles.

It is true that California agriculture is, on the whole, distinctive. Carl Taylor and his colleagues classify most of the state as part of the western specialty crop region consisting of semiarid and desert lands that have been brought under irrigation and produce such crops as almonds, apricots, asparagus, cantaloupes, grapes, and lettuce (Taylor et al. 1955:339–43, 434–45). California specialty-crop agriculture depends on migrant farm workers to such an extent that the harvest season there is unlike that of any other part of the country, and the farming is so intensive and the crops require so much specialized care that the farm is often either a relatively small family affair or an enormous enterprise owned by a very large corporation (Goldschmidt 1946, 1947).

Yet Starkey is not part of the specialty-crop region. The portion of the state in which it is located is devoted primarily to grain and cattle— which is one reason it resembles a community in North Dakota or Nebraska.

But whatever the crops, agricultural technology and the industrialization of farming are as advanced in California as anywhere in the world. A California community is a logical choice for research in a rural town that is fully modernized, in no way depressed or backward. Starkey was accordingly ideal for the study of the effects of urban-industrial values on the rural community.

Part **I** Before 1940

Chapter 1 Economic Development

STARKEY WAS ESTABLISHED in the 1880s and 1890s, when a sudden influx of settlers came to acquire farmland. Before that time the region was quite sparsely populated. The native Indians, who had originally been hunters and gatherers living in small, impermanent villages, had virtually disappeared long before, largely because of disease introduced by Europeans. The Indians' demise was an indirect result of the Spanish missions, for the "brute upshot of missionization, in spite of its kindly flavor and humanitarian root, was only one thing: death" (Kroeber 1953:888). By the time of Starkey's settlement the Indians had left little trace of their earlier occupancy other than a few stone artifacts and rock paintings.

In the latter part of the 1700s a Spanish mission, the mission Saint George, was established less than twenty miles coastward from what is now Starkey. The mission fathers oversaw the raising of cattle and sheep and the growing of such farm products as wheat, barley, corn, and fruit. But the activities of the padres had comparatively little effect on the lands in the immediate vicinity of Starkey, which were too distant to be used for anything more than the occasional grazing of sheep and cattle.

In 1822 California became a part of Mexico, then a sovereign nation independent of Spain. Shortly thereafter, in 1833, the Mexican government undertook the secularization of the church's holdings in California. This entailed converting the missions into parish churches— transfering them from the hands of missionaries to parish priests, releasing the neophyte Indians from the supervision of the friars, and making the church's agricultural lands available to Indians and other settlers. Secularization brought an end to the mission system; the mission Saint George soon was virtually abandoned and its local influence terminated.

Shortly after the missions were dispossessed, the effects of another era of California history were felt in the Starkey region. This was the era of the large Mexican land grants, or ranchos, on which enormous herds of semiwild cattle were raised. Most of the ranchos—which have become famous for their fiestas, rodeos, and lavish hospitality—were located nearer the coast than Starkey, but one was situated nearby and eventually formed the northeastern boundary of the community. This Mexican land grant amounted to over 25,000 acres, most of which consisted of rolling and lightly wooded range land. The establishment of this rancho brought westernization one step closer to the Starkey region, although its impact was not immediate, for neither did the estate bring significant changes to the landscape nor did it add substantially to the human population.

A final historical episode preceded the influx of settlers and the establishment of Starkey. This was the period of large American cattle ranches.

Between 1846 and 1848 Mexico and the United States were at war, and when the conflict was over the Mexican government ceded its North American holdings. In 1850 California was admitted into the Union as a state, and the same year saw the creation of the county of which Starkey is a part.

After 1850 large tracts of unclaimed land in the county were purchased from the American government by private citizens. Land speculation may have been the long-term goal of the buyers, but the short-term plan was to use this property as range land for cattle and sheep. During the 1860s and 1870s four of these holdings, varying in size from 15,000 to nearly 40,000 acres, were purchased in the vicinity of Starkey. Shortly before this time the Mexican rancho near Starkey had passed from the hands of its original grantee into those of a wealthy American family. These five holdings now dominated the Starkey region, and they continued to do so until the arrival of the settlers in the 1880s. They gave this region a feeling of the American West, for the ranches were manned by hired cowboys; the countryside was dotted by grazing cattle moving freely across the unfenced range land; and the yearly cycle of events was punctuated by roundups, brandings, and cattle drives.

The workers on the large cattle ranches were not the only inhabitants of the region at this time. On the dry hills there occasionally grazed large, itinerant flocks of sheep cared for by sheepherders who made use of the broad stretches of land that were still unclaimed. In addition, a small number of settlers had appeared. In the mid-1870s the county was surveyed for the first time, and on the survey map are recorded the names and dwelling sites of three people who do not appear to have had any connection with the large cattle ranches mentioned earlier. Virtually nothing is known of two of those people; possibly they farmed, but it is more likely that they were semisedentary sheepherders making free use of government-owned land.

The third person, Benjamin Sharp, was to become well known to the settlers of the 1880s and 1890s. He was the only one of the three to eventually acquire title to the land he occupied. A reserved and solitary man, he had grazed his flock of sheep in the Starkey region since at least 1860. Later he established a small farm along the river below what is now the town of Starkey. His farm was irrigated by an artesian well, and in addition to a small herd he grew abundant crops of wheat, fruit, and vegetables. These he shared willingly with newcomers and travelers, who could hardly miss his land since it was on the main route leading through the area.

Sharp's solitariness and reserve helped establish him as a legendary figure. Some people said that there was something strange about his past, and that although relatives occasionally came to visit he was never happy to see them. According to one story, he had left his wife and moved to the Starkey region because he was convinced that she had been unfaithful to him.

The only commercial center in the region before the influx of settlers was at Howard, approximately seven miles from the present town of Starkey. Situated along a natural route between the Central Valley and coast, Howard was a stopping place for travelers, although it also served the local inhabitants. It consisted of a combination roadhouse and store, which were begun perhaps as early as the 1850s, and a post office, established in the early 1870s. It is significant that

Howard did not also have a school. This was still a region of cowboys and sheepherders, the nearest school being well over a day's ride on horseback away.

The larger region of which Starkey is a part was also lightly inhabited. The county is divided in two by a low mountain range running parallel to the coast. The coastal portion of the county, a long, narrow strip of land, was devoted largely to dairying. Although it is by far the smaller of the two parts, it was the more heavily populated. In 1880, before the arrival of settlers in the Starkey region, the entire county contained fewer than 10,000 people, and over 75 percent of them lived in the narrow coastal section. Several small towns were situated on or near the coast, the most important being Saint Thomas, originally the site of an old Spanish mission and since 1850 the county seat. Saint Thomas was to grow substantially following California's entry into the Union—from a few hundred inhabitants in the 1860s to over 2,000 in 1880. It was the chief commercial center in the county, and when the Starkey settlers eventually arrived they relied heavily on the merchants of that town, making at least one trip there each year to acquire provisions.

The sparsely populated interior section of the county consisted mostly of large ranches, and it had nothing to compare with Saint Thomas. A few people lived at Saint George, where the mission, now in ruins, had been built years before, and where a saloon and a few stores could be found. And not far from there was Oak Flat, which during the 1860s and 1870s was nothing more than a small health resort featuring hot springs. Both of these places would soon become bustling farm towns, but that would have to wait until the influx of settlers into this part of the county that occurred in the 1880s.

The influx took place at a time when significant population changes were under way in the state, and particularly in Southern California. The Americans in California were originally concentrated in the north, since the gold fields were located in the northerly portions of the Sierra Nevadas. San Francisco was the leading city during the first few decades of statehood, and the Sacramento and lower San Joaquin valleys were the main centers of agricultural production. But the 1870s saw a gradual flow of people into Southern California, largely as a result of beliefs about the curative properties of the weather in that part of the state. By 1876 the railroad had been extended to Southern California, and during the 1880s a real-estate boom of enormous proportions was under way. The population south of the Tehachapi Mountains increased accordingly (Caughey 1970:336–51).

The county in which Starkey is located is too far north to have been part of the Southern California real-estate boom.[1] Starkey's growth was an indirect effect of these developments. As the population of Southern California increased, the Southern Pacific Railroad undertook to connect the two ends of the state with a railway line running near the coast. Although this line was not to pass through Starkey, both Saint George and Oak Flat were situated along the projected route, and by the early 1880s these two communities had become small railroad towns.

This part of the state was now linked with San Francisco, and in a few years, when the coastal route was completed, it would be linked with Southern California as well. The railroad made the local farmland far more attractive than it had been before, for it would no longer be necessary for the farmer or rancher to haul his goods across difficult mountain passes to coastal ports, to be shipped from there by ocean-going vessels. Agricultural goods would soon be taken to Oak Flat or Saint George and shipped by rail to San Francisco.

The influx of settlers into the Starkey region continued throughout the 1880s. It consisted chiefly of homesteaders. The population of the county jumped 76 percent between 1880 and 1890, almost solely owing to the sudden flood of people seeking farms in the inland portion. Some of the newcomers planned to gain title to land only to sell it again, but a substantial number came to settle permanently, hoping to piece together small cattle ranches or to raise grain.

The 1880s were a busy decade for the Starkey region, for almost every week saw the arrival of someone new looking for unclaimed land. Most of the choicest property—the level land located along the river banks—was already in the hands of the large cattle ranches, whose owners had purposely sought to dominate the rivers when acquiring their holdings. Any level land that was still available was claimed almost at once by newcomers. In addition, one of the cattle ranches had been purchased and subdivided by a land speculator, and those parcels were sold almost immediately. By 1890 virtually all the land that could be used—including the outlying hill land, much of which was too steep for farming and was good only for pasture land—had already been claimed, and the countryside was soon marked by an even pattern of homestead shacks.

It was several years before agricultural production was in full swing, however, inasmuch as the newcomers worked outside the community for at least part of the year. Several nearby localities had been settled shortly before, and they needed hired help, especially during the harvest. Employment could also be found in the dairies near the coast, and the Southern Pacific needed men with teams to help in constructing the railway. Some people went as far as the Central Valley to find work.

Apparently, the chief reason so few of the newcomers set immediately to work on their land was that most of them had little if any capital—those who hoped to farm typically did not have all the equipment or draft animals they needed, and those who intended to raise cattle normally had only the beginnings of a herd. What is more, many did not plan to remain but were looking forward to selling either their claim or its relinquishment to someone else, and they did no more than the minimum required to maintain their land.

The life of the early settlers was difficult. The people had to construct fences, houses, and barns; plow virgin land; and above all, acquire water. Rainfall in this portion of the state is relatively light, so the region is dry for much of the year. A narrow strip along one of the valleys was favored with artesian wells, and consequently a handful of the newcomers had sufficient water for some irrigation. Most of those with land along the river bottoms had adequate water for personal use, since the rivers flowed year round during this period; yet the water supply was not sufficient for them to engage in anything other than dry-land farming. Many of the settlers situated farther back in the hills were forced to haul water by wagon most of the year. Springs were quite few, and in many places the water table was too low to make hand-dug wells practicable.

Because of these conditions, subsistence farming was virtually impossible. Orchards were difficult to grow and gardens had to be small. One elderly woman relates that even the dirty dishwater was poured onto the small family garden. Nearly everyone had chickens and hogs, and most had at least one milk cow that was bred, providing the family with veal. But this was hardly sufficient to support a family. A substantial portion of the food that was needed—including beans, dried fruit, and flour—was purchased at one of the several general stores to be described in the next chapter. In most cases these purchases were made on credit, which enabled the settler to persist at least for a while.

Another problem was that in most cases the land a man could acquire from the government was insufficient for his needs. Each claim for government land was for 160 acres, or a quarter-section. But an individual could make one claim each under the Homestead Act, the Preemption Act, and the Timber Culture Act,[2] and could thereby acquire as much as 480 acres. Few people around Starkey were able to obtain this much. Most acquired only 160 acres; many got 320; but virtually none were able to manage the full 480. It was particularly difficult to meet the requirements of the Timber Culture Act, so Timber Culture claims were usually unsuccessful, and in any event most people were unable to find more than two vacant quarter-sections that were close enough together to claim.

It took well over 1,000 acres to feed a sufficient herd of cattle to support a family. Farming required less: a family needed only about 200 acres of grain to make a living. But a majority of the settlers did not acquire even that much, and most of those who did could not cultivate all of their acreage because much of it was too steep. Those whose land was situated along the river valleys could farm their entire holdings, but the property of those who settled in the surrounding hilly regions was a mixture of gently rolling hills, portions of which were cultivable, and steep canyons, which were not.

The small size of most holdings became even more troublesome later, for at about the turn of the century the practice of summer fallowing was instituted. This is a method whereby a plot of ground is left fallow every other year in order to increase the water content, and hence the productivity, of the soil. Summer fallowing raised the minimum amount of total crop land needed per farm to 400 acres. Since it was not at all unusual for a farm with that much cultivable soil to contain an additional 400 to 600 acres that were too steep for tillage—though still usable as pasture land—successful family farms had to include nearly 1,000 acres in most cases. After about the turn of the century farms of that size were the rule, not the exception.

When substantial agricultural production finally got under way in the late 1880s and early 1890s, two kinds of enterprise prevailed, cattle ranches and dry-land grain farms. Cattle ranching required a comparatively large piece of ground, and the newcomers who engaged in this type of operation bought much of the land they needed from others who left. The enterprise consisted of breeding a herd of cows and raising the offspring until they were three or four years old, at which time they were driven to cattle pens at either Oak Flat or Saint George. From there they were shipped by rail to slaughter. The drive took two days for those whose land was near Starkey, and somewhat longer for those situated in the valleys and canyons farther east. The major events in the yearly round were the roundup, branding, and the drive to market. During the rest of the year the rancher devoted his time to looking after his herd.

The large ranches that were in operation before homesteading each employed a bunkhouse full of cowboys, perhaps as many as fifteen in some cases. The owners of almost all of these ranches were absentee, leaving the day-to-day decision making in the hands of hired foremen. These large holdings were devoted mostly to cattle, but substantial portions were also farmed as leasehold by local residents.

The settlers' cattle operations were far smaller. Often two or three kinsmen, perhaps brothers, ran the ranch together, and in some cases the members of single families did so. Extra help was sometimes needed for gathering, branding, and driving the cattle to market, but the help that was required was for short periods and usually took the form of labor exchanges. As a result, the ranchers in a particular vicinity were usually involved in a network of reciprocal work relationships with neighbors and kinsmen.

A majority of the settlers were grain farmers. Although farming took less land, it required more equipment, including a grain wagon, a plow, a seeder (which was installed on the rear of a wagon), a harrow, and a header. The latter is a broad mowing machine that cuts the grain and deposits it in a wagon alongside. During the 1890s the grain was threshed and sacked by a large threshing machine. The farmer did not own a threshing machine; rather, he hired the services of one that was moved laboriously from farm to farm. The machine threshed all the grain in the Starkey area within a couple of weeks, and it was then hauled to another locality by a large team of horses. Once the wheat and barley were harvested, threshed, and sacked, it was loaded onto the heavy, lumbering grain wagons and taken to Oak Flat; there it was sold and shipped away by rail.

Before the turn of the century all the farms were small enough so that most of the work could be done by the farmer himself. The labor of an additional person was required for short periods, such as during seeding. This extra labor was typically provided by members of the family; in some cases a man was hired. A crew of six was normal for running a header, and if they were not family members they were paid wages. The threshing machine required twenty or more men, but they were recruited and paid by its owner, not by the farmer. Hired labor seems to have been far more common among farmers than among cattle ranchers.

The farmers engaged in exchange relationships when they lacked teams or equipment. For example, if a man had a grain wagon but did not have a full team, he struck an exchange with a neighbor who had a team but no wagon, and together they hauled their grain to Oak Flat. It was also common for several farmers to pool their resources in the purchase of equipment and to exchange their labor in using it. If four or five farmers purchased a header conjointly they assisted in harvesting one anothers' crops. Exchanges of this kind were regarded as temporary, stopgap mesures, however; all farmers looked forward to the day when they would be free of such encumbrances.

Although agricultural production was well under way during the 1890s, the decade was not a prosperous one for the Starkey settler. One problem was that economic conditions were poor throughout the country. The nation was in the throes of a depression for several years following the business collapse of 1893, and the effects on California agriculture were considerable. There was also a series of dry years during this period. According to one account, the winter of 1897–98 was so dry that the grain did not even sprout, and local newspapers report the closing of a number of banks in the county the following year.

The hard times were reflected in the value of land: one settler paid $12 an acre for hill land in 1889, but ten years later he "couldn't have given it away." Its selling price had dropped to about $2 or $3 an acre.

The Bradford store in Saint Thomas, from which the early settlers bought most of their supplies, felt the economic squeeze as well. Since many settlers could not pay their accounts, the store was unable to pay its creditors, and it survived only by acquiring a fairly sizable loan. Many of the farmers became so desperate that they simply turned over their land to the store and moved away, and others sold out to the storekeepers at a low price. As a consequence, the Bradfords acquired considerable acreage near Starkey. This land today forms part of a ranch owned by their heirs.

One notable effect of the adversities of the 1890s was the development of a population outflow from the Starkey region: whereas the 1880s witnessed a constant flow of settlers into this part of the county, the 1890s saw many of them leave again. A large number never intended to remain, but it seems likely that many others who wanted to stay could not do so because it was too difficult for them to manage on the land they had acquired. Figures are not available to show the portion that left during the 1890s, but it is likely that at least half of those who had arrived during the previous decade did so.

The people who were most seriously affected by the adversities of the 1890s were engaged chiefly in cattle raising. Technological developments had not yet advanced to the point at which the cattle rancher could have supplemental feed hauled to his property during a period of drought. Nearly all his cattle feed grew within the borders of the ranch, and in a dry year at least a portion of his herd starved to death. Nor was it feasible to move the cattle to regions where feed was more plentiful. In 1897–98, for example, the only area in which feed could be located was in the Central Valley. But the trip was all but impossible to make, since by the time the need to move the animals was apparent they were already too weak to travel by hoof.

The farmer was somewhat less affected by the adversities of the 1890s, since his investment was chiefly in land and equipment, which were not perishable, and he could go elsewhere temporarily to work for wages if his crops were poor. At least one farmer traveled all the way to Oregon to support his family in the 1890s. The farmers' plight was still very serious, however, especially for those who were burdened with debt.

The fact that the crisis of the 1890s was felt more strongly by the cattle ranchers than by the farmers had an important result. It virtually eliminated cattle raising as a major form of economic activity on all but the large ranches (those that had preceded the influx of settlers), and it established this locality as a community of farmers.[3] By the end of the decade virtually all of the newcomers who had attempted to engage chiefly or solely in cattle raising had given up their land. Many of the grain farmers did so as well—as is manifest from the amount of property that passed into the hands of the Bradfords—but at least some of them did survive the hardships of this decade.

Starkey was in the process of becoming established during the 1880s and 1890s, but this process was virtually complete by the turn of the century. What had been a frontier community was now simply a farm community, and a mood of normality had replaced the earlier sense of challenge and hardship.

The period from about the turn of the century to 1920 was one of comparative prosperity for the Starkey farmer, just as it was for the farm population throughout the country. This was the "golden age" of American agriculture. Since the Civil War American agriculture had suffered from serious economic disorders, but by about 1900 the prices of agricultural commodities had finally begun to rise and farmers had a chance to make an adequate living. A mood of optimism began to emerge among the rural population, partly because the continued growth of the cities seemed to spell an increasing demand for farm products, and this, coupled with the end of the American frontier and of agricultural expansion, meant even higher prices and more prosperity in the future. The value of farmland also continued to rise; this bolstered not only the farmer's confidence but his net worth and credit rating as well.

The prosperity of the period from about 1900 to 1920 had important economic consequences in Starkey, for it facilitated a pattern of upward mobility. It was possible for a young, penniless newcomer to begin at the bottom and, with a combination of luck and hard work, climb to the top of the agricultural ladder (see Hatch 1975:23–26).

The term *agricultural ladder* has been in use among agricultural economists and others since at least the early part of this century to describe the sequence of steps by which the individual acquires farm ownership and financial security (see especially Spillman 1919). It is conceived of as a temporal sequence of steps and is normally used to describe the "typical" or "ideal" career pattern. But the progressive rungs of the ladder may also be used to classify the members of a farm community at a given point in time and thereby describe the system of social stratification.

At the bottom of both the agricultural ladder and the social hierarchy in Starkey were the landless wage earners. For the most part these were young, unmarried men who were saving to acquire a farm. A handful of jobs were available at the stores in Starkey, and work could be had for brief periods by joining the county road crews. Some young men were hired to assist on the large cattle ranches, and some workers even left the community temporarily to earn money—to work in the dairies situated near the coast, for example. But most of Starkey's young men found work on the local farms. Every established farmer needed help at least occasionally, especially during the harvest, and by the second decade of this century some employed a hired hand year round.

The next step up the ladder was to acquire a farm. The prospective farmer did not need to purchase land to begin with, since ample acreage was available for lease—the depression and drought of the 1890s had driven many of the earlier farmers away—and the lease payment was not due until after the first crop was harvested. But the person who was starting out did have to acquire a team and the necessary equipment. Typically he could not afford all that he needed, and to make up for what he lacked he entered into exchange relationships with other farmers. Exchanges of this kind were a handicap, however, for they required that the farmer leave his own work periodically to help others, and in the long run they were a heavy burden on his time and energy. So the beginning farmer was distinguished by the fact that he was both undercapitalized and overworked.

As the farmer became established, his operation developed in several ways. He acquired enough horses or mules and equipment for his own needs, thereby freeing himself from exchange relationships. He also set out to purchase land—often in a piecemeal fashion and on credit. This property may have been his original leasehold, but frequently it was a better-situated plot that had become available. The farmer also increased the amount of land he cultivated. By now he probably had a wife and family, and he had to farm at least 400 acres (200 acres a year) to support them. If he had the chance and was financially able to, he acquired even more land.

At the top of both the agricultural ladder and the social heirarchy were the farmers who were fully established. They owned all the equipment they needed and made a comfortable living from their farms. They were distinguished by the fact that they owned two teams, not one, employing a full-time hired man to run the second team. The breaking point between those who hired full-time help and those who did not was an annual harvest of about 300 acres (or a total of 600 acres of cultivable land).[4]

The differences among the levels of the social hierarchy were very real. The successful farmer enjoyed a degree of wealth and a sense of security that colored his everyday life and set him apart from the man at the bottom. This was hardly an egalitarian community. Nevertheless, the different levels did not coalesce into distinct, exclusive, and self-conscious strata, for upward mobility was common and each level blended gradually into the next.

The nonexclusive character of this pattern of stratification is illustrated by the relationship between hired man and farm owner, which was more like a relationship between colleagues at different points in their careers than one between members of different social classes. The hired man often lived with his employer, eating from the same table. Frequently he came from a family living nearby, and his father had a farm not unlike the one on which he was employed. The worker also looked forward to the day, not too distant, when he himself would own a farm.

The agricultural ladder in Starkey provided the skeletal framework for the hierarchical ordering of community members, for it supplied the image of economic success within the community and a standard for measuring achievement. It was a standard that seemed both attractive and promising. The aspiring individual saw the opportunity for advance, since land was available and agricultural prices were relatively high. But the image of success was a modest one. Although upward mobility was possible, its outer limit was the ownership of a two-man farm. There was little prospect—and apparently little impulse—for becoming a land baron or a millionaire.

Farm prosperity came to a sudden end in 1920 with the onset of the agricultural depression. The demand for agricultural commodities during World War I had stimulated American agriculture enormously, with the result that farmers throughout the country expanded both acreage and production. Land values rose during and immediately following the war, and many farmers, buoyed by the optimism of prosperity, expanded their holdings at inflated prices and went on to purchase newer and more expensive equipment. Farm debts rose. The adverse effects of this trend became manifest in the second half of 1920, when prices for farm commodities began to tumble because of oversupply, and the value of agricultural land started to decline. That entire decade would prove to be an unprosperous one for American agriculture.

The impact of the agricultural depression on Starkey is clear. Few if any farmers were forced off their land, as happened in other parts of the United States, but upward mobility was severely curtailed. Land was available for lease to the aspiring young man, but the price his crops could bring was insufficient to cover the initial cost of the machinery and other items he needed to begin operating. There was also little chance of purchasing land in view of the depressed conditions of agriculture, so even the farmers who were partially established were severely limited in their movement up the ladder. The farmer's attention was directed toward holding on, not climbing, and the earlier pattern of mobility was replaced by one of motionlessness.

Conditions became even more severe after the stock market crash of 1929. As before, the hired hand saw virtually no chance of striking out on his own. In addition, several Starkey farmers lost their property during the worst years of the Great Depression, and the economic condition of the ones who did not was highly precarious throughout the 1930s.

One result of this state of affairs was the progressive mechanization of farming, since mechanization offered the prospect of greater efficiency. In Starkey the switch to tractor power took place within a brief period of three or four years—during the late 1920s and early 1930s—because of the obvious advantages of the tractor. Increasingly larger farms also became necessary, in part because larger acreages were needed to maximize the benefits of the faster and more efficient machinery, and in part because the narrowing margin of profit made it necessary to increase the volume of production in order to receive the same dollar income. By the late 1930s the amount of crop land needed to support a family in Starkey was double the amount required before 1920—now 400 acres had to be harvested each year. Owing to the practice of summer fallowing, the farmer had to have a total of 800 acres of crop land.

The process of mechanization and the increase in the minimum amount of farmland required were tantamount to the addition of new rungs to the agricultural ladder, and the farmer was forced to resume climbing. If he did not, his economic position became more precarious, not less, and he suffered a comparative drop on the social scale as well, since there were others who did increase their holdings and update their equipment during the 1930s.

The agricultural ladder remained the chief measure of a person's social standing in the community, although changes were under way. During the 1920s the difficulties besetting agriculture may have seemed short term and remediable, and the aspiring but landless young man may have held his hopes in abeyance without abandoning them altogether. But the 1930s brought a new set of conditions. The man with property was not much better off than the farm hand, and this must have demoralized those who otherwise would have wanted to move up the ladder. But an even more serious problem was the increase in farm capitalization that was taking place—including both the increasingly expensive machinery and the larger holdings that were required. When prosperity returned it would be harder than ever to start at the bottom, for the most difficult step—acquiring land and equipment to begin farming—was becoming an increasingly wider stretch. A gap was beginning to appear between the farm worker and the landholder, although it may not have been evident to the people in Starkey at the time.

As important as farming was in the community, it was not the exclusive source of employment, and this was more and more true as time passed. Starkey's occupational heterogeneity was increasing.

The commercial businesses in Starkey illustrate this process, for the first local establishments—to be described later—were initially part-time undertakings. These were begun by settlers who had acquired land near the center of Starkey Flat and had built their small businesses where the corners of their farm property met. But by the turn of the century Starkey had two stores, a hotel, a blacksmith shop, and other establishments, each of which required the full-time attention of their owners and in some cases full-time employees as well.

In 1910 an oil company built a small maintenance facility about four miles from the town center. The facility included three dwellings for a permanent staff and their families, as well as a boardinghouse for occasional work crews. A second oil facility was constructed in the 1930s only a mile and a half from the town, and this, too, included a small cluster of family dwellings and a boardinghouse.[5]

The people living at these facilities did not play an important role in Starkey, for not one of them emerged as a prominent member of the community and most apparently were not very active in its social life. Some attended church, and the children attended the Starkey schools, but these people seem to have been regarded as outsiders and to have conceived of themselves in the same light. Perhaps this was due largely to their mobility. These families normally did not remain in Starkey for more than a few years, after which they were transfered elsewhere by the company.

The schoolteachers also contributed to the occupational heterogeneity of Starkey. Before 1910 or 1920 the teachers blended smoothly into the farm population, for they were usually from rural backgrounds, were typically young and unmarried, and did not bring families with them into the community. It sometimes happened that the women teachers soon married Starkey residents and were fully absorbed into the local life. But with time the schoolteachers became more professional, for the occupation was increasingly viewed as a career. At the new high school, especially, many of the teachers were men accompanied by their families, and they tended to identify more strongly with their profession than with the farm population.

The occupational heterogeneity of Starkey was further increased in the early 1920s, when a state highway was constructed through the town. The highway brought with it the need for a regular, full-time crew of men, together with a permanent facility for equipment. The facility—which included a house for the foreman—was built next to the high school. By the late 1920s the state road crew consisted of nine men, most of whom had families.

This growing occupational heterogeneity helped change the social complexion of Starkey, since it meant that an increasing number of local people could not be easily classified according to the rungs of the agricultural ladder. And yet the farm population was still the dominant element in the community and the agricultural ladder still supplied the measure of social position for most people. The dominance of agriculture in the local social system is reflected in the fact that the leading community organization during the late 1920s and most of the 1930s was the Farm Bureau rather than the Rotary, Kiwanis, or Lions Club.

Chapter 2 The Crystallization of Community

THE STARKEY FARMERS were not as dependent on one another as agriculturalists sometimes are in other parts of the world. The preference in Starkey was to pay wages for extra help and to buy whatever equipment was needed, thus avoiding the reciprocal obligations of exchange labor. To be sure, all the farmers occasionally found themselves out of barbed wire or nails, or in need of a particular kind of tool, and to save a trip to town they borrowed from someone nearby. This form of borrowing was relatively incidental, however; it was a matter of convenience, not necessity. The economic independence of the farmers appears even greater when we consider the marketing of goods, for the local agriculturalists felt little economic competition with one another. The prices they received for their grain and beef reflected the current state of the world market and were virtually unaffected by the productivity of their neighbors.

What served to integrate the farm families was less their economic relations with one another than their mutual associations with a number of commercial and social centers. Each family conceived of itself as a member of a discrete community, which in turn was conceived of as part of the hinterland of more extensive communities. This pattern of community relations constituted the basic framework for the social organization of the interior of the county.

Each of these communities was defined in relation to its hub, which could range from a solitary one-room schoolhouse to a small town. The significance of the hub both in the community's actual existence and in its definition of itself is manifest in that the community bore the name of its hub, and when the hub came to an end—when, for example, the solitary schoolhouse closed—the community soon ceased to exist as a distinct entity with a social life of is own.

In this chapter I discuss the development of social and commercial centers in the general region of Starkey, the nature of the communities that formed around those centers, and the nature of the relationships among those communities.

Between the period of settlement and World War II the communities in the inland portion of the county could be classified into three general types according to size and function.[1] First were the railroad towns like Oak Flat, which were focal points for the region. I will discuss the railroad towns shortly. Second were minor service centers that were not situated along the railway. I call these farm towns inasmuch as they served the daily needs of the nearby farm families. Farm towns were located ten to fifteen miles apart, and by about 1900 or 1910 they consisted of at least one or two stores, a blacksmith shop, a hotel, a post office, a saloon, a school, and a church. Each had no more than a handful of houses—perhaps twenty at most—for the majority of the community's members lived on the surrounding farmland. In spite of their dimunitive size, the farm towns regarded themselves as independent communities and not as satellites of the railroad towns.

The third type of community was even smaller. It was referred to locally as a district, since it represented the crystallization of social sentiment among those who lived within the boundaries of a single school district. The hub of these communities was an isolated one-room schoolhouse; some districts eventually added a post office and later a community hall. As a rule these communities conceived of themselves as satellites of the nearest farm town or railroad town.

Starkey was a farm town, and associated with it were several satellite district communities, the number varying somewhat over time. To understand the distribution of the small social hubs and the nature of the relationships among these communities it is necessary to describe the local configuration of the land.

The farm town of Starkey is situated on Starkey Flat, a triangular alluvial fan covering nine or ten square miles (see Map 1). This level expanse was formed by the confluence of two rivers, and these have cut narrow valleys that converge at this spot. The waters skirt one edge of the Flat and continue along a third valley. Starkey Flat thus marks the

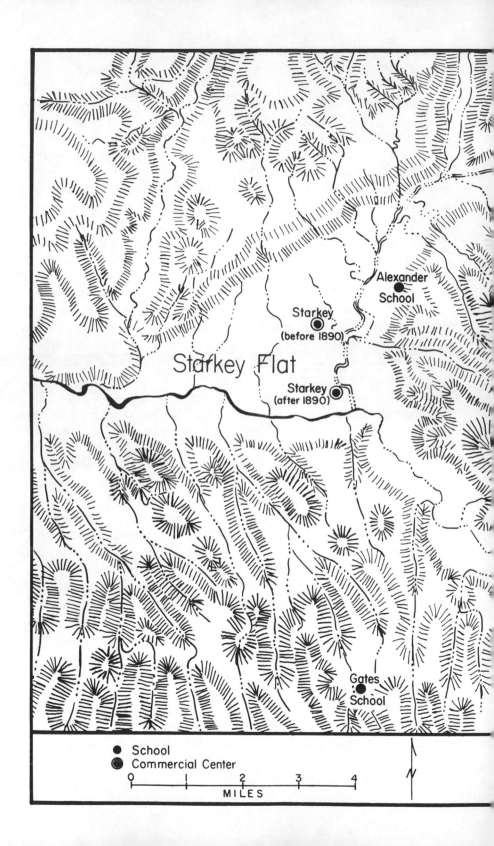

Alexander
School

Starkey
(before 1890)

Starkey Flat

Starkey
(after 1890)

Gates
School

● School
◉ Commercial Center

0   1   2   3   4
MILES

N

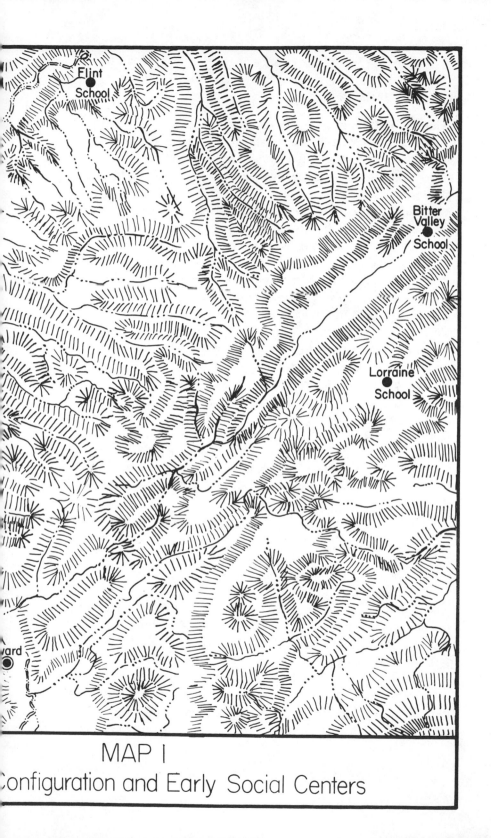

MAP I
Configuration and Early Social Centers

intersection of three river valleys, each about a half-mile wide. Surrounding the Flat and the river valleys are rolling, grass-covered hills several hundred feet in height, and etched through the hills is a network of steep, narrow canyons that eventually join the river valleys at almost right angles.

Human travel is severely constrained by this pattern of drainage. Movement is easy on the Flat and along the river valleys, and somewhat slower, though still feasible, along the canyons. But it is all but impossible for a person to travel at an angle across the system of canyons unless he does so on foot or on horseback, and even then progress is slow and laborious. Most of the people in the vicinity of Starkey lived in the hilly reaches, and their movement was channeled directly to the narrow valleys and from there to Starkey Flat.

During the period of settlement in the 1880s a small social and commercial nucleus was developing at nearly the exact center of the Flat. The businesses were fledgling ones unable to supply all the homesteaders' needs, so the Starkey center attracted only incidental trade at first, the major purchases being made at Bradford's store in Saint Thomas.

The first concern to be established on Starkey Flat was the saloon built by one of the earliest homesteaders on one corner of his property. This establishment was patronized chiefly by sheepherders and cowboys working on the large ranches, but it also provided food and lodging for passers-by, and by mid-decade it served as the post office as well. The saloon was never well regarded by the majority of the settlers because of their feelings about alcohol—many would not even enter the building to pick up their mail—and it soon closed.

By the end of the 1880s the saloon no longer existed, but near the same spot there was now a small, unpretentious town center made up of a cluster of unpainted, board-and-batten structures. One of these housed a combination post office and store where pastries and patent medicines could be purchased. The postmaster was an elderly bachelor, somewhat eccentric and very devout. A second store sold groceries for the most part, although some dry goods were also kept in stock. Third was a small drugstore owned by a local homesteader who also supplemented his income by working as a photographer. The fourth structure housed a small blacksmith shop. Last was a one-room school-house, crudely built and furnished with home-made desks and benches.

During the 1890s at least some of the settlers were becoming established on their land, and the relationship between customer and store was changing. The people were still heavily dependent on store-bought goods, for none of the settlers could engage in subsistence farming. And they still depended heavily on credit. But most of the people now produced butter and eggs in quantities beyond their needs, and by the 1890s the surplus was used to barter with the Starkey establishments. A substantial portion of the store bill was apparently settled in this way. What is more, more goods were now purchased in Starkey rather than in Saint Thomas. Each week the local stores sent a wagon to Oak Flat loaded with the agricultural goods that had been traded to them, and from there the goods were shipped by rail to San Francisco and other markets. The wagons returned to Starkey with new supplies to be sold to the farmers and ranchers. The payment of store bills with eggs and butter was a trait that persisted among many Starkey residents until about World War II, though it progressively diminished in importance.

The commercial center at Starkey grew slowly during the 1890s, and its location on the Flat was shifted. In 1890 a town site was surveyed and laid out by a land company hoping to make a profit on town lots. The new spot for the town center was about a mile and a half from the original one; this site was on the southeast corner of the Flat at nearly the point where the two rivers converge. Most of the buildings from the former town center—the blacksmith shop, school, and post office—were moved there, and more buildings were soon erected. An elderly resident has drawn from memory a map of the new town as it was in about 1900.[2] At that time it included nine houses, two butcher shops, two general stores, two blacksmith shops, a combined hotel and saloon, a Chinese laundry, the post office, the school, and a church.

The town's appearance was typical for the time and place. Except for a butcher shop built of adobe—a material that served to maintain cool temperatures during the hot summer days—the buildings were all made of rough wood, and most were unpainted. The post office and

stores had high false fronts, and most had a broad plank porch stretching the width of the building. The streets were unpaved and were
usually either muddy or dusty, depending on the weather.

Another person has drawn a map of Starkey as it appeared when
he arrived there as a boy in 1912 (see Map 2). At that time there were
approximately 35 structures in the town. Only 13 of these were houses;
another 6 were barns used to store feed and stable horses. The church
was probably the most impressive of the buildings in Starkey, with its
high, peaked roof and steeple and its freshly painted walls. By contrast,
the elementary school—important as it was to the local residents—was
one of the least impressive, for it was the same small, dingy, one-room
building that had served Starkey's earliest settlers.

There were two stores in town, both selling food, dry goods, and
general merchandise. One of these was quite small and was run by its
owner, who employed a full-time clerk to assist him. The other was
larger and more successful. It was owned by two brothers, one of whom
served as manager. They employed a clerk (who also served as freight
man, driving the wagon to Oak Flat once a week) and a young woman
who acted as clerk and bookkeeper. Both of the stores were gathering
places throughout the work day—which extended into the early evening—for most residents came to town at least once a week to shop.

The hotel, one of the few two-story structures in town, was nearly as
impressive in appearance as the church. Its significance to the community was declining in 1912, however, largely because Starkey's county
supervisoral district had voted dry by local option the year before and
the saloon had been forced to close its doors. The hotel was run by its
owner and his wife, along with their son and daughter-in-law.

The post office acted as a center for the dissemination of local
news, since representatives from nearly every household periodically
stopped there to pick up their mail. The blacksmith shop was another
important gathering spot during the day. The blacksmith was gregarious and well liked. Both farmers and townspeople gathered at his shop
to wait while he shoed their horses or repaired their machinery, or
perhaps to visit with someone else who was waiting.

A man living on the outskirts of Starkey owned equipment for
drilling wells. While his business did not stimulate the gathering of

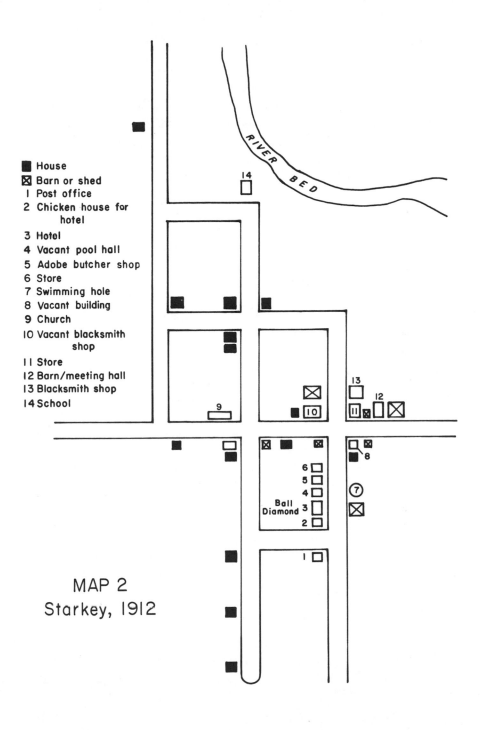

House
Barn or shed
1 Post office
2 Chicken house for hotel
3 Hotel
4 Vacant pool hall
5 Adobe butcher shop
6 Store
7 Swimming hole
8 Vacant building
9 Church
10 Vacant blacksmith shop
11 Store
12 Barn/meeting hall
13 Blacksmith shop
14 School

RIVER BED

14

13

12

11

10

9

Ball Diamond

6
5
4
3
2

7

8

1

MAP 2
Starkey, 1912

community members, it was an additional element in the commercial activity of the town.

Several forms of recreation were available. There happened not to be a pool hall in Starkey in 1912, but one had closed shortly before and another would open in the near future. There was a baseball diamond in a vacant lot behind the hotel, and this attracted sizable crowds on Sunday afternoons. Across from the hotel was a small irrigation reservoir that was used as a swimming hole. It had been made by digging a deep depression in the ground and lining it with cement; the water was supplied by an artesian well. A community hall, referred to as Turner Hall, was also located in town. This was a two-story barn, the lower portion of which was used to store feed, the upper portion being used for plays, dances, and public meetings.

A variety of events and undertakings conducted during the late nineteenth and early twentieth centuries illustrate the growing sense of community in Starkey. Perhaps the most significant of these was the construction of the church. Two separate congregations were holding services during the 1880s: a group of Methodists, who had met in the schoolhouse on the Flat since the beginning of homesteading, and a group of Presbyterians, who had begun using a schoolhouse in the hills nearby shortly thereafter. Both congregations decided to pool their labor and money in the construction of a single church building once the town was laid out. Although it would be a united effort, the Methodists would hold the deed to the chapel because they had obtained financial assistance (a $200 loan and a $250 gift) from their national organization.

A campaign to raise money for the project was initiated in 1891. It included box socials, cake and ice cream sales, and the solicitation of donations. By summer of that year enough had been raised to begin construction, and when the harvest was over several farmers began hauling the lumber to Starkey from Oak Flat. They had to drive their heavy wagons to the railroad town in order to sell their grain, and after doing so they simply loaded the redwood boards for the return trip. Although a carpenter was employed to superintend the job, people who were interested in the project donated their labor whenever possible.

The church was used by the two denominations on alternate

Sundays. The preacher for each group was a circuit rider who served at least one other community simultaneously and traveled to Starkey every second sabbath to conduct services.

A variety of other events illustrate the sense of community that was developing in Starkey. For example, dances were held periodically at the hotel, and debating club meetings, potluck suppers, and yearly harvest festivals were staged at the schoolhouse in town.

The two primary social events of the year were held on May Day and Christmas Eve. The Christmas Eve celebration was preceded by festive preparations in which a group of people drove a wagon into the hills to cut a suitable pine tree. The tree was set up inside the church and decorated. Families soon began to arrive for the celebration, bringing a few presents to be opened during the evening, and a short religious program was presented. Small sacks of candy and oranges were later distributed to the children.

Each May Day the members of the community dressed in their finest clothes and congregated at a particular spot on the banks of one of the rivers to enjoy an ample and very decorous picnic. The wild flowers were usually in bloom at this time, adding to the festive atmosphere. After the meal was over the people engaged in community singing, listened to poetry readings by schoolchildren, and were usually entertained by a skit or play. Ball games, sack and foot races, and other contests were held. A Maypole was wound later in the day, and a May Queen was chosen from among the schoolgirls.

As time went by, the town center went through a gradual process of evolution. In 1915 the Starkey elementary school was replaced by another, larger one, with finished wood on the outside and plaster within, that contained two classrooms. The blacksmith shop was transformed into a garage as the gasoline engine replaced the horse, and gasoline pumps soon appeared in front of the stores. Somewhat later a small cafe was added to the roster of businesses in town. Turner Hall was replaced by the Community Hall, a larger, more suitable building that contained both a stage and a separate dining room; it was constructed by cooperative effort. Later a town park and swimming pool were built in similar fashion.[3]

But growth was limited. Even in the 1960s there were fewer than

100 houses in town, and the local population was never sufficient to warrant a bank, drugstore, or newspaper. These were available in Oak Flat but never in Starkey.

The school on Starkey Flat was not the only one in the vicinity by the close of the 1880s, for by then three other one-room schoolhouses had been constructed in the outlying regions nearby (see Map 1). One of the schools, the Gates school, was located in the hills to the south. The canyons leading out of that district led directly onto the Flat, thereby strengthening the bond between the families of that region and the central hub developing on the level ground. Two more schools, Flint and Alexander, were situated at different places along the river valley that leads to Starkey Flat from the northeast, and these districts served the families living in the adjacent hills.

Each school represented a separate district, a legal entity demarcated by formally defined boundaries, overseen by a board of three trustees elected from among the local residents, and supported by local taxes.

The school's significance went beyond educational matters, however: the school districts developed into self-conscious communities. In part this consciousness came about because the schools served to unite the local residents in cooperative and collective action, for work days were held periodically to maintain the school buildings and yards. The schools were also in constant use as community meeting places. Church services, box socials, potluck suppers, plays, and dances were frequently held in the small structures. It is important to note that opportunities for entertainment and social life were quite limited at this time. Travel was time-consuming and difficult—roads were little more than wagon trails, and they were intersected by a barbed-wire gate at the property line of every farm through which they passed—so the opportunity for travel beyond the immediate neighborhood was limited. The events taking place at the nearby schoolhouse supplied the major respites from the loneliness and drudgery of the settler's life.

Even though the outlying districts were distinct, they were also identified as part of the larger community of Starkey because of their association with the small center that was developing there. The residents of the outlying hill regions shared the commercial and postal facilities of the central hub on the Flat, and most of the people living in the surrounding hills occasionally attended dances and other social events at the Starkey school, the most central of the four.

The unity of this larger Starkey community would continue to grow through time, and it would do so for several reasons. One was the gradual improvement of both roads and transportation. As the gates disappeared and the roadbed became graded, graveled, and eventually paved, and as the automobile came into vogue, a trip to Starkey could become a daily event. The central hub acquired a growing significance as the point of articulation among the several districts and as a focus of activity and common interest.

Another factor contributing to the growing unity was the fact that the number of districts was reduced by the closure of several of the outlying schools. As the schools lapsed, the social distinctiveness and cohesion of the districts dissolved and the local significance of the central hub at Starkey increased. The main reason for the schools' closure was the population decline following the depression of the 1890s, for by about the turn of the century two of the outlying schools no longer had sufficient enrollments to stay open. The few children remaining in the district south of the Flat (Gates) now attended the Starkey school, whereas the two schools situated in the valley northeast of Starkey (Flint and Alexander) were merged into one (the Alexander school). Prosperity had returned by the beginning of the new century, but whatever population increase this may have brought, it was still not enough to warrant reopening these schools.

Another cluster of districts was located to the east of Starkey. At first these apparently did not identify with the small social and commercial center growing on Starkey Flat, but eventually they, too, became part of the farm town that was emerging.

The first of the eastern districts was Howard, the hub of which was located in the valley running southeast of Starkey Flat. During the period of settlement the original roadhouse and store at Howard was transformed into a general store supplying the growing farm population, although the establishment continued to serve as a stagecoach stop for a number of years. The small post office at Howard occupied a single room attached to the store, and a blacksmith shop was built next door. A school was soon located a short distance away.

A settler arriving in the 1880s would have found it difficult to guess whether Howard or Starkey was to become the more important center, but already by the 1890s the former roadhouse was slipping behind. Unlike Starkey, Howard never enjoyed enough trade to support two stores; it never had a church or hotel; and it never witnessed the growth of a residential section of more than two or three houses. The only major addition to appear after the 1880s was a community hall. The buildings at Howard were occasionally updated, and the original schoolhouse was eventually replaced by a newer one, but Howard's growth was quite limited.

Howard was not only eclipsed by Starkey but eventually absorbed as well. The store at Howard continued to serve the residents in the vicinity after the turn of the century, but it was smaller than the two stores in Starkey, and by 1900 the people of the Howard District were buying much of what they needed in the larger community.

Howard's social life also shifted toward Starkey. The Howard school provided a center of interest and a series of social events, especially during the early decades of the century, and in the 1920s the Howard residents built their community hall by collective effort. Nevertheless, as the use of the automobile became more and more prevalent the Howard residents went increasingly to Starkey Farm Bueau meetings, church services, dances, and the like. By 1940 the community hall at Howard lay unused, and the store would soon be converted into a cafe catering chiefly to highway traffic. By the beginning of World War II the main focus of the community was its one-room school. This still provided a focus of interest and a sense of distinctness, but the community's autonomy was far less marked than it had been in the past.[4]

A series of hills stretches to the northeast of Howard, and these are dissected by a number of canyons that lead almost directly to the site of the former roadhouse. Two more districts were located in that hilly and remote area, and although it is not clear how closely the residents of that region identified with Howard late in the nineteenth century and early in the twentieth, it is certain that they were dependent on the store, blacksmith shop, and post office located there.

These two districts, Lorraine and Bitter Valley, were linked together in people's minds and were closely associated in fact. Collectively they were referred to simply as Lorraine, a usage that I employ here. The closeness of the association between the two districts is manifest from the fact that the schools often combined in presenting programs such as the Christmas pageant.

During the 1890s a post office was opened next to the Lorraine school. The mail was first delivered by stagecoach to the post office at Howard, and letters and parcels addressed to people living in the hilly districts to the northeast were then transported to the small outlying postal facility. In the early 1920s a community hall and a separate dining hall were built by collective effort near the post office and school, and these were heavily used for such events as public dances (followed by ample suppers cooked by the women of the community), plays, and community meetings.

The community of Lorraine exhibited an active social life until about 1950, and it retained a degree of social independence from Starkey during that period. Until perhaps as late as the 1940s, if a Lorraine resident were asked whether his or her community was a part of Starkey the reply would be no, and the respondent would mention a variety of facts to emphasize the point. For example, during the 1920s Lorraine had its own baseball team—Starkey's main rival in the regional league—and its own civic organization. Like Starkey, Lorraine started its own Farm Bureau Center in the early 1920s, entered its own float in the annual Homestead Celebration parade in Oak Flat, to be discussed later, and so forth.

But Lorraine's autonomy was already threatened by the 1920s, when the Starkey high school was established. Lorraine was within the area served by the Starkey high school, and children from Lorraine would attend that institution if they wanted to pursue their education beyond the eighth grade. A greater and greater emphasis was being placed on achieving a high school diploma, and the link between Lorraine and Starkey—and the dominance of the latter—became increasingly pronounced. The Lorraine post office closed in 1930, and this served to diminish the importance of the small hub. And of course this remote community center never had a store, so the residents were dependent on Starkey and Howard for even the most incidental purchases.

Not even Starkey could supply all the goods and services needed by the residents of Lorraine—or of Starkey, for that matter. The people of the entire region had to deal at least occasionally with commercial centers of a higher order. In particular, they had to trade periodically with the merchants at one of the nearby railroad towns. Purchases of such major items as farm machinery and lumber were made at the railroad centers, where banks and barbershops could also be found and where grain and beef were taken for shipment. The inhabitants of the inland portion of the county made, at the very least, several trips a year to the nearest railroad town.

Four railroad towns were distributed about six to ten miles apart along the railway line, and together they served the entire inland portion of the county. While the railroad was under construction each of them enjoyed a brief boom period when it had the advantage of being at the very end of the line, but the next town was soon reached by the advancing railway and the moment of enthusiasm and glory passed.

All four railroad towns started as equals, but within a few years Oak Flat began to outstrip the others in importance. Yet Oak Flat remained a small town. In the late 1880s its estimated population was only about 800, and in 1910 it was less than 1,500. In 1940 it still had not reached 4,000.

The hinterland of Oak Flat (see Map 3) shared a sense of unity. The population of this part of the county apparently was not more than about 7,000 in 1940,[5] so it was possible for the members of each of the constituent localities to know a great deal about the others. These were hardly isolated, self-contained communities. Their interrelatedness was enhanced by similarities in farming methods, and the people occasionally met by chance and exchanged news on the streets or in the stores of Oak Flat. The residents of one community sometimes visited friends and relatives living in nearby localities, thereby learning firsthand what was taking place there.

The closeness of the bond linking the outlying communities with Oak Flat was manifest from the tendency for the merchants of the larger town to know even their most distant customers by name. The cstomers also tended to be aware of the scandals and other internal affairs of Oak Flat, and in that sense to share in the community life of the railroad town.

The smaller communities did not conceive of themselves as mere appendages or satellites of Oak Flat, however. Their sense of indepen-

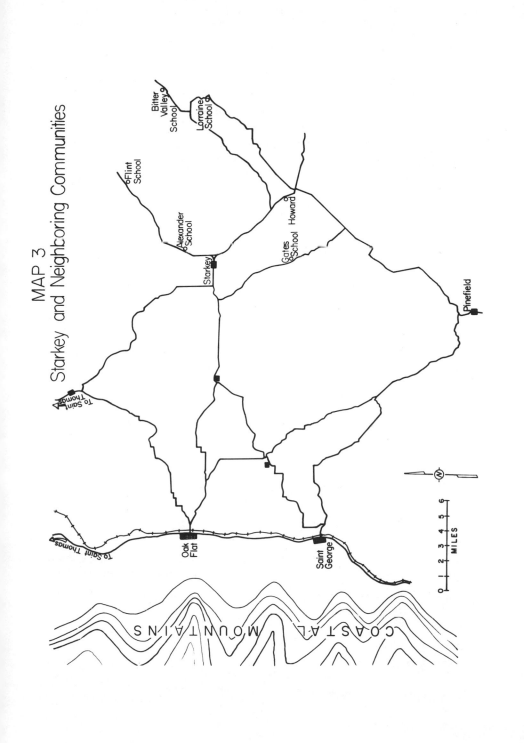

MAP 3

Starkey and Neighboring Communities

dence was both exhibited and fortified by a general feeling of resentment toward the railroad town—a feeling that the latter was prone to take advantage of its preeminence and that it viewed these outlying localities as parochial and countrified.

The several facets of the relationship between Oak Flat and Starkey were given concrete expression in the high-school system. The Starkey elementary schools gave instruction through the eighth grade, and until well into the twentieth century few families undertook to send their children beyond that level. Those who did so in Starkey's earliest years made arrangements for their sons and daughters to live with relatives in Saint Thomas, where there was a high school. Soon after the turn of the century a high school was established in Oak Flat, and once this was accomplished a handful of students from Starkey continued their education at that institution. Since Oak Flat was too distant for the children to make daily trips back and forth, they still had to live away from home during the school year.

High-school instruction was first begun in Starkey in 1920, when a branch of the Oak Flat school was opened there. The classes of the new school were held in the barroom of the hotel, which had closed some time earlier. Fourteen students were enrolled the year the school began, and by 1924, when a full four-year course was first offered, there were thirty-one students and two teachers. Several additional teachers traveled from Oak Flat once a week to give instruction in special subjects. As the student body and faculty grew, the bedrooms upstairs were converted into classrooms. Finally, in 1925, a new school building was constructed.

The subordination of the Starkey school to the parent institution was manifest in several ways. For example, a commencement program was not held in Starkey. The Starkey graduates received their diplomas at a combined ceremony held at the Oak Flat school. The Starkey student body shared a small section of the Oak Flat school annual. Most significant, the Starkey teachers were supervised and promoted by the Oak Flat principal, who oversaw the routine operations of the outlying school.

The Oak Flat high-school system was governed by an elected board of five trustees; two were selected from among the residents of Oak Flat and one from each of three outlying communities within the school district's boundaries. Starkey was one of the communities within the district, and one of Starkey's residents was regularly elected to the board.

Starkey was never satisfied with its position as part of the Oak Flat high-school system, and occasionally its dissatisfaction took the form of vocal opposition to school policy. This discontent and resentment became manifest in 1936, when the Starkey high school succeeded in severing its relationship with the parent institution and becoming an independent unit headed by its own board of trustees.

Several reasons were cited for the change, including the prospect that withdrawal from the larger school district could result in lower school taxes for Starkey landowners. But the main argument, expressed to me by one of the leaders of the movement and corroborated by others who lived in the community at the time, was that "Starkey was in a secondary position, getting the discarded desks, worn-out buses, and so on." It was felt that Starkey was not receiving fair treatment. It is difficult to assess the validity of this complaint, but it is clear that it was mixed with resentment and indignation over the community's subordination to Oak Flat. This resentment was expressed by one community member when he remarked that "we thought that Oak Flat only thought they were better than us because they were bigger." The movement to establish the independence of the Starkey high school reflected in part the local feeling of community autonomy.

The relationship between Oak Flat and the communities of its hinterland was given expression in graphic form by an annual festival, the Homestead Celebration, that was begun in the early 1930s. The event was conducted in Oak Flat, being organized and carried out by the town's civic organizations. The men of Oak Flat and of the outlying communities were exhorted to grow beards for the occasion, and during the last few days before it took place any man who was caught clean-shaven was thrown briefly into a makeshift jail. The windows of the firms in Oak Flat were lined with old pictures of the town and of its dependent communities; there were photographs of early settlers, farmhouses, farm equipment, crops, schools, and stores.

The day of the event was declared a local holiday and the businesses not only of Oak Flat but of its entire hinterland were closed. Large crowds of people traveled to the town from throughout its sphere of influence. An article in the Oak Flat newspaper in 1938 described the event as a "unique celebration, where the people of the town play host to the people of the surrounding country."

The first attraction of the day was a parade made up of entries from the entire region. Outlying communities, including Starkey and Lorraine, normally entered floats in the parade. A typical entry was a scene constructed on a wagon bed and depicting the rigors of pioneer life. Families sometimes entered, riding horseback and dressed in early-day costume. Old farm equipment, grain wagons, and even a small herd of cattle were included in the parade.

A free meal was served at noon in the Oak Flat park, located at the center of the town. Enormous quantities of beans and beef were provided by one of the community organizations, whose members also cooked the food in open barbecue pits. Nailed to trees throughout the park were signs bearing the names of each of the small communities; members of each community congregated and ate at the tree marked with its name.

Every year a leading citizen from Oak Flat or from one of the outlying communities was chosen to occupy the honorary position of marshal, and the Farm Bureau of each community selected a local high-school girl to run for the title of Belle of the Homestead Celebration. The winner of the latter contest came from a different community each year, for selection was based on the principle of rotation, not competition.

The distinctness of each community was graphically represented by the Homestead Celebration, for each locality had its designated spot in the park and each selected its own entry for Belle of the Homestead Celebration, among other things. The preeminence of Oak Flat was also expressed, since the latter was the site of the event and its civic organizations hosted the affair.

The friction between the smaller communities and Oak Flat was also evident. This was manifest in an article written by a Starkey resident and published in the Oak Flat newspaper in the mid-1930s. The article noted that some cynics thought the event was a means to promote business for the merchants of the larger town, but the fact that the firms closed for the day, the writer argued (without sarcasm), showed that the spirit behind the festivities was something other than crass commercialism.

Starkey's relationship with Saint Thomas was more distant than its tie with Oak Flat. For example, although most of the residents of Starkey had at least a few relatives, friends, or acquaintances at the county seat, the merchants there knew the names of only a few of the people from this portion of the county. Yet Starkey's association with Saint Thomas was very important, as is manifest from the role of the Bradford store during the period of settlement. By about the turn of the century commercial establishments closer to home were adequate for most needs, and it was no longer necessary to make the long trip to Saint Thomas to purchase supplies. Still, a variety of other forms of business had to be conducted at the county seat. It was in Saint Thomas that leases and land sales were recorded, taxes were paid, and voting was administered. The superintendent of county schools had responsibilities toward every school district in the county, and his office was in Saint Thomas.

Saint Thomas was also the locus of important political decisions. At the head of the county administration were five county supervisors, each elected by the constituents of a different district. Starkey was part of one of those districts—along with several other nearby communities, including Oak Flat—and was represented by a supervisor on the County Board.

Among the most important decisions made by the supervisors were those concerning the allocation of funds for road work. All the major roads in the county were originally county owned, for it was not until the 1920s that a nationwide road-building program transformed a few of the most important routes into state-maintained thoroughfares. Even after this program was completed, however, most residents lived some distance from the main highways and had to depend heavily on the county road system, which always seemed undernourished.

By controlling allocations for road work, the county supervisors played a very significant role in the lives of the farmers, for whom the task of transporting farm goods to market could be lightened substantially by the improvement of a road where it climbed a difficult grade, or by the addition of a bridge at a key point along the way. Early in the century the issue of road work was important in another way as well, for the county road crews—both road bosses and assistants—were originally farmers and farm workers who supplied their own teams and equipment and undertook the work as a means of augmenting their incomes. The supervisors appointed a number of road bosses and assistants throughout the county, and a usual item at each regular meeting of the Board was the authorization of payment for the work that had been done by these men during the past month. Although road work was only a subsidiary source of income for the road crews, it frequently was a very important one, especially for young farmers who were just starting out and needed cash.

Saint Thomas was the largest and most important town in the county, and yet it was little more than a rural community itself, for in 1940 it had a population of less than 10,000. The United States as a whole was rapidly becoming an urban nation during the first half of this century, but this process was far more advanced elsewhere than in the county of which Starkey is a part.

In sum, soon after the influx of settlers in the late nineteenth century a system of service centers appeared in the inland portion of the county. These were distributed in a fairly orderly pattern according to very practical considerations. Each emerged in response to such basic needs as educating the young, shipping farm produce, and buying food to supplement what was grown at home. The service centers varied in size and importance according to their role in the network, from the isolated, one-room schoolhouse in a remote canyon to the small railroad towns, especially Oak Flat.

Yet there was another side to these centers besides the practical one of serving the settlers' needs. The families living within the sphere of influence of a center entered into social relations and soon were knit into a definable community with its own internal affairs and dynamics. These communities became the basic components of the regional social organization, in that a considerable portion of an individual's social relations were conducted within the context of the local group. What is more, these communities were articulated into a larger structure consisting of a complex of relations of dominance and subordination, attachment and distrust; events and affairs that included more than one community were shaped to a degree by the nature of the relations between the communities involved. This is illustrated by the Homestead Celebration, which graphically illustrates the role of Oak Flat in relation to its social hinterland, and by the hostility emanating from the Starkey high school toward Oak Flat when the Starkey institution was still a branch of the Oak Flat school system.

Chapter **3** Starkey's Social Life

THE CENTRAL HUB of each community played a key role in its existence. The hub drew the local families together, creating a system of
social interaction among them, and served as a symbol by which one
community was distinguished from another. Equally important as the
hub was the social life associated with it. In the opinion of community
members, social affairs were the cornerstone of the locality, giving it
distinction and demonstrating its worth.

Rural sociologists have made detailed studies of certain patterns
of social life in rural America—the average number of organizations
per community, increases and decreases in different types of organization, regional variations in social life, and the like. These writers tend to
regard community affairs largely as a form of recreation. In a study of
rural church life in the middle west in the early 1920s, Benson Y. Landis
(1922:42–43) noted that twenty years prior to his research the people
had not yet formed many social organizations. This, he wrote, was
because they were "busy getting started or settled, or developing their
farms." Presumably there was too much to do to engage in recreation.
But by the time of Landis' study the schools and local organizations,
including the lodges, were a major focus of recreational interest. Similarly, in a book on rural social trends J. H. Kolb and Edmund de S.
Brunner (1933:242) remark that social and recreational organizations in
rural communities "are usually associations, formal or informal in character, designed to help individuals or groups secure more of the
amenities and the enjoyments of life."

Recreation undoubtedly plays an important role in the social life of
rural communities, but viewing local affairs chiefly in that context limits
understanding and leads us to underrate their significance. In Starkey

these affairs should be seen in the context of a local system of values and ideas that collectively form a folk theory or folk sociology by which the people represent their community to themselves and by which they interpret the events that take place there. I refer to this system as the folk theory of community.

Central to this folk theory was the notion that a community is something more than a set of independent individuals, for the concept implied a degree of cohesion and cooperation in events and undertakings of common interest. A community was thought to exist only when a group of people acted together in some way. This idea was not exclusive to Starkey, for it runs deep in western social thought.

The local concept of community in Starkey was not value free, for it contained an ideal that seems to have colored most local events. It was assumed not only that a community *does* exhibit cooperation, cohesion, and collective action but that it *should* do so. Communities are strong or weak according to the nature and extent of their common social life, and regions that lack a community life altogether—and therefore are not communities—lack merit.

The evaluative aspect of the folk theory of community was expressed in a form that has been widely observed in American localities, both urban and rural. This is the pattern of boosterism or the spirit of local improvement. This in turn seems to be related to a notion with a venerable history in western society—the notion of progress.

The concept of progress was a fundamental ingredient of the beliefs of homesteaders and other settlers on the American frontier in the nineteenth century. The historian Merle Curti (1959:116–18) has sketched the characteristics of this idea among at least some of the rural people of Trempealeau County, Wisconsin, during the several decades before 1900, when the area was being settled. The people there conceived of the frontier as a place of opportunity where free land was available and a man could advance himself. It was believed that frontier conditions were uniquely suited to foster such attributes as independence, energy, and perseverance—the very qualities on which progress depended—and that in this respect the frontiersman was superior to the people living in the settled East. Such technological developments as the railroad, the telegraph, and electricity also lent weight to the notion of progress.

The emergence of towns on the frontier was especially suggestive of the advance of civilization. Areas that had once been untamed were transformed by the railroad and plow, and small villages seemed to spring up everywhere. These were thought of as standing at the very beginning of a trajectory of growth, for each of them aspired to become a metropolis—or at least a center for trade and shipping. This process of growth was not left to the vicissitudes of fate, however, for virtually every town undertook programs to stimulate its own advancement and improvement.

Lewis Atherton (1954:330–57), in a historical study of small towns in the Midwest, has supplied a clear picture of the spirit of impovement that prevailed there:

Men enamored with the idea of progress established country towns in order to share in the blessings which lay ahead. To them, the present was superior to the past, and the future held even greater promise. For the town itself, progress meant growth, growth in population and real-estate values. Everywhere, associations of businessmen crusaded in behalf of local progress [1954:330].

Booster groups emerged bearing such names as Business Men's Association, Improvement Association, Retail Merchants' Association, Board of Trade, Commercial Club, and later, Chamber of Commerce (p. 332). These organizations sought to bring factories into town—often by offering bonuses or subsidies; they undertook programs that would improve transportation, induce population growth, encourage trade with hometown businesses, and foster hometown loyalty.

Atherton and others (e.g., Veblen 1923a:418) have stressed the commercial element in small-town boosterism. In Atherton's account the ends usually sought by booster groups were higher real-estate values, jobs, and economic prosperity for the merchant. But normally the local spirit of improvement contained another element as well. This was the notion of cultural uplift, for the intellectual and moral betterment of the community was regarded as an indispensable part of its development (see Wright 1955:81–122, 226–36). The frontier community wanted to become not only as wealthy but also as sophisticated and refined as its counterpart in the East. Page Smith (1966:162, 169) notes that after the Civil War community organizations began to flourish in the small towns in America, and that among the most common organizations to appear were debating, lecture, and library societies. These groups were of an "improving" nature, for they were "designed to draw the community together and to elevate it."

The spirit of improvement seems to have undergone fundamental changes in the twentieth century, largely because the fortune of the small American community has suffered considerably and its optimism has faded. Most country towns stopped growing long ago and began losing their sons and daughters to the city. The small community acquired the reputation of a stifling, drab, and backward place, an image that was solemnized in Sinclair Lewis' *Main Street.* The spirit of improvement lost much of its ambitiousness, often becoming merely a self-conscious adulation of the hometown.

But in many localities an important element of the nineteenth-century spirit of improvement survived (see Moline 1971). This was the sentiment that the community should not be allowed simply to "happen"—that its development, however limited, should not be left completely to chance but should be taken firmly in hand. Small-town boosterism in the twentieth century may be a pale reflection of what existed before 1900, but the continuity is clear.

The spirit of improvement that prevailed in Starkey before 1940 was far more modest—and realistic—than that which characterized the country towns of the late nineteenth century. A number of major collective achievements were undertaken in Starkey, and in part these may have been motivated to promote the commercial welfare of the community. An example was the successful attempt to have a highway routed through the town, thereby increasing business and ensuring the improvement of roads leading to and from the community hub. But Starkey conceived of itself as a farm community rather than a business center, and it had little aspiration for commercial development. Community activities were generally directed toward improving and increasing the noncommercial attractions of the locality: constructing a community hall, a park, a swimming pool, and the like, rather than enticing manufacturing firms to locate there.

The chief focus of Starkey's spirit of improvement was not commercial but social. According to the folk theory of community, a crucial characteristic of a progressive, enterprising town was an active social life. Even if it was impossible to grow in size and to challenge the economic and political hegemony of Oak Flat or Saint Thomas, Starkey could show that it was a wide-awake, go-ahead town by exhibiting a vigorous community spirit. A locality that did so was thought to be healthy and wholesome—it was a creditable place to spend one's life and to raise children[1]—whereas a town lacking these characteristics was stagnant and unwholesome. Throughout its history Starkey is said to have had activities and events in which "everyone" participated. The term *everyone* is clearly an exaggeration, but a significant one. It is not a statement of fact but the expression of an ideal and a form of community boosting. What is more, social pressure was apparently applied to those who failed to appear at these events. At least in theory, participation in local events was a "contribution" to the community and was rewarded with esteem.

The inadequacy of viewing the local social life as a form of recreation is patent. The desire for recreation may have been an important motivation behind the community members' participation, but the desire to make Starkey a strong and vigorous community, together with the social pressure to "contribute" toward that end, was equally if not more important.

In addition to the idea that Starkey ought to exhibit a vigorous social life, the folk theory of community contained another component, which might be termed the focus on moral uplift. Most of the settlers were very religious in outlook, and in their attempt to create a self-respecting community they saw themselves as engaged in a struggle against disreputable forces. An early manifestation of this sentiment was mentioned earlier: the first commercial establishment on Starkey Flat, a saloon, was a source of moral concern to the newcomers and was soon forced to close. I will discuss the focus on moral uplift in detail later in the chapter.

Starkey's theory of community is manifest in the local self-image, for it was felt that the town was reasonably successful in achieving a high level of social life and moral uplift. According to this self-image, Starkey was unusual in its ability to pull together in the pursuit of common ends—such as the construction of a community hall—and to sustain an active community social life. These attributes seem to have been noted by the members of neighboring communities, for Starkey was viewed by others as a particularly cohesive and lively town with more community spirit than most. Starkey was also thought to adhere to notably high moral standards. By contrast, Saint George was viewed as a shameless and unprincipled community. One person remarked, "If someone said to me they were from Saint George I'd have thought they came from an evil, loose environment." It was in Saint George that prostitution was allowed to flourish during World War II (in truth not because of local indulgence but because a military base had opened nearby). But the social events in Starkey were thought to be dominated by the church and to be both wholesome and respectable, as is illustrated by the severe restrictions placed on drinking by the force of public opinion.

The statements that follow reveal the self-image that prevailed in Starkey. The first is that of a person who lived in the community most of his life. He was a student in the Starkey schools during the 1940s, and his remark refers to that decade:

Starkey always did maintain a total community. It had everything but a clothing store or a drugstore. The basic needs for life were there, it was self-sustaining that way. It also had its social life. Other places had to send their kids out to high school, no other place this size had a high school. . . . Starkey had a highway. It had everything. I used to think we were at the crossroads of the world here. . . . In many ways Starkey was a leader in what a small town can do. They had a high school, Conservation Club, they had all these things, they proved what people could do even though they were a small community. I know what it was—it was that all the other towns but Oak Flat thought Starkey was better than them.

The following is the view of a man who moved to Starkey as a young adult during the early 1930s:

[These small communities in the vicinity of Oak Flat] are all the same in that they are quite old, and they have old-timers who have lived there through all the years. They have people of the second and third generations living in them. This is the common denominator. . . . [But] Starkey is flavored by the church quite a bit; the others have had churches which have been an influence, but Starkey's church has been more influential than theirs. [Several of these small communities] have always been pretty rough. . . . Starkey has more community spirit than the other communities. Probably all the communities feel the same— that their community has more spirit. It's true that all these communities have a bond and a tie that the larger towns lose. But Starkey got together and got itself a park. Saint George couldn't get together to do this. . . . All the towns around here have a drinking element. Up until recently, when the old-timers got too old to fight, they have kept liquor out of Starkey. Until recently a liquor license had never been acquired in Starkey.

The next statement is that of a Starkey farmer who was born in the community at about the turn of the century:

[The small communities in the vicinity of Oak Flat] are similar in that the old-time families have stuck around for so long. . . . But the thing that Starkey had on them all is that Starkey has had more key men [community leaders] than all of them put together. You could take [all of these small communities], pick the twelve best men, and Starkey would be on top.

A variety of annual or occasional social events served to reinforce Starkey's self-image as a community-spirited and active town. These were events in which "everyone" is said to have participated. They were explicitly referred to as community events, implying that participation or attendance was a contribution to the community.

The May Day and Christmas Eve celebrations continued to be the annual events of greatest importance after the turn of the century, although both seem to have lost much of their standing by 1920. By then a variety of other activities had emerged.

One of these was baseball. Starkey had its own team, which belonged to a league made up of ball clubs from a number of nearby communities. Home games were played on Sunday afternoons on the diamond behind the hotel, and the sidelines were crowded with specta-tors—especially if the game happened to be with either Lorraine or Oak Flat, Starkey's major rivals. Even out-of-town games attracted Starkey spectators, for those with automobiles sometimes packed picnic lunches and followed their team to what they hoped would be a hometown victory. A manager handled all the arrangements with the other teams, and he was formally in charge of the ball club. In addition, a captain assigned the team members to their respective positions and was responsible for decisions relating to the game. The manager's position was always held by Brian Green, one of the most successful leaders in community affairs, whereas the position of captain rotated among the team members. Dances were occasionally held to raise money for equipment and uniforms.

The high school also began supplying a series of important com-munity events after its founding in the 1920s. High-school basketball and baseball teams played in league competition with other schools in the county—including the Oak Flat and Saint Thomas schools—and these games enjoyed a wide following in Starkey. The high school occasionally presented plays and concerts in the Community Hall, where it also held commencement exercises. Baccalaureate services were conducted in the church. A "community fair" held in 1940 provides a glimpse of the role played by the high school in Starkey's social life. The fair was organized by the students and held on the school grounds, but all the community organizations participated by providing exhibits and concession booths. According to the school annual, approximately 1,200 people attended, some of them members of nearby communities.

Attendance at high-school events was not restricted to the teachers and the students' parents, for a sizable cross-section of the community was usually present. These were conceived of as "community events." One person illustrated the matter of attendance with the following example: an old bachelor might not go to a school play or to commencement exercises by himself, but it would not be unusual for a neighbor to offer to take him, and he would probably accept.

The growing importance of the high school in Starkey's social life was due in part to the increasing emphasis on secondary education, but Tony Giles, the high-school principal in the 1930s and 1940s, was also a factor. He was unusually adept at mobilizing community support—he became one of Starkey's primary leaders—and managed thus to focus local attention on school athletic events, plays, concerts, and the like. His wife was also remarkably enterprising. She taught music at the high school, and the orchestra and chorus began an active program of public performances in the community under her direction.

Another event that grew to prominence during the 1920s was the Ladies Aid Bazaar, held each year in the Community Hall to raise money for charitable causes. Well in advance of the event the women prepared crochet and embroidery work that would be offered for sale at the Bazaar, and on the day of the event they prepared a chicken pie dinner to be purchased by those in attendance. After dinner the women usually presented a play.

In the mid-1930s a few of the Methodists undertook a Christmas program in the sanctuary of the church, and within two or three years the audiences were so large that the production had to be moved to the

Community Hall. By the end of the 1930s this was one of the two major events of the year (the other being the Ladies Aid Bazaar). Although this was originally a church-oriented affair, planned and staged chiefly by church members, it was also a community affair, as is manifest from the name it bore in the high-school annual. The school always had a Christmas party, which was designated as a school event; the latter was explicitly distinguished from the Community Christmas Program sponsored by the church.

The format of the performance varied somewhat from year to year, although a religious pageant was always presented. The pageant usually consisted of a series of narrated scenes depicting the Nativity, accompanied by selections sung by the Sunday School children; the high-school chorus provided entertainment during scene changes. After the pageant Santa Claus—played by one of the community leaders—gave small sacks of candy and oranges to the children, and then he presented "joke gifts" to the adults. (One year, for example, he gave a fire extinguisher to a merchant whose store had recently burned to the ground.)

In addition to these annual or periodic events, Starkey's social life included a variety of community organizations whose primary goal was to promote the interests of the community. The voluntary associations thus became the vehicle for the local spirit of improvement.

Several organizations existed in Starkey before and immediately following the turn of the century, but except fot the church none of them played a significant role in local affairs and all have vanished virtually without trace. The first strictly secular organization to leave its mark on Starkey was the Pleasure Seekers, begun in the mid-teens.

Since the turn of the century dances and other events had been held occasionally in Turner Hall, the barn that doubled as a community meeting place. But some people desired a more organized social life, and in 1914 a small group of "younger people"—the unmarried people who liked to dance—began their own organization. "There was nothing at that time but the church, and the young people in Starkey wanted something social." So they instituted the Pleasure Seekers in order to provide community dances and other recreational events, including plays and, on at least one occasion, a Christmas program in Turner Hall. Both the name and the organization were "snickered at by the old people," however. Within a short time the members also began to feel that the group was "a useless thing," and their enthusiasm began to flag. As a result, at one of the regular meetings it was proposed that the club should "reorganize and become something for everyone in the community,not just the young people." [2]

In the spring of 1919 a number of posters were placed in store windows advertising a general community meeting. According to the minutes of the meeting, its purpose was to consider the creation of an "Improvement Club such as other towns have," and a leading goal of the group was the construction of a community hall. Turner Hall had become unusable: The building was so unstable that it shook when people danced in it, and since it was nothing more than the upper floor of a barn it was quite cold during the winter. Perhaps it was also felt that Turner Hall was too undignified for a community like Starkey, a sentiment that may have been stimulated by plans to build community halls in nearby towns.

Building the structure was the club's major preoccupation but not its sole concern, for the group's mission included the general improvement of the community. The bylaws of the group list the following goals:

1. The purpose of this club is to stimulate and concentrate the public opinion and public spirit of the people of Starkey and the surrounding vicinity, for the upbuilding and improvement of the same in every way possible.
2. To raise funds for and equip as our funds may justify, a public building that will be to Starkey a Civic Centre.
3. To improve and beautify the streets by grading and planting trees, and any other improvements that may appear at the time necessary.

At the third meeting of the organization an Observation Committee was appointed; this was defined in the minutes as "a committee which observes and brings before the club any matters that may need attention, that will discuss subjects of general interest and promotion of improvement in Starkey."

During its first few years the Improvement Club initiated or became involved in a number of programs of general interest. For example, in 1919 the organization provided Starkey's entry in the Oak Flat Armistice Day parade. According to the minutes, "A motion was made, seconded and carried that the Improvement Club take up the matter of Armistice Day preparations and carry out Starkey's plans for entering into the parade in Oak Flat." The minutes for 1920 also reveal several discussions regarding plans for the new high school in Starkey, and on one occasion the county superintendent of schools attended a meeting of the Improvement Club to discuss the issue with the community. During the same year the minutes expressed the group's concern about the Starkey cemetery, the deed to which was held by the Methodist Church. The grounds were in need of attention, and it was felt that trees should be planted. The club voted to try to have the county assume jurisdiction over the cemetery and ensure its upkeep by levying taxes for this purpose. The club circulated petitions within the community requesting the supervisors to accept this proposal, and then succeeded in bringing about the change. At one of the Improvement Club meetings it was proposed that the group try to get a branch of the county library located in Starkey; this project too was successful.

The club played a major role in several May Day celebrations. According to the minutes for 1921, "A committee was appointed by our president to talk to the people of the community in regard to having a May Day picnic here in Starkey, to find out how the people felt about a picnic this year." The picnic was held, and the Improvement Club provided the Maypole and appointed a cleanup committee. It also put on a play, and in the evening it held a dance for which it charged an admission fee.

The Starkey Improvement Club quickly became the springboard for community-wide programs of action. According to one Starkey resident, it represented the "organized outcrop of what went on informally before the club existed."

The construction of the Community Hall had to wait until 1923, when sufficient funds had been raised to proceed with the project. Plays, dances, socials, and dinners were held in the Starkey grammar school to make money, and donations were solicited from community members. The total cost of the building was about $4,500, and when construction was begun probably not more than half that amount had been raised. The rest was provided by a bank loan.

Construction required a considerable amount of collective effort. At least one full-time carpenter was hired to supervise the task, but most of the work was donated. The dance floor alone was 40 feet wide and 80 feet long; the building also included a stage, two anterooms, and, beneath the rear half of the building, a basement that served as a dining hall. Farmers, farm workers, pump station employees, and store workers donated their time and equipment, excavating the basement, hauling lumber from Oak Flat, and assisting in construction. The high-school boys spent much of their physical-education time working on the building.

After the hall had been completed, money was raised to pay the bank loan, primarily by conducting public dances after which hot suppers were served. Other communities throughout the county had clubs similar to Starkey's, and they too were building or had built halls and were conducting public dances to pay for them. These events attracted people from well beyond the host community, and Starkey's were no exception, for they were advertised several days in advance in the Oak Flat newspaper and movie theater.[3]

The dances were money-making events and not community affairs, and this sometimes led to problems, since Starkey was a more sober community than some of its neighbors. A number of the participants at the dances drank bootleg liquor, and some became quite boisterous. The dances soon became unpopular within the community, but they were continued as an economic necessity.

The membership records of the Improvement Club show that the number of dues-paying members was high at first but fell off sharply. Nearly 120 people were on the rolls at the beginning, although many apparently conceived of their first month's dues payment as an expression of support for the organization and not as a commitment to participate in its affairs. Within three months the membership had dropped to about 90 people, and it continued to decline by 5 or 10 members a year until 1925, when it fell to a mere 23. By 1927 only 13 stalwarts remained.

It is impossible to say how many people attended the monthly meetings, although as many as 50 to 70 probably did so on occasions when plays or other forms of entertainment were presented. Clearly, however, most of the meetings did not attract large crowds, and the main community events in Starkey—those that drew the greatest numbers of people—remained occasional affairs such as the Ladies Aid Bazaar.

The importance of the Improvement Club should not be assessed from attendance figures or membership lists, neither of which are as revealing as the projects that were undertaken by the group. At least at the beginning, the Improvement Club was conceived of as the legitimate instrument for conducting the affairs of the community, and people who devoted little time to its organizational details were usually concerned about what it did and how it proceeded. What is more, the community leaders were represented on the organization's elected board of directors. They used the Improvement Club as a vehicle for their leadership roles and in turn gave the group an effectiveness in dealing with local affairs that It would have lacked otherwise.

By the mid-1920s, however, the Improvement Club had lost most of its authority, partly because it had been eclipsed by the emergence of yet another organization, the Starkey Farm Bureau.

The national Farm Bureau movement, which was largely a response to difficulties faced by American agriculture in the 1920s and 1930s, sought both to establish cooperatives among farmers and to influence farm legislation at the state and national levels. The Farm Bureau was given official support by the government through the Extension Service, a hybrid organization drawing sustenance from the U.S. Department of Agriculture and the land grant colleges. The Extension Service had been created by Congress for the improvement of farming through education, and county farm agents were appointed in each county to carry out this program. When the Extension Service undertook the sponsorship of the Farm Bureau, the farm agent became directly involved in the local Farm Bureau centers within his county, and he performed his educational services within the framework of the county Farm Bureau organization.

During the early 1920s the Farm Bureau was becoming organized in the county in which Starkey is located, and every small community nearby soon had its own center. The directors of each, together with the farm agent, whose office was in Saint Thomas, formed a county-wide board of directors.

Late in 1921 "the people of Starkey met to organize a Farm Center," as the minutes of the first meeting note. Officers were elected, and the center was soon under way. The meeting was apparently instigated by several leaders in the community, all farmers, and they were the ones who were elected to office.

Meetings were held monthly at the Community Hall once that had been built, and the organization attracted fairly large crowds at least some of the time.[4] Like the Improvement Club, however, the Farm Bureau was unable to sustain widespread public interest in its regular meetings, and the major community events continued to be annual affairs such as the Community Christmas Program. It seems likely that the Farm Bureau would have had an even shorter life span[5] if the farm agent had not been so determined in his efforts to stimulate local support for the group. According to one of the leaders. "It was always hard to keep it going in Starkey. I never felt Starkey had much enthusiasm for the Farm Bureau."

At each meeting the farm agent usually led a discussion about some matter related to farming, such as new varieties of grain or how to prevent cattle diseases. Candidates for political office and members of other Farm Bureau centers sometimes spoke. Occasionally a skit or play was performed by members of the organization or their children, but more frequently the high school orchestra, chorus, or string ensemble performed. Talent from outside the community was sometimes arranged for by the farm agent. According to one Farm Bureau member, "The greatest attraction of the Farm Bureau was the social part." Another remarked,

At first the whole family went to the Farm Bureau, into the early 1930s, as I remember. The women put on a big feed in the basement, and there were games for the kids. The meeting came first. There were people hanging around talking until 12:30 or 1:00 in the morning. And the farm agent was always the last to leave, even though it was a two-and-a-half-hour drive to Saint Thomas [where he lived] then.

In principle, the Starkey Farm Bureau was an organization of farmers, and it was oriented toward serving their needs. Membership provided such economic benefits as lower gasoline prices, group rate insurance, and access to a cooperatively owned seed-cleaning machine. But the Farm Bureau was not solely a farm group. An employee of the state road crew remarked that his family frequently attended and that it was not uncommon for other nonagriculturalists to do so. The high-school principal, Tony Giles, was an active participant during the 1930s and 1940s, for according to the minutes he frequently made announcements and assisted with organizational matters, although he did not hold formal office.

What is more, the Farm Bureau did not direct its attention exclusively toward the farmer and his problems, for it focused on community improvement as well, and it became the chief organized means for doing so. According to the minutes for 1922, almost an entire meeting was devoted to the new high school (which at that time was part of the Oak Flat school system):

The members discussed different phases of the Starkey High School and decided that they would make every effort to obtain another teacher in our high school next term. Henry Turner, [a Starkey resident and] High School trustee, spoke on the expense of the other teacher and pledged his support in every way. Charles Thomas also addressed the meeting in behalf of the Lorraine patrons of the High School.

In 1926 a committee of Farm Bureau members was appointed to oversee the planting of trees and the pouring of concrete walks at the high school, and later, in 1930, the organization voted "to set out trees and shrubs in the cemetery." In the late 1930s a committee was appointed to "ask the County Supervisors about getting a place fixed near Starkey for dumping garbage," and letters were sent to "local business concerns" informing them about a discussion of the "garbage subject" to be held at the next meeting. When the Homestead Celebration was begun in Oak Flat its instigators decided to solicit the community's support and participation, and they attended a meeting of the Starkey Farm Bureau to do so. During the 1930s the Farm Bureau also assumed responsibility for the maintenance of the Community Hall: it purchased and installed a furnace and, later, a curtain for the stage; hired a janitor and paid his salary; repaired the roof; and so forth.

The Farm Bureau had become the leading organization in the community. One person remarked, "Prior to the Farm Bureau there were the Pleasure Seekers and the Improvement Club. The Farm Bureau became the central social activity in Starkey, encompassing all these other organizations." Another said, "The Farm Bureau took over the role of maintaining the community."

In the 1930s yet another organization began in Starkey, and it provides a striking contrast with the ones discussed so far. On the one hand, unlike the Improvement Club or Farm Bureau, it was never conceived of as a community organization—it never enjoyed widespread support, did not attract widespread interest, and was not considered a legitimate vehicle for the management of local affairs. On the other hand, this group was closely associated with a segment of the community that had a reputation for contrariness, an issue that will be discussed shortly. In spite of these facts, however, the group seems to have been drawn inexorably toward programs of community improvement.

This organization was the Starkey Women's Club, begun in 1934 by Hazel Joseph. Mrs. Joseph was an active and effective leader, but her morals were considered questionable by many members of the community because she ran bars in both Howard and Starkey. The women who joined the club were, for the most part, looked upon with disfavor by what I call the Starkey establishment.

The Women's Club was affiliated with both a county and a state association of women's clubs, and a portion of the members' dues supported the larger associations. In addition, visits to and from other clubs occasionally took place, and a few of the members from Starkey periodically attended regional conventions held elsewhere in California.

Originally one of the chief goals of the group was the cultural uplift of its members, for meetings included talks or discussions about such topics as the opera, theater, or literature.[6] At one meeting in 1935 the following readings were presented: "Ibsen, the Man and His Plays," "Norwegian Music and Grief," and "The Story of Peer Gynt." "The Peer Gynt Suite" was then played as a piano duet. At the next club meeting it was suggested that if it was not always possible "to have speakers with us at our meetings, we should study different subjects, such as opera and different parts of our country." One person remarked that the Women's Club "started out as the intellectuals in Starkey." Another stated that it was "Starkey's first attempt at society. Some of the members were educated, they wanted something above the Ladies' Aid. It was an intellectual group."

The interest in intellectual matters soon abated, and by 1937 the minutes show little evidence of the earlier desire for cultural uplift. Rather, two other concerns had come to dominate the organization. One was the desire for social entertainment. Immediately following the business meeting the members entered into conversation and were served refreshments. The other was raising money, for the Women's Club was deeply involved in public-spirited projects. A large share of each business meeting was devoted to planning such money-making events as card parties, dances, dinners, food sales, and raffles.

Among the deeds undertaken by the Women's Club were contributions to such charitable institutions as welfare organizations, orphanages, and homes for the aged, all located outside of Starkey. But these contributions represented an insignificant fraction of the expenditures of the group, which concentrated most of its attention on improvements within the community itself.

The Women's Club—and particularly its president, Mrs. Joseph—played a key role in acquiring the Starkey park. The minutes of the organization reveal a series of discussions concerning the matter, and the negotiations that took place between Mrs. Joseph and the park's donor were followed in detail by the members. The acquisition of the park was a major community undertaking and will be discussed at length in another chapter.

Once the park had been acquired, the Women's Club proceeded to build a clubhouse on the grounds. Although this structure would belong to the club, it would also be available for public use and was conceived of by the members as a contribution to the community. But the organization had little success in convincing other community members of the legitimacy of the project. Most people seem to have regarded the proposed new building as a private matter concerning the club alone and not as a community venture at all. It is significant that in the records of the Women's Club the building was always referred to simply as the Clubhouse, never as the Community Clubhouse.

The women's group was under severe strain to pay for the building, which cost a little over $2,000 to construct. Bonds were placed on sale, but surprisingly few were purchased. Public dances, held at the Community Hall, were the principal sources of revenue, but they were boisterous events attracting large numbers of people from out of town, and they enjoyed little favor within Starkey. According to a person who belonged to the Women's Club, "It got to be a rather bad crowd, going into people's yards and throwing beer bottles around. The community didn't like the dances, but what other way is there to raise money?"

Construction of the Clubhouse was begun in January 1939. Work proceeded at a halting pace, since each new step had to wait until sufficient money had been raised. It soon became clear that at that rate it would be a long while before the building was completed, so a bank loan was acquired, and finally, in the summer of 1940, the building was done—although the dances were continued for another several years in order to pay for the structure. The labor was provided almost solely by a hired carpenter. Unlike the Community Hall, the Clubhouse attracted virtually no collective effort whatever, and the high-school students played no part in its construction.

The Women's Club undertook other projects. It provided funds for a septic tank and a drinking fountain at the Community Hall, the work being done, according to the minutes, by community members. The organization also attempted to have an additional traffic officer assigned to the highway that ran through town, and it helped pay the power bill for the Christmas lights decorating the trees in the park.

The Women's Club was quite willing to contribute to the improvement of Starkey, but in doing so it was all but rebuffed by the community. It was not a community organization in the same sense as the others.

I will return to the Women's Club at the end of this chapter, but before doing so it is necessary to turn to a feature of the local theory of community mentioned earlier—the focus on moral uplift—and then to discuss what I call the establishment division.[7]

The focus on moral respectability seems to have centered largely on the issue of alcohol, for drinking was conceived of as a major source of evil. Early in this century one of the leading figures in the drive against liquor in Starkey was Agnes Thompson, who was referred to locally as Aunt Agnes. She was a large, forceful person, a midwife who delivered more than seventy children in Starkey, an active member of the Methodist Church, and the epitome of rectitude. Aunt Agnes was openly at odds with those who used alcohol and was the spokeswoman and symbol of the nondrinkers. John Wright, the hotel owner, was seen as her arch-opponent and as the representative of the drinking element in Starkey. He was a very genial and gregarious man but was also an atheist who enthusiastically defended his beliefs. Wright was known as the saloon keeper because he ran a bar in his establishment. The saloon attracted mostly young, unmarried men—cowboys and other hired workers—as well as out-of-towners.

Two anecdotes concerning Wright and Aunt Agnes were still told in the community in the mid-1960s. Both stories had symbolic significance, for they expressed a general principle behind local organization: the division between drinkers and nondrinkers. On one occasion Aunt Agnes' retarded son, a young adult, was discovered drinking in the saloon, and she reputedly charged into the barroom, struck Wright on the face, grabbed her son by the arm, and took him home. On another occasion a confrontation of a different kind occurred. When Starkey's supervisoral district voted dry by local option in 1911 the saloon was forced to close. Wright held a small party for his customers immediately before the new law took effect. Aunt Agnes appeared at the gathering, shook his hand, wished him luck, and abruptly left. It is worth noting that Wright, who symbolized the drinkers, comes out second-best in both tales.

The local norms regulating the use of alcohol were clear-cut. In theory at least, drinking was not done at all by respectable people, although some may have taken small to moderate amounts in private. One person remarked that "the nondrinkers used to completely dominate Starkey."

Restrictive drinking norms were apparently quite common in small towns across the country, and turn-of-the-century community studies throw light on the patterns found in Starkey. One of these studies was conducted in a small Indiana town called Aton (a pseudonym). According to Sims (1912:106–7), there were few businessmen in Aton

who dare to enter a saloon on a business errand, to say nothing of drinking. To do so invites suspicion and severe criticism. The attorney who defends the violator of the liquor law is severely censured. Liquor would be tolerated at no public function. A few cases where it is brought to homes in private packages are looked upon as "disgraceful practices for respectable people." The occasional drinker is not considered a worthy citizen, and few will repose confidence in him. The young man who dares to drink loses the esteem of "right-thinking people," and is "a nobody." No church member would think of using liquor as a beverage.

James M. Williams (1906:188) wrote an account of a late nineteenth-century country town located in the northeastern part of the United States in which he remarked on "the intensity of the abhorrence of the saloon-keeper, of the intemperate man, of the moderate drinker, and, in fact, of any person who stopped short of total abstinence."

In Starkey, even though most people adhered to the norm of abstinence in public, drinking was still done. One person commented that "during Improvement Club days there were a lot of people who were drinkers on the sly, but when it came down to an issue they sided with the non-drinkers. But then there was also the hard-core drinking group." Another stated that

drinking never came out in the open. The drinkers drank in a drinking shack somewhere or in a parked car. But they would never do it publicly. Today you'll hear people defend drinking—Bradford, for example. In those days, though, a person wouldn't defend drinking, unless perhaps he was in the drinking shack. But he wouldn't defend it in the open, the community would squelch it quick if he did. At the Improvement Club dances the drinkers would go outside to drink.

Another person explained the drinking patterns with the remark, "It used to be that public drinking was limited to inside the bar, outside the dance hall, and quietly at brandings."

Even those who were among the regular drinkers in the community adhered to a definite set of norms, for they drank in such a way that their tippling was not visible to nondrinkers. Normally they drank at the saloon in the hotel until that closed, and then at the bar when that opened in the 1930s. Some of the men attending community events had bottles in their coat pockets and would step quietly outside to drink. At dances they concealed their bottles in the trunks of automobiles, and several at a time would saunter out into the dark to imbibe. A shack on the outskirts of town was sometimes used for drinking parties by a small group of men. But once the individual was back among nondrinkers— when he stepped out of the saloon and onto the streets of Starkey, for example, or when he returned to the Community Hall after quietly taking a drink—he behaved as soberly as possible.

The Methodist church—which was strongly committed to the principle of temperance—was conceived of as a highly influential force in local affairs. For example, a person who had arrived in the community during the 1930s remarked that "the church pretty well had the say of everything when I first came," and others referred to the church as the center of the community.

The Methodists were credited in local thought not only with keeping drinking to a minimum but also with creating a generally moral atmosphere at such events as Improvement Club and Farm Bureau meetings, which were regarded as wholesome affairs for the entire family. Sims expressed a similar belief in his study of Aton. He wrote (1912:99, 104) that "if the unusual pressure [from the church] . . . were removed, many would freely indulge in forbidden things"; "as great numbers have come into the church, morals have improved" (see also Atherton 1954:255).

But the supposed importance of the Starkey church was not reflected in the size of the gatherings on Sunday mornings, for except on such occasions as Easter the sanctuary was seldom full during worship services. Shortly after the turn of the century most of the Presbyterians had moved away from Starkey, and those who remained joined the Methodists to form a single, united congregation. At the core of this congregation was a small nucleus, never more than twenty people, who were especially devout. They were quite fundamentalist in viewpoint, for they opposed dancing in addition to liquor. These were the most dedicated church goers, and they undertook most of the routine duties associated with running a parish. A somewhat larger number of people were less strict in their religious views and less active in church affairs but frequently attended weekly services. This group gradually merged with a far larger body of residents who seldom attended on Sunday mornings but were regarded as church supporters.

In truth, the Starkey Methodists did not wield the organized sanctions that would have been necessary for them to exert the influence attributed to them. The church could seem influential only because it expressd the moral principles to which a majority of the community already adhered.

The church did tend to dominate local affairs in one sense, however: it played a key role in a substantial number of social events in the community. In this respect the similarity between Starkey and Aton is again notable. According to Sims (1912:64, 110), "The church is easily the most dominant social force in Aton, leading reforms, promoting improvements, and directing pleasure"; a majority of the "pleasurable functions" in the Indiana community—including parties, receptions, dinners, and musical concerts—were held under church auspices.

Among the Starkey social events directly associated with the church were the Christmas Program and the Ladies Aid Bazaar mentioned earlier. A large portion of the children of Starkey also attended Sunday School, many of them unaccompanied by their parents, who were apparently more interested in giving their children a religious upbringing than in their own salvation. One person remarked, with some exaggeration, that "every kid in town went to Sunday School."

The Ladies Aid was associated with the Methodist Church, although it enjoyed a degree of independence and was not a mere appendage of the congregation. The membership of the Ladies Aid included many other women besides those who were actively involved in the church—it had about 100 members throughout most of the 1930s and 1940s, although meetings were seldom attended by more than 20 or 30 people. One person offered the following description of the organization: "It truly was an organization of church women, but other people joined, too. A lot of them weren't church members, and they didn't come to many of the Ladies Aid meetings." Those who seldom attended meetings were called upon to assist with such activities as the annual Bazaar, which required a considerable amount of collective effort. The Ladies Aid also undertook an active role in the social life of the community, for, in addition to offering the Bazaar each year, the group apparently played a part in planning and organizing such events as the May Day picnics and the Christmas Eve celebrations at the church.

The local importance of the church is also signified by the role it played in funerals, for the death of a community member automatically brought the church into action. Originally the body was prepared for burial by members of the community and a small group of people remained with it around the clock. By the late 1920s, however, the automobile and the highway had made it possible to take the body to a funeral home in Oak Flat, and it was not returned until shortly before the funeral began.

Soon after the death occurred, a group of men gathered at the Starkey cemetery to dig the grave. A few got to be regarded as the "regular" gravediggers, although others inevitably assisted. Help was never wanting. So many were on hand that a person sometimes had little chance to dig, and those waiting their turn would sit in groups around the grave talking.

Regardless of what the relationship between the congregation and the deceased may have been, the funeral was always held in the church, and the services were conducted either by the minister or by Arnold Donelson, an active member of the church who was a particularly gifted speaker and a major community leader. A small choir made up of a few of the most devout church members sang at these events— "they were always asked, and would have been disappointed not to have been asked." The funerals in Starkey were as widely attended as they were solemn.

Funeral rites created the appearance of unity in Starkey, yet this was deceptive, for an important effect of Starkey's spirit of improvement was the development of a deep-seated division in the community. This was perhaps inevitable, since any concerted attempt to better the locality would naturally lead to differences of opinion over just what constituted "improvement" and how to achieve it, while an emphasis on moral respectability would tend to produce disagreements over standards of conduct. In spite of Starkey's image as a cohesive community with a strong local *esprit*—and a marked ability to achieve collective undertakings—its people were very much at odds with one another.

The two opposing factions or segments of the community were not solidary, cohesive groups and did not engage in acts of open hostility. Rather, the animosity dividing them tended to remain submerged— opponents normally restricted their attacks to the private sphere of gossip, where scandal and ridicule could be used effectively and with a degree of safety. The community had a deceptively placid appearance on the surface.

I will refer to this factional division as the establishment–nonestablishment division, and the two alignments will be referred to as the establishment and the nonestablishment. These are not the terms the community members themselves would employ, for they used such expressions as "detractors" and "contributors," or "those who tried to run the community" and "those who refused to be cowed." The difficulty with using the local expressions is that they are hardly neutral. For example, the terms *contributors* and *detractors* are biased in favor of the establishment, or toward the "contributors." [8]

The two sides of the division agreed on a number of issues, such as the importance of a strong community spirit and of local improvement programs. But they differed fundamentally in their interpretations of the way in which local affairs were conducted. The two sides had opposing folk theories concerning the very organization of Starkey.

What distinguished the nonestablishment from the establishment was the view that local affairs were dominated by a certain segment of the community. The nonestablishment held that in the Improvement Club, the Farm Bureau, the Ladies Aid Society, and virtually every other community organization or event, the opinions of a vaguely defined and loosely coordinated group of individuals prevailed. It was also felt that this coterie was highly judgmental, for these people were censorious toward anyone who happened not to contribute—such as a woman who did not donate needlework to be sold at the Ladies Aid Bazaar—and unsparing in their criticism of anyone who disagreed with the way local affairs were conducted.

The establishment exhibited a diametrically opposite viewpoint. They felt that the affairs of the community were managed well and in a democratic fashion, and that the disagreement that emanated from the "detractors" in the community manifested the recalcitrance and negativeness of their personalities. The "detractors" were "born opposers" who would never be satisfied with the way things were done; they would rather sabotage than help, rather criticize than applaud. The following statements illustrate the establishment viewpoint:

There was always the opposition to constructive things in Starkey, the clique as it was called [I could find no other evidence that the term *clique* had been applied to the "opposition" in the past]. It was the same group that would try to run someone out of the country. It was a negative influence, always there for its own share, however. It opposed anything progressive. Perhaps these people were inhibited when it came to speaking, so their opposing things salved their feelings. . . . The clique never had cohesion. It was always opposed to trying to build things in the community. Myrtle Wilson, for example, was always an agin'er. She was self-admittedly against things. She just liked to oppose. These people, if you put them together, could never create anything. They could never make an organization a success. Frances Green[9] was in the clique. She couldn't stand to see things run smoothly.

There were those who had no constructive criticism, and so they were against things. They were strong-willed people, and strong-willed people can't get together. They are going to set up dissension right off the bat.

The roots of the establishment reached into the church. The small nucleus of very devout and conservative church members was not a major force in the community, to be sure, because they devoted most of their efforts to the church itself. Few of them participated in the Improvement Club during its peak of influence in the 1920s, for example. But those who were members of the establishment—those who thought the community was democratically run and did not share the misgivings of the "detractors"—either were regular worshipers at the church or counted themselves among the Methodists' well-wishers and supporters. In short, to be part of the establishment was also to be associated with the church.

On the other hand, the nonestablishment was decidedly hostile toward the church. A person who had lived in Starkey since before the Depression expressed the nonestablishment view of the church when he commented,

There was always a certain amount of people who didn't like the church. In some cases it was so conspicuous that, years ago, it became a byword around here that you don't want to deal with a church member or he'll get the better of you. They figured they'd rather not work for a churchgoer, because they'll get the best deal. . . . It's that way somewhat today.

I named three deceased community members and asked whether they had been opposed to the church people. He replied,

Yes, they were like my dad. They used to complain about the ministers. The church people used to ask my dad why he didn't go to church, and he would start arguing with them. My dad was about as opposite from the church as you can get without being an atheist.

An incident that occurred during the mid-1930s is illustrative. It was reported to me by one of the most devout and conservative members of the congregation, Edgar Smith, who began by remarking that "the Johnsons were hard, old characters." The Smith family was on its way home from church services one Sunday morning when they saw Mrs. Johnson rush out of her home and wave for them to stop their car. She was hysterical, shouting that her husband was about to kill her and her child. Smith noted that he could smell liquor on the woman's breath and that she was very drunk. In spite of her fear, she suddenly became reluctant to accept help: "When she saw who it was [in the car] she didn't want to say anything, she probably figured I wouldn't have any sympathy for her because I'm in the church. But I told her if she needed help, I couldn't leave." As it turned out, Mrs. Johnson was not in as much danger as she thought,[10] but her reluctance to accept Smith's help illustrates both the feelings that some people had toward the church and the way church membership intruded into the community's social system.

The local norms against the use of alcohol were another aspect of the establishment–nonestablishment division. Those who were aligned with the church were either nondrinkers in fact or so circumspect about their drinking that they were regarded as nondrinkers. On the other hand, anyone who was known to drink and was at all indiscreet in doing so soon felt the force of public opinion and became alienated from the church because of its "control" over standards of public conduct. The drinkers in Starkey tended to be anti-church in their opinions; they also adhered to the nonestablishment theory of community according to which a vaguely defined coterie of people who were aligned with the church dominated the locality.

The following statements illustrate the role of drinking as an aspect of the establishment division:

At one time [during the 1920s and 1930s] some people wouldn't go to Betty's house if they knew her sister [who was a drinker and a "wild" woman] was there. She was an outlaw to them then.

There was always that faction of drinkers and nondrinkers. But it wasn't really a faction, they were just separated.

This thing was always in the background, nothing definite. The Community Christmas party used to be held in the church [during the 1930s], and some of the people would have a bottle with them and get to feeling pretty good. Later on there would be whispers. A few of the [people] on both sides would overlook these things, but there would be hard feelings for a while.

By law, an agency of the State of California must license businesses that serve alcoholic beverages, and during the 1930s and 1940s the churchgoers circulated petitions around Starkey in the hope of persuading this agency to either deny or revoke the licenses of the successive proprietors of the Starkey bar. The petitions were never successful, but they heightened the animosity and crystallized the division between drinkers and nondrinkers. One of those who passed around a petition during the mid-1930s commented, "There was a petition against Mrs. Joseph's bringing in the bar, and this put me against her. We got along, but we were never good friends." Apparently most of the community members signed the petitions, either because they opposed the bar or because their refusal would tacitly indicate association with the drinkers. One person stated that "At the time the petition [against Mrs. Joseph] was passed there were more against than for her. It wasn't very popular not to sign the petition." [11]

It is surprising that some nondrinkers in Starkey were by no means aligned with the church. For example, Frances Green associated socially with several drinkers, but she herself was a nondrinker and an outspoken opponent of alcohol. In spite of her agreement with the Methodists over liquor, however, she was one of their most caustic opponents. In each case of this kind the anomaly can be explained by another principle: those who were both anti-church and pro-temperance are described (by members of the establishment) as "detractors" rather than "contributors." These seemingly anomalous individuals were members of the nonestablishment on grounds other than their feelings about alcohol, and their animosity toward the church was simply a manifestation of their nonestablishment leanings.

Starkey's social life may have been dominated by the establishment, as the nonestablishment believed, but at least two organizations in the community appear to have been in the hands of the nonestablishment. One was the Grange, which existed from the 1920s to the 1940s. Although its records are not available, it had a small membership that apparently consisted exclusively of nonestablishment people, and it seems to have had the local image of a nonestablishment group. One person remarked to me, "I always thought the Grange was a little in opposition to the Farm Bureau," and another, when questioned about the Grange, commented, "You mean the dissenters!" It is significant that the Grange seems to have attracted little attention in the community and that it left little mark on community life, unlike either the Improvement Club or the Farm Bureau—both of which were decidedly establishment oriented.

The Women's Club was also associated with the nonestablishment. The materials on this organization are rich and provide considerable insight into the nature of the establishment–nonestablishment division.

I have remarked on the failure of the Women's Club to win support in the community. One of its members commented,

The community never supported the Women's Club, they always seemed to fight it. If it wasn't for the Women's Club there would be no park; and the Club got the Clubhouse, but people were still against it. Maybe they didn't like the people who were behind it.

The following are comments made by members of the establishment when shown a list of the Women's Club members:

Many of these people had husbands with a problem with booze. Many of them were drinkers themselves, and often apt to get drunk. These people that drank were loose in moral standards. Still, a few, such as Myrtle Wilson and Frances Green, had a strict moral code. A lot of these women would have been on the other side everything else being equal, but because of their husbands' drinking they were associated with that side. Mrs. Barclay fits with this group, she was always opposing. She would never help out if Henry Turner [an establishment leader] was there first. Florence French would have been vociferous on that other side.

These are renegade people.

There were rough women in the Women's Club—rough as they come—such as Mrs. Joseph, Mrs. Johnson.

I asked one of the women who had once been a member of the club if the organization were composed of drinkers; she replied, "They weren't the drinkers, several members weren't drinkers. We were the nonchurch group. The people in the club were broadminded about drinking, though; we didn't hold it against a person if he or she drank a little."

The community members' evaluations of the instigator and leader of the club, Mrs. Joseph, are illuminating. Several establishment people gave the following descriptions:

Mrs. Joseph was working all the time, was energetic, always going. But she was questionable. She came into the community on her own terms—she wouldn't have been invited in.

Mrs. Joseph was the head of the drinking crowd, she was kind of looked on as the saloon keeper. At first they lived at Howard, where they had the restaurant and bar, and then they came to Starkey where she ran the restaurant. She was an able person, but hard to peg socially. Evidently she wasn't well accepted in Starkey. She was good-hearted, though. She wasn't here long.

[She was] a big old madam. She didn't have the highest morals. She lived in the parsonage,[12] and one day she had the high-school graduates in and gave them all a drink.

On the other hand, one person who had been a member of the Women's Club remarked, "A lot of people held it against her because she drank a little wine. She used to live in the parsonage next to the church, and was forced out of there. She started the girls' 4-H Club in 1934, and [one of the church members] took it from her."

The lack of community support embittered the club's members, who spent considerable effort "for the community's benefit." One member commented, "It was an uphill job paying for the Clubhouse." The dances that were given to help pay for the building were disliked in Starkey because of the unruly crowds they attracted, and this further antagonized the Women's Club members: "If the community had supported the Women's Club dances we wouldn't have had to advertise [in the Oak Flat newspaper] and we wouldn't have had so much riff-raff there."

The members of the organization regarded their Clubhouse project as a contribution to the community, but others apparently took a more cynical view; according to one person, "Maybe the Women's Club built the Clubhouse just to show the church they could do something. That's the way most things seem to get done, to show someone else they can do it."

In sum, although Starkey began as a small commercial hub, it soon became a focus of social activities as well, and of course this was part of its role as a service center—the town was a convenient location not only for a general store and blacksmith but also for recreation, club meetings, and church services. What is more, it is possible to discern an ideological dimension to this social life, for the affairs that took place were cast in an idiom of improvement or boosterism. An active social life was thought to be the mark of a meritorious community, so even if Starkey could never grow to the size of Oak Flat or compete with it commercially, it could at least prove itself a commuity-spirited place. Participation in local affairs was thus a way of boosting the hometown. The idiom of improvement is also evident in the form the town's social life took, in that collective undertakings were usually directed toward making the community a better place to live. There were projects to improve local recreational and public facilities, the town's appearance, and the like. The community organizations were also drawn toward the goal of community improvement.

This is not to say that everyone pulled together in pursuit of these goals, for differences of opinion were evident in local affairs, and particularly on the issue of drinking. Starkey was sharply divided between a church-oriented, abstinent establishment and a somewhat more indulgent and clearly alienated nonestablishment.

Chapter 4 Patterns of Leadership

THE LOCAL SPIRIT of improvement contributed to the deep rift between the establishment and the nonestablishment, but it also prompted the rise of a set of people who were quite effective in planning community undertakings and in mobilizing support for them. Throughout most of Starkey's history a few individuals enjoyed the position of community leader, and their leadership role exhibited several distinct features.

One of the chief problems confronting the leader was that of dealing with the animosities and prejudices separating the establishment from the nonestablishment. If an issue such as the acquisition of the park was not to become mired in controversy, potential jealousies and misunderstandings had to be spotted in advance and coped with. Again, if a person was to manage a community undertaking successfully, he had to avoid the stigma of being an agent of either the "church people" or the "detractors."

Characteristic of the leadership patterns in Starkey was a lack of material power; the leader had no compelling sanctions. For example, land titles were recorded at the county seat and rights of ownership were enforced by the government, so it was impossible for a leader to bring an individual into line by threatening to force him off his land. Nor could a resident be frozen out of work: a worker who lost favor with one farmer could normally find a job with another over whom the first had no direct influence. The principal sanction that was available was gossip and scandal, for it was the pressure of public opinion—and the threat to a person's reputation—that were used against the recalcitrant individual. But even this sanction was seldom employed by the leaders; rather, they diplomatically avoided gossiping about others. When a person scandalized a fellow community member, he himself became controversial, and this was precisely what the leader tried to avoid. Instead, the main technique at the leader's disposal was persuasion.

The Starkey residents had little difficulty naming the community leaders of the past, for at almost every period in the community's history a small number of men have been consciously recognized as occupying this status. Other community members sometimes performed leadership roles in restricted contexts; for example, Mrs. Joseph spearheaded the acquisition of the park and was known as an energetic and effective organizer, even though she was never considered a community leader in the strict sense. The line between the leader and the nonleader was therefore somewhat flexible. What set the true community leader apart from the others, however, was that his leadership ability was one of the distinctive elements of his local reputation: if he were being described to an outsider, his role as a leader would be among the first of his attributes to be mentioned.

The Starkey residents tended to distinguish between two types of leader. The first they commonly described as "someone others would go to for advice," whereas the second was usually termed a "pusher" or "doer" and was described as a person who could "get things done in the community." The two roles—which I refer to as that of the notable and that of the pusher—were not mutually exclusive. Although some community leaders performed only one of these roles, some performed both simultaneously.

The basis of the notable's role was prestige, for he was considered both successful and capable, a person whose achievements proved his good judgment. Most notables were successful farmers, and their views on agricultural and economic matters were respected. Their views about community affairs were also thought to be noteworthy, and their support lent an issue the stamp of respectability. The role of the notable was therefore a symbolic one: he did not necessarily bring his influence to bear in direct, face-to-face relations, but he helped legitimize programs that were conducted by others. For example, community meetings were usually called to launch important projects, and the presence—and support—of several notables at those meetings was arranged for beforehand. An example of the notable's role occurred while I was living in Starkey in 1966. The school board had decided that it was necessary to raise school taxes, but the approval of a majority of the voters in the community was needed before the increase could be implemented. The board called a small meeting to determine how to go about presenting the proposal to the community. It invited several notables—all of whom had once been school board members—to this discussion. A tacit purpose of the meeting was to enlist the verbal support of these people, for their views could then be cited as evidence for the needed tax increase.

The pusher's role was more substantive than symbolic, for he was both active and skillful in promoting and managing community programs of action. Perhaps his most distinctive characteristic was that he occupied a central position in the community's informal communication system and was adept not only at molding public opinion but at discovering where discontent and dissent lay. He spent a considerable amount of time discussing community matters with Starkey residents at the post office stores, and local events.

A second attribute of the pusher was what might be termed the art of conducting community affairs or the art of public management. A guiding principle behind the planning of a program of action was the need to both overcome resistance and generate support, and a variety of techniques were at hand to accomplish this. For example, one of Starkey's leaders remarked that a way to ensure support for a program was to enlist the help of those who were likely to oppose it, because "they would more readily support the project if they felt they were in on the planning."

A third attribute of the successful pusher was that he enjoyed broad support in the community. He was gregarious and likable and was able to ingratiate himself with his fellow residents. And he avoided partisan commitments. One person said, "Something would happen and people would take up sides; the real leaders would have no part of either side." The pusher also had to tolerate personal criticism. A man who had once been a community leader made this point:

Any time someone tries to do something someone's going to resent it. If someone's going ahead, making some money, people will try to kick him down a little. A leader's got to get along with that type of person, to see animosities and not put his foot down when someone growls at him a little. That's one good thing about Bill Donelson. He can overlook remarks and what have you.

The pusher's motivations also had to be beyond reproach, for he could not be effective if people believed that a desire for personal gratification was the primary reason for his community undertakings. Because of the tendency toward distrust and rivalry among community members, however, the image of disinterestedness was difficult to maintain, and it is likely that none of Starkey's leaders remained untouched by incriminations. A supporter of Brian Green commented that the latter "did more for this community than the rest [of the community leaders] combined." But another person remarked, "Brian Green was either well thought of or [was considered] a louse. He was hero-worshiped by some, others didn't like him at all." A third person commented that Green "was an opportunist, he didn't give a damn about Starkey. He was a false leader—he wouldn't do a thing for Starkey if he didn't get his name in the paper for it. He was like the Women's Society today."

The issue of the county's political system is beyond the scope of this study, but it is worth noting that the Starkey leadership articulated with the larger political organization. The Starkey leader could usually exert some influence at the county level: His leadership at home was recognized by the elected officials, who were therefore responsive to his requests. In addition, a Starkey resident who was not a community leader but happened to have the ear of the officials at the county seat was occasionally called upon to use his influence in the community's behalf. Such a person tended to acquire at least a qualified reputation as a leader.

Before 1910 a number of Starkey residents stood out from the others for their influence and prestige, but it is not at all clear to what extent any of them was conceived of as a community leader or even whether the role of community leader had yet become crystallized in local thought. The data are scanty, although it seems possible that Starkey was still too young for the appearance of distinct leadership patterns.

The situation was quite different after about 1910, however, for between that year and 1930 five community leaders emerged.

The first was Henry Turner, who had come to Starkey as a young man during the 1880s when his father claimed a homestead in the hills near town. During the late 1890s Henry and an older brother took a team of horses to a railroad construction site elsewhere in the state and got a job. They worked on the railroad for several years, saving their money, and shortly after the turn of the century they were able to return to

Starkey and purchase one of the local stores. Although their business prospered, their partnership was shaky, and they sold the store in 1913. Henry then acquired a small dairy farm on the outskirts of the community hub. He was not poor by any means, but he was not among the wealthiest or most successful members of the community.

After running his dairy for a few years Turner was able to leave most of the work to his sons and devote much of his time to community affairs, for he spent a portion of nearly every day at the community hub. On most afternoons he could be found at one of the stores, the post office, or the blacksmith shop talking with whomever had come to town. He continued to be active in this way until shortly before his death in 1925.

Turner was not a churchgoer, but he was a nondrinker and was considered a supporter of the Methodists.

The second community leader was Arnold Donelson, who had come to Starkey in the 1880s as a homesteader. Unlike many of the settlers nearby, he did not lose his holdings during the depression and drought of the 1890s, and when prosperity finally came after the turn of the century he was able to make an adequate living from his farm. By 1910 he owned enough acreage to require the labor of two teams and a hired man. But his good fortune did not last long. He attempted to expand his holdings during the late 1920s because his sons needed work, and in doing so he went too far into debt and soon lost virtually all his land. He died almost penniless in 1935, several years after suffering a stroke that left him both speechless and bedridden.

Donelson earned a comfortable living from his land prior to his misfortune, but like Turner he was not one of the wealthiest farmers in the community. One person remarked, "Arnold never felt money was important. He would drop a job to preach a funeral service, for example." He was a gifted speaker and a charismatic leader, and again like Turner, he left most of the farm work to his sons and the hired man, spending a large share of his own time at the community hub. What is more, his leadership abilities were not restricted to the community of Starkey. As a result of his work in the Farm Bureau and his attendance at Farm Bureau meetings in other towns he became known throughout the county, and in 1922 he was elected for a term to the state legislature.

Donelson was a devout Presbyterian, although he attended the

Methodist services and was frequently called upon to deliver sermons and funeral eulogies at the church. He was "dry," but he "got along with the alcoholics as well as the church people." The following comments illustrate his reputation in the community:

He never let personal things affect his fairness, he never discussed people.

Arnold was a bright man, a good man. . . . He was good to be in charge of a group or the head speaker for something.

Arnold was a good reader, and he could talk, like all the Donelsons. He stood up and said what he thought, whether you agreed with him or not. Both Arnold Donelson and Henry Turner probably read a lot, newspapers, etc. And they thought a lot, probably.

The third influential was Ben Harlow, a local farmer who was just beginning to assume a leadership role when he was killed in an automobile accident about 1920. Had he not died when he did, his importance in community affairs would soon have equaled Turner's and Donelson's.

The fourth influential, Peter Jensen, was a European immigrant who was among the early homesteaders in Starkey. He was notoriously frugal and hardworking, and soon after the turn of the century he was one of the wealthiest farmers in the vicinity.

Jensen spoke with a heavy accent, and because of his rustic dress and crude manners he was considered quite boorish. One person remarked, "He didn't speak very well. He didn't speak very much. He was looked on as an oddball member of the community." But he had a lively interest in community affairs and the time to devote to them. The following exhibits his local reputation: "Many people looked on him as an old, dumb foreigner. . . . In the community of Starkey he didn't carry much weight. But at the county seat you had to consider him, he had the property and paid the taxes. Anything that involved the county he could influence." Jensen was a drinker and "anti-church."

The fifth community leader was Brian Green. Green's father had bought land near Starkey after the turn of the century, and in 1918 Brian moved to the community in order to take charge of the farm. During the first few years he had little time for anything but work, yet in the 1920s he began spending an increasing amount of time at the community hub, leaving the farming to his hired man. He was gregarious and a skillful leader, and he played an important part in Starkey's social life almost until the time he left in the early 1950s.

Green was regarded as a drinker. He was discreet in his tippling— for example, he was never drunk in public—but he made no attempt to conceal the fact that he drank. His wife, though a nondrinker, was decidedly nonestablishment, and he also associated with a group of people who were outspokenly opposed to the Starkey Methodists. And yet he enjoyed a friendly relationship with the church people: "Green drank, and consorted with the other drinkers. But he also got along with the other group, such as Arnold Donelson and Henry Turner." The following statements illustrate his local reputation:

Brian was doing things for the community almost from the time he came here. For example, he was in on the Improvement Club, he was also in the Farm Bureau. In fact, he was a county man, known throughout the county, primarily through the Farm Bureau. He was always willing to serve as a representative for something in the community. He could speak beautifully, he could get up in front of any group.

Brian was even-tempered. He thought things through. He was a great arbitrator.

Relations among the five leaders were amiable, and they frequently worked together in local affairs. There is no evidence that they ever engaged in political competition or were thought of as rivals.

Green was set apart somewhat from the others, for he did not always work as closely with them as they did with one another. One reason was that he assumed importance later than the rest; he had barely emerged as an important figure before they had ceased to play significant roles in the community. But there was another reason for his separation. Green traced his principal social ties to the "anti-church" segment of Starkey, and he looked toward the nonestablishment in his private life. He moved in a somewhat different social circle than the others. It is true that Jensen was "anti-church" and a drinker, but his personal relations with Turner and Donelson were much closer than with any member of the nonestablishment.

Turner, Donelson, Jensen, and Harlow constituted a distinct coterie, for they frequently engaged in programs of action as a group. The relationships among them are clear. The most influential, both within the community and among themselves, were Donelson and Turner. One person remarked, "Arnold and Henry were the two spokesmen for this area. They always spoke out on defending principles and in presenting facts and figures. In any group there are some who are organizers and leaders, and some who are supporters but don't want to lead."

Harlow's leadership role had not reached maturity when he died. Jensen, on the other hand, occupied an unusual position. He wanted to be a leader, and he put in the time and effort to become one, but he lacked the personal qualities required in a leader. He also remained subordinate to Donelson and Turner. A Starkey resident characterized Jensen's relationship with the others by remarking that Jensen "would do a lot of spouting and spewing, but [he] would come around to Henry's and Arnold's way of thinking."

Among these five leaders at least two, Donelson and Turner, were notables. They enjoyed considerable personal esteem, and their judgment was widely respected in the community. But what distinguished all of these men from other members of the community was their role as pushers, in that they were actively engaged in promoting and coordinating community undertakings (although Jensen, by himself, was never very successful in doing so). One person, referring to Donelson, Turner, and Green, stated that "if you needed anything with the school they were willing to help. They were willing to help with anything, in fact." Another remarked, "They were for the good of Starkey."

One of the manifestations of their role as pushers was that each of these five men spent a portion of nearly every day at the Starkey hub. They were at the center of the community's informal system of communication and were successful at "getting things going, like rodeos and barbecues."

For example, the May Day picnics had little if any definite organization; but each year the affair was held at a different location and prizes were acquired for the winners of the various events. The Ladies Aid apparently had a hand in arranging these matters, but much was accomplished through casual conversations among Starkey residents, with the community leaders playing a key role. One person remarked, "Beforehand people talked about the picnic and it got around where it was going to be. Then everyone congregated at the right place." During World War I the community erected a flagpole on a street corner near the center of town. I questioned one person about how the matter was handled, and he said,

The community flagpole probably got started by four or five people standing around talking. That's the way things got done then. . . . Lots of things were hashed over when digging graves or at wakes. It seemed that there was always the same people digging graves and sitting at wakes and helping the unfortunate—for example, Arnold Donelson.

In the early 1920s a barbecue was held in Starkey to celebrate the completion of the new highway through the town. One person commented, "There was no organization behind the barbecue, it was a community-wide thing. Arnold Donelson or Henry Turner probably were the leaders behind it."

The role of community leader could be demanding, and the case of the new highway is illustrative. In 1921 the state highway that was to pass through Starkey was still in the planning stages, and the state road department intended to have the thoroughfare built on the opposite side of the river from town. The local people felt that it would be to their advantage to have the roadway cross the river and pass through the community hub instead, primarily because the river was impassable for short periods each winter and the highway would require the construction of all-weather bridges. Turner, Donelson, Jensen, and Harlow decided to pursue this issue, and for several months they devoted a significant amount of their time to it. In particular, on a number of occasions they drove to the county seat as a group, both to argue the case before the state authorities and to press for the support of the county board of supervisors. As a result of their persistence the officials finally acceded to the change.

The community leaders—especially Donelson and Turner—were occasionally called upon to bring sanctions to bear against others or to undertake what one person called the "maintenance of discipline" in Starkey. When a person flagrantly violated the local moral norms one or both of these men were called upon to speak to the individual. The following illustrate this aspect of their role:

People would always go to Arnold or Henry as leaders. The community looked down on those who kicked through what was right. If it got around that so-and-so was going to run off with someone else's wife, or was stealing horses, they would go to Arnold or Henry and ask them to go to the persons involved. The others would go, too, but behind Henry or Arnold.

People came to Henry Turner when someone was doing something they shouldn't. He would tell them to move out.

I have been able to discover but one instance of this feature of leadership. One Sunday afternoon a group of "toughs" was standing outside the pool hall talking. The leading member of the group, Henry Turner's younger brother, was a drinker and a decisively nonestablishment person. The small gathering of men decided to play a practical joke on Aunt Agnes' young retarded son, and they began by asking him to demonstrate how fast he could race. He ran a short distance. They called him back and suggested that if he greased his body he could improve his speed. He was about to do so when a bystander summoned Arnold Donelson, who was at the Methodist church nearby. According to a secondhand account, Donelson came out of the church and "read quite a speech off to the toughs. They talked back at first, but the longer he talked the more they realized how cruel they were and they all shuffled off." In another account of this incident Donelson's ability as a speaker and the force of his personality were emphasized. The way he dealt with the situation was compared with the way another person, Charles Collins, might have proceeded. According to this account,

Charles Collins was a strange fellow, but he always stood by the cause. Had he been the one to confront the toughs that were making Aunt Agnes' boy look foolish he wouldn't have talked them into leaving the boy alone. He wasn't the speaker of Arnold Donelson's ability. He would have pulled a knife and challenged them.

It was largely because of Donelson's verbal ability that he, like Turner, was called upon to deal with situations of this kind.[1]

The records of Starkey's formal associations further illustrate the leadership roles of Donelson, Turner, and Green, for these men were active participants in community organizations and were frequently elected to office in those groups. For example, all three were elected to the board of directors of the Improvement Club, along with two other community members whose leadership roles were less pronounced. Arnold Donelson was the primary force behind the formation of the Starkey Farm Bureau late in 1921, and he and Green were immediately elected president and vice president, respectively, of that organization. Fred Jensen's name appears frequently in the Farm Bureau minutes, suggesting that he was by no means a passive member. But he was not elected to office—which shows once more that he lacked the personal qualities necessary for a successful leader.[2]

The county Farm Bureau was a vehicle for the development of leadership roles beyond the limits of the local community. The county-wide organization became a major political force in this part of the state, and the president of each community farm center was an *ex officio* member of the county board of directors. I have noted that Donelson's activities in the county-wide organization culminated in his election to the state legislature in 1922. Brian Green was active in the county Farm Bureau, and he too acquired influence well beyond Starkey's borders. By contrast, because of Henry Turner's failure to become involved in the Farm Bureau his influence remained strictly local in scope.

Turner and Harlow were dead by the mid-1920s, and a few years later Donelson was penniless and bedridden. By that time Peter Jensen was about 70 years old and was no longer able to take an active part in the social life of Starkey. Of the five men who had emerged as community leaders between 1910 and 1930, only Green was still important during the 1930s. But he was joined by several new influentials.

The first of these was Tony Giles. Giles moved to Starkey in 1930 to serve as the high-school principal, and he remained in that position until he left the community in 1947. He was a nondrinker and was clearly aligned with the Methodists, although neither he nor his wife attended Sunday services.

Giles was a friendly, outgoing person, and he was active in community affairs almost from the moment he entered Starkey. He was also a gifted organizer. For example, in 1946 he conceived the idea of holding a Memorial Day celebration to honor the men who had returned from overseas, and he personally stimulated local interest in the undertaking, planned it, and carried it out. The following are some typical comments about his role in the community:

Giles was a driver, a go-getter. He was always trying to do things, and people liked him. When you get to know a lot of people, and they like you, and you do a lot of things, then you tend to have influence.

I can remember potlucks and school affairs, Tony and his wife were right in there all the time, hopping around, making coffee and so on. They're doers, they get things done.

Giles was a pusher, so was Bill Donelson, Arnold's son [who will be discussed later]. They were always doing things. For example, Giles got the swimming pool.

I never had a feeling Giles did anything in a selfish manner. This includes his wife, too.

Giles and his wife were for the community. He was the backbone of the community.

The second new leader to appear in the 1930s was Jerold Whitman, the son of an early Starkey settler. Whitman began farming his father's land early in the century and soon won the reputation of a capable and energetic worker. His holdings increased steadily, and although prosperity was beyond his reach during the agricultural depression of the 1920s or the Great Depression that followed, by the mid-1940s he was among the most successful farmers in Starkey (see Hatch 1975:26, 31–32, 34). He was also considered one of the most upright members of the community. He was a nondrinker and was definitely aligned with the church, although he seldom attended Sunday services.

Whitman was shy and found it quite difficult to assume the role of leader. But with a keen interest in community affairs and enormous determination he set out to overcome his social awkwardness, and although he never became an effective pusher he was frequently involved in local undertakings spearheaded by others. For example, because of his personal prestige he was frequently called upon to offer support for programs that were in the planning stage. His leadership role was chiefly that of the notable rather than that of the pusher. The following illustrate the reputation he acquired as a leader:

Jerold knew everything that was going on, but he was living out there in the country. I can't think of him taking any leadership or initiative, actually. He might come and speak at graduation exercises or the Farm Bureau. . . . He wasn't too much a leader right here, but he was in there backing up anything that was going on. He could put pressure on [the county officials in] Saint Thomas. People would say, "Jerold, let's go to Saint Thomas and put some pressure on," and he'd go. . . . Jerold wasn't a pusher himself, but he was always willing to help.

Jerold Whitman was always short and timid, he was scared to speak. At the Farm Bureau meetings when he spoke his voice quivered. He got over it—he never became a good speaker, but he got so that he could stand up in front of a group of people   .Jerold was always community minded. He was a high-school trustee for years. And once you got involved, you carried an aura of responsibility. It lifted a person up socially.

Jerold Whitman was . . . someone others would go to for advice.

He was a well-read man, he had a sharp mind.

A third person to emerge as a leader during the 1930s was Bill Donelson, one of Arnold's seven children. Bill began farming in the early 1920s by leasing a small plot of land near his father's, but he was soon forced to relinquish the property and work for wages. During the 1920s he held several jobs both within the community and elsewhere, and in 1931 he accepted a position as manager of the entire farming operation of one of the largest ranches in Starkey.[3] He received a percentage of the profits that were made on the farmland, and during the agricultural boom of the 1940s he became a moderately wealthy man.

Bill Donelson was regarded as an extremely capable businessman and a highly successful farmer. One person remarked, "It seemed that every year he made the right decisions and made money while other people were losing." His success was the source of ill will from at least some people, who believed that his good fortune was due in part to questionable business practices. A friend and supporter gave the following explanation of this animosity:

One thing about Bill is that he drives a hard bargain. If he is buying grain, for example, he'll offer the price he thinks it should bring. If you're a good fellow, or if you're having hard times, it won't matter, he won't offer you any more. It isn't that Bill's done anything wrong necessarily, because he sticks to the straight and narrow. But he drives a hard bargain.

As young men Donelson and his brothers were drinkers, and they acquired the reputation of ruffians. But this phase was short-lived, and by the 1930s Donelson was known for his business acumen and his uprightness. He had become a nondrinker and a vocal opponent of the use of alcohol. He and his wife were among the most active members of the Starkey church. He was unequivocally aligned with the establishment.

Donelson was a gregarious, well-spoken, charismatic man, and he mixed easily with all segments of the community. Even those who were critical of him saluted his sociability and leadership capacity, for he found the role of pusher quite congenial and devoted much of his spare time to it. The following illustrates his reputation as a leader: "Bill Donelson has always been probably the first man to enter my mind as someone to go to [to get something done in the community]. . . . Bill is a good organizer, he gets behind something and pushes. He can create interest."

By the 1930s a change had taken place in the leader's role. The roads had been improved, and most households now had an automobile or a truck. Some even had a telephone. Information was no longer channeled through the community hub to the extent that it had been before, and the leaders did not spend as much time there during the day as their predecessors had. On the other hand, community events such as school programs and Farm Bureau meetings became relatively more important as channels of communication. The hub had not completely lost its importance, to be sure. As late as the mid-1960s Donelson could often be found lingering at the post office at midday, speaking with residents who had come to pick up their mail.

As in the past, relations among the Starkey leaders were amicable. During the 1930s the two dominant and most effective leaders were Tony Giles and Brian Green. Bill Donelson was an energetic pusher, but his reputation was being won more slowly than Giles's, perhaps because his job often kept him away from the community hub. Whitman was far more reserved than the other three and older—he was 60 in 1935. He did not play as active a part as the others.

A telling example of community leadership during the 1930s was the way the Starkey high school achieved its independence. When the local high school was a subsidiary of the Oak Flat school system the Starkey resident who was regularly elected to the board of trustees was Henry Turner, and after his death in the 1920s Jerold Whitman took his place. Starkey's irritation at Oak Flat's dominance over the local school had festered for a number of years when, in 1935, Whitman and Bill Donelson went to Giles, the principal, and asked him to see what could be done about severing the tie. Giles contacted one of the state senators. The senator told him that the first requisite was to file a petition requesting the change, and that this must be signed by two-thirds of the voters of the school system—which included not only the voters of Starkey but also those of Oak Flat and the other small communities in the high-school district.

The project was soon under way, and after considerable effort the required number of signatures was obtained. Giles (whom I had the chance to interview during one of his visits to Starkey in the mid-1960s) stated that Donelson "was the one who put it over, working untiringly passing the petition around Oak Flat. He knew a lot of people there and he got them as well as others to sign." Giles was also active in the project, although in a somewhat different capacity. In Giles' words, "I never stopped letting them [the Oak Flat school officials] know they weren't treating Starkey right. I think one factor [behind Oak Flat's willingness to sever the tie] was that they got tired of my complaining to them."

An influential resident of Oak Flat who was a lawyer and a member of the school board was persuaded to publish a notice in the town newspaper urging people to sign the petition.

State law required that any new school system had to have a minimum enrollment of 100 students, and Starkey's student body was slightly below that figure. Consequently, the senator—who had been following the issue closely—introduced a bill into the state senate excepting Starkey from the law, and the bill passed.

Once the Starkey high school had achieved autonomy it was headed by a five-member, locally elected board of trustees. From 1936 until the mid-1940s Brian Green, Jerold Whitman, and Bill Donelson were among the board members, and it is likely that Giles would also have been elected if he had not been principal.

The acquisition of the park is a further illustration of local leadership patterns. At a meeting of the Farm Bureau in 1933 the farm agent happened to be sitting next to Giles. The farm agent mentioned that federal funds from the WPA, a New Deal program, might be available to the community for the construction of a park, and that it would be worthwhile to look into this possibility.[4] Mrs. Joseph, the president of the newly formed Women's Club, was sitting nearby. The principal mentioned to her that this might be a worthwhile project for her organization, and she agreed.

An open field across the main road from the high school seemed ideally suited to this plan. This property was part of one of the large ranches that had existed before the arrival of homesteaders, and its heir was a wealthy San Francisco woman who had never lived in Starkey. Mrs. Joseph traveled to San Francisco to request that she donate the parcel to the community, and although the owner was willing, she stipulated that the county must hold title to the park.

Mrs. Joseph relayed this information to Giles, and Giles went to Green to suggest that they attend a meeting of the county board of supervisors to request that the land be accepted as a county park. Giles and Green then spoke to Donelson, who agreed to accompany them.

The board was reluctant to accept the financial burden of a new park, but after lengthy discussion it finally agreed to do so if Giles himself would take charge of the park's construction without pay. The supervisors were willing to maintain the park once it was finished, but they wanted the community itself to develop it. Giles consented to their terms.

The community's support now had to be enlisted. Green, Donelson, and Giles set to work generating enthusiasm for the project by speaking informally to community members. Next Giles called a community meeting, which he chaired, for a public discussion of the issue. As a result of the meeting a committee was selected to oversee the project, and Giles was elected chairman. The other members consisted of representatives of each of Starkey's organizations, including the Methodist Church, the Farm Bureau, the Grange, and the Women's

Club. Thus both sides of the establishment–nonestablishment division were formally involved in the undertaking.

The actual direction of the park project was provided by Giles himself, the committee being no more than a figurehead. It did not hold a single meeting, and if a matter arose that required the consultation of the committee members Giles spoke to them individually as he met them in town. I asked Giles to explain the purpose of this group. He said, "To get the work done you've got to include everyone. By selecting the committee we were able to include the most people." The committee's true purpose was to provide legitimacy, not leadership, for the project.

The project was begun in 1936. Several farmers brought equipment to level the land, and others drove their trucks to the Central Valley to pick up trees that a nursery there had donated. The trees were planted by members of the community, as was a large lawn, part of which was to serve as an athletic field. Another community member was enlisted to drill a well. In a few months the project was completed.[5]

Another major community endeavor was under way within a few years. Even before the park was completed people began discussing the need for a swimming pool to enhance the town, for as early as 1935 mention of a proposed "community plunge" appeared in the minutes of the Women's Club. When the park had been completed, it became the logical place for the new pool.

This project was formalized early in the 1940s, when Giles and several other Starkey residents attended a meeting of the county board of supervisors to propose that if the county would provide materials and financial assistance the community would build a pool. The supervisors did not think the task could be done as cheaply as the Starkey delegates thought, and they were reluctant to accept the proposal. But after extensive debate they relented, and the park committee was immediately put back to work. As before, the committee turned out to be a figurehead, the actual leadership being provided by Giles.

The pool project required far more collective effort than the development of the park. A carpenter was hired to superintend the building of the concrete forms, but the rest of the labor was donated by Starkey residents. Several community members brought their tractors to town to excavate the hole; a group then acquired used wood for building forms, and others removed nails from the planks. Cement was transported from the Central Valley by community members, and sand was hauled from the riverbed near town. Steel rods for reinforcement were acquired from a demolished bridge elsewhere in the county, and this material had to be brought to Starkey by truck and straightened by hand. Within four and a half months—by late August of 1942—the project had been completed, and the pool was opened with considerable fanfare. The cost to the county was only $1,600, which included payment for cement and for the carpenter's labor.

The key to the project's success was Giles, for he and one of the high-school teachers devoted the entire summer to the undertaking. Each evening they drove to the homes of community members to solicit a crew for the next day's work, and the following morning they were on hand to labor alongside the others.[6]

One characteristic of all the successful leaders in Starkey was their personal prestige, for these men were thought to be among the most outstanding members of the community. Even their severest critics conceded their local eminence.

It is important that this prestige did not derive chiefly from economic or financial standing. Only two of the Starkey leaders, Whitman and Donelson, were ever noted for their financial success, and their material accomplishments did not come until the 1940s. In one respect financial success was incompatible with leadership, for the truly effective leader had to sacrifice his own economic advancement at times in order to devote himself to community affairs.

The prestige of the leader was a manifestation of the force of the local spirit of improvement. A person's social standing was not based exclusively on his economic achievements, and an account of the agricultural ladder by itself does not provide an altogether accurate picture of the local social hierarchy. The values embodied in Starkey's spirit of improvement supplied an additional and very significant set of criteria for assessing community members.

A relationship between leadership patterns and the establishment–nonestablishment division becomes clear in this context. For a number of reasons, some people acquired a reputation for obstructionism and moral unworthiness, and they felt the sting of local disapproval.

Their actions were being assessed by the same criteria as those of the leader, and they responded with hostility toward what to them was a judgmental, discriminatory in-group.

In short, the patterns of local leadership and the cleavage which cut through the community were part of a single system and were rooted in the booster ideology. This is a matter that I pursue in more detail in the next chapter.

Chapter 5 Principles of Local Organization

BEHIND NEARLY ALL the facets of Starkey's social life—the interactions between people who met casually in town, the community events and organizational affairs that took place, the patterns of leadership—two chief principles (or values[1]) appeared. These were the principle of community participation and cohesion on the one hand and that of individual economic achievement on the other. These principles gave direction to behavior by providing goals that each person sought to achieve. They also constituted criteria for assessing behavior and for measuring one person against another.

These two principles have been given extensive treatment in Page Smith's historical study of the small town in America. In his analysis they correspond to two main forms of community, which he calls cumulative and covenanted towns. The type community of the covenanted variety was the New England Puritan town, colonized by people of common belief who set out to create an ideal and sacred society. "At the heart of the Puritan community," Smith writes, "was the church covenant, forming it, binding it, making explicit its hopes and its assumptions" (1966:3). The covenant was a written document signed by the community's members; it was a compact with God and with every other member that established the town as a congregation. The covenanted community was characterized by the principles (Smith uses the term *values*) of solidarity and cohesion: the covenant made this a community in which each member had a moral obligation to cooperate, cohere, and share (pp. 3–16).

The cumulative town is a foil for Smith's analysis. The type locality seems to be the agricultural community of the Midwest extolled by Frederick Jackson Turner (1958). This was a locality formed by the accumulation of settlers claiming government land, a locality that fostered individualism and competition. The town that resulted was not the product of a conscious plan, for it "grew by the gradual accretion of individuals, or, sometimes by rapid but disorderly accumulations of fortune seekers" (p. 30). What the members of the cumulative locality had in common was not a selfless devotion to the common good but simply personal material interests. These towns were commercial and service centers, not communities. They were convenient places to attend church and school, perhaps to enjoy an evening of recreation, but above all to conduct trade. They were "oriented toward commercial values"; "they gave free rein to 'rugged individualism,' to the often recklessly acquisitive interests of their citizens" (p. 33).[2]

Whereas the New England covenanted towns prevailed during the early history of American society, the cumulative community became increasingly common in the nineteenth century with the opening of the western frontier. As settlers began to spread across the land, small towns seemed to spring up everywhere, many of them in a fortuitous, cumulative fashion. What is more, there has been a trend in America away from the principles of cohesion, egalitarianism, and community welfare. Even the most strongly covenanted towns have tended over time to slip in the direction of individualism and competition, and thus to resemble cumulative towns.

Smith suggests that communities in which the qualities of covenanted towns are either weak or absent tend to seek what he terms *covenant substitutes* (p. 26). Temperance was such a substitute, for at one time it had the capacity to unify many American communities (pp. 27, 30, 156). Another substitute was religious revivalism (pp. 46ff., 67, 77), and another was opposition to slavery (p. 51). Smith also suggests that community organizations—including booster or improvement societies—were often covenant substitutes. The proliferation of these community associations, he remarks, "can best be explained in terms of an effort to recapture that sense of personal involvement which had been so strong in the original covenanted community" (p. 174).

Starkey was formed as a cumulative community, for the settlers who claimed the land sought to achieve personal security and advancement rather than to promote the common good. The town itself was fortuitous both in origin and in growth. It sprang almost entirely from the individual entrepreneurship of blacksmith, storekeeper, and hotel owner. But soon there emerged something resembling Smith's concept of the covenant. The locality came to be conceived of by its residents as a distinct social entity, a community standing apart from other communities nearby; and the hub itself, the small town center, constituted a physical symbol of this social entity. What is more, the growing sense of unity became manifest in the form of a folk theory of community: Starkey regarded itself as a cohesive, vigorous, and upstanding town, and it thought of these characteristics as good. The people of Starkey had something in common, a mutual orientation toward the collective goal of making their town a progressive and meritorious place to live. A person did not necessarily have to forgo his or her own material interests for the sake of community improvement, but the collective goals should receive their fair due.

Not everyone fully agreed on the exact nature of the goals that Starkey should pursue. For example, a conflict of opinion existed over whether certain moral attributes—notably temperance—were desirable. People also quarreled over how social events and programs should be conducted, and some were less active in social affairs than others. But they do not seem to have been divided on the belief that a progressive and meritorious community was an active and cohesive one.

It is in the context of the principle of participation and cohesion, and the underlying ideology of boosterism and improvement, that one of the key features of Starkey's social life is to be understood. This is the tendency for events and organizations to be inclusive rather than exclusive. According to Atherton (1954:186, 216, 290ff.), in nineteenth-century midwestern communities, formal organizations like churches and lodges tended to admit all comers, but the twentieth-century pattern is to exclude certain portions of the locality on class or other grounds. The nineteenth-century pattern he characterized as one of "togetherness," the twentieth-century pattern as one of social fragmentation. In Starkey, however, there is no evidence for a pattern of exclusion in such organizations as the Farm Bureau or the Improvement Club. On the contrary, these groups sought to extend their membership as widely as possible and to represent and carry out the public will.[3]

In addition to supplying collective ends for the residents to pursue, the principle of participation and cohesion also provided criteria for assessing the behavior of others and for allocating social prestige. Reputations—both good and bad—were won through involvement in social affairs, so what a person had at stake in the community life was his or her standing in the locality. For example, those who were active and effective in conducting local affairs—such as Arnold Donelson, Henry Turner, Brian Green, and Tony Giles—enjoyed considerable local eminence for the roles they played. Each was criticized, sometimes bitterly, for trying to dominate community life, but they were never disparaged for wasting their time foolishly or dabbling in frivolous issues.

On the other hand, those who felt alienated from local affairs and were prone to criticize the way they were conducted were themselves criticized. Their feelings of alienation and bitterness increased accordingly, and they became known as "detractors" and "agin'ers" by the establishment. A person who did not fully adhere to the prevailing moral norms, especially the principle of temperance, often chafed at the pressure of public opinion and became associated with the "agin'ers." Consequently, the Starkey church became a symbol and focus of the division between the establishment and the non-establishment.

It was not only the "agin'ers" who tarnished Starkey's image as a cohesive, lively town with a vigorous community spirit. Although community members may occasionally speak of a time when "everyone" participated, in fact this golden age never existed, for in every period a number of people were either too busy to become active in community life or disinclined to do so. For example, Carl Andersen (see Hatch 1975:25–26) was a hardworking farmer, a bachelor until he was almost 50, a good neighbor, and a congenial man. But he seldom found time to attend local events. Nonparticipants of this kind were disparaged only mildly as long as they were not critical of the way local affairs were conducted—they were said to be community supporters in word if not in deed—and as long as they did not allow themselves to drift into the social life of a rival locality, such as Oak Flat. The local prestige of nonparticipants was certainly not enhanced by their failure to become involved, however, and their aloofness was considered uncommendable at best.

The second principle behind community organization—individual economic achievement—was also an important criterion for evaluating people, assessing their social standing, and determining their local reputation. In particular, the agricultural ladder supplied both a framework for measuring an individual's accomplishments and a hierarchical ordering of community members. Carl Andersen may not have contributed much to the community, but he had a very distinct image in Starkey—and beyond—as a farmer. He began at the very bottom of the agricultural ladder early in the century, when he arrived in the region as a young Scandinavian immigrant, but through hard work and sound business practices he became one of the most successful farmers in the community. He was meticulous in his work, and his farm was a model of perfection—he seldom allowed himself to slip behind in the seasonal routine, his fields were always well tended, and his fences, buildings, and equipment were kept in prime condition. Because of his success as a farmer and the very high quality of his work, Andersen enjoyed an excellent reputation.

Important as the economic hierarchy may have been to local residents, differences in wealth among community members were not marked and the stratification system did not harden into a set of distinct strata separated by deep cleavages. For example, the life styles of farm owner and farm worker were not dissimilar. There were no opulent houses, no equivalent of the "brick mansion . . . at the edge of town—a house with a turret surrounded by wrought iron work, set well back among tall evergreens" (quoted in Smith 1966:206). The only "mansions" in Starkey were located on the large cattle ranches that had existed before homesteading began. These now served as ranch headquarters and bunkhouses for hired hands; none was used as a family residence by the absentee ranch owners. Without exception, the family dwellings in Starkey were small, wood frame structures. To see even a modest version of the brick mansion a person had to travel to Oak Flat, and for a mildly impressive example one had to go all the way to Saint Thomas.

The fact that the social–economic hierarchy did not harden into distinct classes is also manifest in that the different levels were not set apart by distinct patterns of moral belief, and in this respect Starkey may have differed from many other small towns in both nineteenth- and twentieth-century America. According to Atherton, the dominant moral code in midwestern towns was that of "a pious, church-going, middle-class society" (1954:72) for whom the McGuffey's school readers were ideally suited (see pp. 65–108). By contrast, the lower class ignored "the dominant code except perhaps for temporary allegiance following revival meetings" (p. 75). This "lower group" below the dominant middle class consisted of "ne'er-do-wells who flout respectability" (p. 249).

The ne'er-do-wells in Starkey do not seem to have constituted a lower-class element in the community, for they were usually young, unmarried farmers' sons working temporarily as farm laborers or cow-boys, and they would settle down to respectable lives once they had acquired a footing on the agricultural ladder and a family of their own. Arnold Donelson's sons were among the most notorious ruffians in the community, but they would eventually become pillars of rectitude. Besides these "young toughs" there were people like John Wright, the hotel owner and saloon keeper, and the beer-drinking Peter Jensen, who aspired (with limited success) to community leadership. Neither of these men could be described as ne'er-do-wells, but they were clearly at odds with the pious, temperance-oriented norms that prevailed in the community. In Starkey, the social division based on differences in moral belief was associated not with the social–economic hierarchy but with the establishment–nonestablishment division.

In Smith's analysis, the values of cumulative towns—individual achievement, business competition, the accumulation of capital, the desire for worldly accomplishments—were incompatible with cove-nanted communities (1966:27). In covenanted towns, according to Smith, "the well-being of the community, or the 'common good,' was more important than that of the individual" (p. 138). The "common good" was safeguarded by a variety of means. In law, for example, the emphasis was on "protection for the community rather than for the individual" (p. 139).

There is little evidence in Starkey of more than minor conflict between the principle of participation and cohesion on the one hand and that of personal economic success on the other. The two sets of standards were alternate avenues of achievement that could be pursued either alone or in combination. Carl Andersen achieved economic success with minimum community participation, and his local prestige was due solely to his agricultural accomplishments. His reputation would have been enhanced if he had engaged actively in community life, but his failure to do so did not mean the loss of his good name. Jerold Whitman offers a striking contrast. He was an excellent farmer, but he also put in sufficient time and energy to become known as a leader. Whitman enjoyed a position of social importance for both lines of activity.

The case of Jerold Whitman is an instructive one. The main reason he was not a more effective leader is that he did not devote as much time to community affairs as was necessary to be a truly outstanding pusher. The role of leader was a demanding one, and Whitman chose to give most of his energy to his farm instead. Arnold Donelson, Henry Turner, and Brian Green, however, chose to sacrifice a degree of economic success for the role of leader. This shows that the principle of participation and cohesion was sufficiently strong to divert at least a few talented people from personal economic advancement. Thorstein Veblen (1923a:418) could complain that boosterism and improvement programs in American country towns were motivated chiefly by the desire for material rewards; he wrote that the town's "municipal affairs, its civic pride, its community interest, converge upon its real-estate values." But this surely was not true in Starkey, where few if any of the programs that were undertaken had even the slightest prospect of financial benefit either for the leaders or for anyone else.

The principle of individual economic achievement was a significant factor behind the local organization because it provided a framework for the hierarchical ordering of community members. It also articulated with and gave support to leadership patterns. The notable was always someone who had proved his ability in the economic sphere, and although the most effective pushers were not the most successful men in economic terms, they were always well established: for example, none of them was a hired farm hand at the time that he emerged as a leader.

But the principle of participation and cohesion was at least as important as the principle of economic achievement. The leadership patterns may have been supported by the social–economic hierarchy, but they were rooted in the principle of participation and cohesion, and the most gifted and successful leaders were willing to sacrifice in one sphere in return for achievement in the other. Similarly, whereas the social–economic hierarchy did not harden into distinct strata, the community principle gave rise to one of the most notable features of the local organization: the acrimonious rift between the establishment and the nonestablishment.

This account of the local organization brings the concept of personal reputation into prominence. Each person in Starkey had a local image about which there was general agreement, for certain attributes were mentioned again and again by various community members when they were discussing that individual. It is relatively simple to portray the reputation of, say, Mrs. Joseph, Jerold Whitman, Peter Jensen, or Arnold Donelson. The attributes that were used to characterize each of these people amounted to a sort of local *curriculum vitae* of accomplishments, personal traits, and other socially significant features.

A person's reputation included a variety of disparate elements, some of which were unique or particularistic, others more general. An example of a particularistic feature is the "boorishness" of Peter Jensen. This was one of the leading elements of his local image, and virtually everyone who spoke of him to me alluded to this trait. It would be difficult to describe his role in the community without mentioning it. But I know of no one else in Starkey to whom the quality of boorishness was ascribed as an outstanding or essential element—although its opposite was thought to characterize a few people, including Arnold Donelson, who was viewed as tactful, articulate, well read, and dignified. Donelson was regarded as the antithesis of Jensen in this regard.

Attributes that could be applied to everyone, or nearly everyone, were especially important in the local social system. These included the principles of community participation and cohesion and of individual economic achievement. On the one hand, they provided a set of goals toward which one could strive in order to achieve social merit, or a set of avenues for personal achievement. On the other hand, they provided a comprehensive conceptual framework for ordering community members. Both constituted standards for assessing the social position of individuals and for making invidious comparisons among them.

This leads to a crucial issue, that of the sense in which Starkey was a community. The town was quite capable of achieving collective goals, as the construction of the Community Hall verifies. But these goals were not very basic, in that they had virtually nothing to do with material rewards, let alone human survival. If Starkey could not have accomplished its collective undertakings it might have had a very different image of itself, but the daily lives of its members would not have been very different.

Yet the people took these undertakings quite seriously—more so, seemingly, than was warranted on purely practical grounds. Why? I suggest that it was because their personal reputations—and social identities—were deeply involved. By and large the people of Starkey cared about one another's opinions of themselves, as is illustrated by the amount of animosity engendered by the censoriousness of at least some members of the establishment: those who became known as "agin'ers" were hardly indifferent to the derogation they received. The community of Starkey was a small-scale network of interpersonal relations of which a prime constituent was the competitive system of social evaluation. What made it a community was the fact that its members were sufficiently important in one another's social universe that their assessments of social position counted very much—enough so that individuals either adjusted their behavior to win their neighbors' respect or became quite angry at their neighbors' disapproval.

In sum, Starkey was a form of reference group,[4] in that the standards of the local community were a primary ingredient in the individual's social frame of reference.

Part **II** After World War II

Chapter 6 Starkey After World War II

I NOW TURN away from the time when Starkey enjoyed a sense of confidence in itself and in its virtues and goals. I turn instead to the community as it appeared after World War II, and particularly as it was in the mid-1960s, when I did fieldwork in the locality. The community now had become far more "modern" in appearance and attitude. The new state of affairs is symbolized by the fact that by war's end no one used butter or eggs to pay their monthly store bill. Now grocery shopping was conducted exclusively through the medium of cash.

Change had always been a prominent feature in Starkey's existence. New forms of transportation, agricultural equipment, methods of financing, and the like were constantly appearing, and associated with these economic and technological developments were a variety of modifications in the social sphere. The spread of the automobile alone had a considerable impact on the community's autonomy.

But World War II promoted further change and hastened effects that had been under way for a number of years. Soon after the German surrender the significance of a variety of fundamental developments was finally becoming clear.

It is ironic that the war helped mask the very changes that would become illuminated once the conflict was over. The reason for this deceptiveness was that wartime conditions were an enormous stimulant in the community, so that local attention was stolen away from developments that were truly basic. Much of the stimulation was economic—the war was very good for business. The farmer in particular enjoyed financial rewards unmatched at any period in the community's past, and the misery of the Depression suddenly turned into incredible prosperity. Past debts were now being paid; property was being added to existing farms whenever land became available; new and better equipment was being purchased—if it could be squeezed out of a war-oriented system of production—and capital assets soared.

Wartime conditions also served to intensify the local social life.[1] The young men of the community who entered the armed forces were given a rousing send-off. Shortly after the bombing of Pearl Harbor a series of community meetings were called on the topic of home defense, reflecting the local fear that the Japanese might soon launch an attack on California, and record was made of every available firearm in the community in case the attack came. A local volunteer militia was organized, composed of about thirty men. They purchased their own uniforms and supplied their own rifles, and together they drilled on the playing field in the park. A round-the-clock air watch program was instituted whereby volunteers manned a plane-spotting station on the school grounds to detect enemy aircraft should they appear.

The stimulating effect of the war is illustrated by the development of the local fire-fighting system. The fire hazard in Starkey is severe during the summer, for then the fields are extremely dry and combustible. An overheated harvester engine is often enough to cause a grass fire, and with proper wind conditions it can burn hundreds or even thousands of acres of farmland. Because food was needed for the war effort, the danger of fire had become not merely a personal matter for the landholder but an issue of national importance. A rumor circulated in Starkey that Japanese saboteurs might try to set fire to the area to help create a food shortage for the Allied countries, and on one occasion it was thought (mistakenly) that a squad of spies had been spotted by the side of the road a few miles from town. Another rumor was that an incendiary bomb attack might be tried.

In order to meet the danger the Fire Control was established in conjunction with both the Starkey Farm Bureau and the Starkey Militia. All the land in the Starkey region was divided into seven fire control districts, each headed by a district leader, a rancher whose job was to ensure that the roadsides were either plowed or burned to protect against fire, accidental or intentional, and to investigate possible fire hazards in his region. At the head of the organization was Bill Donelson.[2]

A small fire crew was also formed. This was instigated by Donelson and state fire-fighting officials. The state paid the wages of one full-time and four part-time firemen and provided a fire truck, which was kept in repair by the militia. Donelson, who lived on the outskirts of the small town, was a part-time crew member and the fire chief. The other members lived in town and were therefore available if an emergency arose. In case of fire, one of the crew members drove the truck slowly down the main street, siren wailing, whereupon the remainder jumped aboard the vehicle as it passed. One of the firemen, Edgar Smith, was the park caretaker, and he served as lifeguard at the swimming pool during the summer. When the fire alarm sounded, a local woman rushed to the park on her bicycle to relieve Smith at the pool while Smith, clad in swimming trunks, ran to catch the truck.

Wartime conditions were a stimulant to the hub itself, helping to give the town the appearance of a bustling, thriving community. The highway that ran through the center of Starkey had become an important link in the statewide system, and the military base near Saint George contributed to a surge in both military and civilian traffic. Seven days a week a constant flow of civilian cars and trucks and military convoys passed through Starkey's main street, impatient to reach the edge of town and resume speed. The commercial establishments in the community were oriented toward highway trade as well as local business, and they thrived. In the heart of town there were now three service stations, a garage, two stores—each with gasoline pumps in front—two cafes, a bar,and a motel. The local merchants may not have been as prosperous as the farmers, but they had little to complain about.

The town center was the focus of considerable local social life during the day. One of the two cafes survived mostly on highway trade, but the other served as a community meeting place. Probably more local business was conducted at the cafe's horseshoe-shaped counter than anywhere else in Starkey: a farmer who wanted to rent or borrow equipment or hire help went there to make his needs known; grain, hay, and cattle could be bought or sold there—not only to local people but to out-of-town buyers as well. The cafe owner and a few of his regular customers were entertaining conversationalists, and a favorite pastime in Starkey was to stop at the cafe, order a cup of coffee, and enjoy the dialog. The fact that the cafe had become a focal point within the community was manifest in an institutionalized form somewhat later, in the early 1950s. A chess club was then active in Starkey, and a chess game was nearly always in progress at the cafe. If a player had to leave before finishing a game, any one of several spectators would be happy to replace him.

Next to the cafe was a service station that was a secondary focal point for the daily community life. When the chess club was active in the early 1950s a second game was usually in progress either in the station's tiny office or in the shade outside. Across the highway from the service station was the garage, which was kept quite busy repairing the family automobiles of local residents, the cars and trucks of passers-by, and farm equipment. While waiting for the mechanic to complete his work the community member walked across the street to the cafe or the service station to visit with whomever was there. He or she would be joined by others who stopped for a few minutes of conversation after buying groceries or checking their mailboxes at the post office.

But not long after the war was over a change became apparent in the tone of the community. The shift may have been coming about slowly over several decades, but it had become a dominant theme by the post-World War II era. It seems to have made a dramatic difference. It was probably as striking a development as the dazzling changes in technology.

Starkey had been a vigorous, self-confident town radiating pride in its accomplishments. The town center was a lively and agreeable place, with its well-equipped stores and shady residential streets. Community affairs were in the hands of an effective team of influentials, at least one of whom was usually in town and ready to visit with whomever chanced by.

But a few years after the war this local self-respect had begun to fall sharply. This may have been associated with changing ideas in the larger society about the merits of small-town life. With the urbanization of American society had come a growing disapproval of rural life, a disapproval that had become manifest in the concept of "hayseed" or "hick." Rural patterns had been in low repute in America since at least the 1920s, when the city's criticism of the country reached its peak (see

Shideler 1973). In the post-World War II period, it seems, the members of Starkey had come to accept this disparagement and to see their locality as a backwater.

An index of the loss of community esteem was the changing attitude toward teachers. By the mid-1960s there was a strong feeling that it was all but impossible to get truly good instructors to come to a community the size of Starkey, for it was believed that well-trained and dedicated teachers would gravitate to the city. "Who would want a job in Starkey?" I was asked. This attitude may have existed in the 1930s, but it seems to have grown substantially after World War II.

The physical appearance of the hub itself came to symbolize the community's malaise and decline. The liveliness that once character-ized the town center had slowed considerably by the mid-1960s, largely owing to the efficiency of the automobile for the local establish-ments were losing an increasing amount of business to Oak Flat and Saint Thomas. The merchant's woes were increased in the early 1960s, when the highway was rerouted to pass along the river bank opposite the community hub. The grocery stores no longer enjoyed the trade of passers-by; the service stations in town either closed or moved to more favorable locations on the new highway; and the garage was moved outside of town to a place where it could cater to through traffic. The restaurant that had attracted most of the local trade burned to the ground in the 1950s and was never rebuilt. In the mid-1960s the bar burned down, and it too was allowed to lapse. Even though one of the grocery stores that had been destroyed by fire was replaced by a new, more modern one, by the mid-1960s there was hardly enough business to support the two stores, both of which were anemic, one nearly to the point of expiring altogether.

The change from a prosperous and bustling little town to a dying one was distressing to most people in Starkey. One person commented,

When the highway was rerouted around Starkey things looked pretty bad for the community. The service stations, of course, closed down. When the store burned down, Fred [the owner] almost didn't rebuild. If he hadn't it would have been very bad for Starkey, because it would have lost its hub. But Fred decided to go ahead and rebuild, which was a very real benefit to the community.

By the mid-1960s portions of the small town appeared decrepit, especially the remaining cafe, the older of the two grocery stores, and the motel. The houses themselves seemed rather old and run-down. The newer and larger homes in the community were now situated on the ranches outside of town, for it was chiefly the landholders who could afford to build new residences or remodel old ones.

Another attribute of the community that was typically referred to by community members in commenting on Starkey's decline, and one that symbolized the local malaise, was the change in moral and religious patterns. By the mid-1960s the Methodist Church—at one time described as the "center" of the locality—was no longer thought to enjoy a central position in local affairs. A similar decline had occurred with respect to the drinking patterns. The division between drinkers and nondrinkers was still marked, as we will see, but it was far less rigid than in the past and was becoming even less so. In particular, the drinkers had become more open in their tippling. There were now community affairs at which drinking took place quite openly.

By the mid-1960s a few of the town's more cynical citizens claimed that Starkey was no longer a community at all, whereas the majority view was that it was declining but had not totally expired. I asked one person if Starkey were declining as a community, and he remarked, "Yes it is. All of this is now almost a part of Oak Flat. All you have to do is take the [Starkey] high school in there and Oak Flat, Starkey, Saint George, and Pinefield would be a community like Starkey was at one time." But after a moment's reflection he added, "Still, Starkey is a community, though."

One community member stressed the growing lack of cohesion in Starkey. He commented,

After the war Starkey began breaking up into cliques, bumping heads. It was altogether different before and after the war. . . . Everybody branched out and bucked heads. If you call someone now and tell him something needs to be done he would say, "Who's doing it?" Before, there were no questions asked, people would just help. There are too many hard feelings [today].

The following comment about a teacher at the Starkey High School portrays Starkey's decline—and malaise—in yet another light: "He spends three nights a week in Saint Thomas. He's almost more a member of that community than he is of Starkey. The people wouldn't have stood for that several years ago." This statement is revealing in two ways. It illustrates the feeling that Starkey no longer had the cohesion it enjoyed in the past, but the resentment implicit in these words also manifests a continuing sense of community.

One factor in particular was emphasized by Starkey people as a cause of the community's decline. This was the influx of newcomers and the proportionate loss of the "old guard." It is impossible to say whether the percentage of newcomers was truly growing or even, if so, whether this had the adverse effects that people claimed it had. But it seems reasonable to suggest that this folk explanation of Starkey's decline was a somewhat inaccurate representation of a state of affairs that was very real: the small-town values no longer commanded the respect they once had. If the newcomers did not always share the community spirit, neither did the old-timers. In a sense, the old family members had become increasingly like newcomers.

A full explanation of the changes that were under way in Starkey would have to touch on a wide variety of factors, and at present, it seems, such an account cannot be written: Although an enormous literature exists on community deterioration—Roland Warren (1972) refers to it as the "great change" in American communities—in fact our understanding of the process is still quite primitive.[3]

What is clear is that these changes in the local group are but one expression of some truly basic alterations in the structure of American society. At one time the American people were organized on the geographic basis of community and region, but increasingly it is a matter of such nonlocal principles as social stratification. Stated in more concrete terms, early in the twentieth century the people living in the area centering on Oak Flat drew their identities largely from their home communities. The local community was the primary arena in which the individual sought to achieve social standing. What is more, a person was identified by others outside the community according to his or her hometown. A Starkey resident shopping at one of the stores in Oak Flat would probably have been greeted by a question that tacitly acknowledged his or her community affiliation: "How is the weather in Starkey today" or "How is the Community Hall coming along?" But after World War II the principle of community began to lose its importance.

For example, by the mid-1960s the Starkey farmer shopping in Oak Flat was more likely to be asked whether he had heard the latest news about farm prices than to be questioned about the current state of affairs in his community. And people in other communities were likely to rival—if not surpass—members of his hometown in the attention they received from him.

Starkey's deterioration and the local malaise were striking features of the community in the mid-1960s and would have been noticed by any observer. But this was only part of what stood out about the locality, for Starkey was far from expiring altogether, and its self-image was not wholly negative by any means. The sting of public opinion could still be an effective sanction, and as will become clear shortly, people sometimes took extraordinary measures to avoid local censure. What is more, community undertakings were still conducted according to patterns that suggest that the locality was an organizational entity.

Perhaps one of the clearest indexes of the persistence of community was a set of somewhat detailed social distinctions having a strictly local definition and focus. If I were to ask a knowledgeable resident about another member of the community—if I were to ask one person to identify the other, to tell me who he or she is—these distinctions would be among those used to place him or her in the social universe.

One set of social distinctions was between old-family members and newcomers. The importance of this criterion is suggested by one woman's response when asked about the major social distinctions in the locality. She replied, "The most important thing is the distinction between new family and old family." Not everyone would have placed this item at the head of the list, but no one in Starkey would have denied that old-family membership was a highly significant matter in local affairs.

Old-family status conferred a degree of prestige on a person, and this was manifest in a number of contexts. For example, on issues of local importance the opinions of old-family members were more actively sought than those of newcomers, and their support was more vigorously courted. A local organization that attempted to sample community opinion would normally focus its attention on the views of the longer-established members of the community on the ground that these people were leaders in public opinion. Similarly, a ne'er-do-well was considered a "town character" if his family was a long-established one in Starkey, but otherwise he was considered a no-good. One man in particular, an antisocial bachelor (and the son of Peter Jensen), had a very unfavorable reputation as a disagreeable, unsuccessful and un-civic-minded person. His property in town was considered an eyesore, and he refused to clean it up even after several requests by the leading community organization. But the elderly bachelor was also considered one of the most colorful of the town characters. Several months after I arrived in the community, one person—who had little personal sympa-thy with the misanthrope—became quite concerned that I had not yet interviewed this man and told me that my study would not be complete until I had done so.

The concept of old-family member was a flexible one, for the definition of the term varied somewhat from one situation to the next. The descendants of the early Starkey settlers (defined here as those who arrived before 1900) were the only ones who were referred to unequivocally and in all contexts as old-family members. Their family histories were tightly intertwined with that of the community, and stories about the community's past—about the hardships suffered by the homesteaders, the construction of the Community Hall, or spectacular fires, accidents, or Hallowe'en pranks—inevitably revolved around their forebears. Their family names had become affixed to the map of the region in that the canyons in which their fathers, grandfathers, and great-grandfathers had homesteaded now bore their last names. Each of these people could trace kin ties to the others, for the several family lines making up this category of residents had become more or less fused through the intermarriage of at least a few sons and daughters in each generation.

Families that had arrived in Starkey after the community was settled (after about 1900) but before the stock market crash of 1929 were considered old families in most contexts. Though they were not pioneers, they shared in much of Starkey's history. Almost all of these people were related by kinship to one another and to the descendants of Starkey homesteaders.

Those who had come to the community during the 1930s were often spoken of as "more or less old family," although they were reluctant to describe themselves as old-family members. A man who had brought his family to Starkey during the Depression said, "We're not an old family in Starkey, and because of that fact I know that people feel about me, in a way, like they feel toward the Negro." Most families that had arrived in the 1930s were related to at least one other family in the community, and some could trace kin ties to the more longstanding members of the locality.

It is difficult to conceive of a context in which people who had moved to Starkey after 1940 would have been referred to as old family in the mid-1960s. They were almost unequivocally newcomers. Few of these people could trace kin ties to the descendants of homesteaders, and many had no relatives in the community outside their immediate families.

The category of "old county family" was a complication in the distinction between old-family member and newcomer. The people of this category were members of old families from nearby communities, such as Saint George and Oak Flat; most could trace kin ties within Starkey, and their families played a role in the history of the county if not in that of Starkey itself. These people were hardly the same as rank newcomers who had recently arrived from the Midwest or Los Angeles, yet they did not fully share in the community's past like the truly old families in Starkey.

In 23 percent of Starkey's households in the mid-1960s either the husband or the wife or both had arrived in the locality before 1900 or could trace direct lineal descent from pre-1900 settlers. These were pioneers—now quite elderly—or their sons and daughters, or perhaps grandsons and granddaughters. Another 10 percent of the households contained a man or a woman (or both) who had arrived between 1900 and 1930 or could trace direct lineal descent from a family that had done so. The number of households falling into the 1930–1940 category, in turn, constituted 11 percent of those in the community, whereas the ones that had arrived since 1940 constituted 46 percent. An additional 9 percent of the local households contained a husband or a wife (or both) from an old county family.

Another figure sheds further light on the category of old family. Counting not only lineal descent but all known ties based on kinship and marriage, however remote, 44 percent of the Starkey households could trace connections to one another and to families that had arrived before 1900. This category included nieces and nephews of early settlers, for example, as well as relatives through marriage (siblings and parents of those who had married old-family members). In other words, a little less than half the community consisted of a single network of kinsmen linked to the early pioneers.

An additional social distinction was asociated with that between old-family member and newcomer. This was commonly expressed by community members as a division between those "who are a part of the community" and those "who are outside of everything in the community." I will use the less cumbersome terms *core* and *periphery.*

The criterion that determined an individual's placement in one category or the other was community participation. A newcomer could become part of the core within a few years by taking an active role in local affairs, a point that was expressed repeatedly. I asked one person about the importance of old-family membership in being considered "a part of the community," and she said,

I feel [that being of an old family] is important, but it's not the most important thing in Starkey. There is quite a number of relatively new families, such as [a family that moved to Starkey during the 1930s], who are just as much a part of Starkey as anyone else. It's a matter of getting in and becoming a part of the community.

Being "a part of the community" in this sense did not necessarily require regular attendance at community affairs. A person could be part of the core by virtue of passive involvement, by which I mean knowing about local matters and regularly engaging in discussions—or gossip—about them. A person who seldom attended community events and belonged to none of the community organizations could nevertheless be part of the core if he or she frequently discussed local matters with friends and relatives.

The members of the periphery were truly "outside of everything in the community" in the sense that they did not have a grasp of local affairs and could not easily identify people in terms of the roles they played in community life.

The distinction between periphery and core was fairly clear-cut in the people's minds, but it hardly produced two distinct groups when applied to living individuals. Many people could not be placed in either category without equivocation, in part because they were involved in some aspects of community life but not in others. In order to convey some idea of the relative sizes of the two categories, however, some attempt to arrive at numerical figures is called for.

The method I have employed is to classify community members according to my own assessment of their knowledge of local affairs. This exercise gave the following results. A little more than half, or 54 percent, of the community members belonged to the core. These were people whom I knew to be aware of the details about major current events and scandals in the community and to hold opinions about them. Nearly one-fifth, or 19 percent, belonged to the periphery. These were people whom I judged to be more or less unaware of even the most basic facts about the social life of the community; they would probably be unable to name the latest social event, for example, and it was unlikely that they would know about recent scandals. About 28 percent of the community occupied an intermediate position. These were individuals who knew about some matters—such as controversies concerning the schools or the current gossip about an important community member—but were ignorant of other major features of social life.

Membership in the core and old-family status were related, since people whose families had resided in Starkey since before 1940 could hardly avoid being involved to some extent in local affairs. Their interpersonal relations within the community were sufficiently extensive and strong to draw them into at least passive involvement. Nevertheless, not all old-family members were clearly part of the core. The antisocial bachelor mentioned earlier is an example. He had strong feelings about many of the community members, and he knew at least a smattering of the most recent gossip. But he had little interest in current community affairs, and by my assessment he falls into the intermediate category between periphery and core.[4]

I have remarked that the deterioration of Starkey as a community and the accompanying sense of malaise in the mid-1960s presented a striking contrast with the state of affairs before World War II. A second dramatic change—one that would have struck virtually any observer—occurred within the social–economic hierarchy.

By and large, agricultural occupations were still dominant numeri-
cally, and they still supplied the principal reference points for assessing social rank. But farming itself had been transformed—a change that
was closely tied to World War II, for the world conflict was a powerful
stimulant to developments that had been under way in agriculture since
before the fighting began. With the changes in farming came changes
in the pattern of stratification.

The major change in agriculture was that the farm enterprise
became a relatively big business. World War II began at a time when
most landholders in Starkey were trying desperately to remain solvent
in the face of the need to expand, but once the United States had
become involved in the war conditions changed almost immediately:
agricultural profits now were considerable, and the debts of past years
were being paid with a single crop. Whoever was in a position to enjoy
the profits of wartime—which is to say those who did not go into military
service and could find land to add to their holdings—soon found
themselves operating a business enterprise of substantial proportions.
Those who were not in such a position—such as elderly farmers whose
sons were called to fight, or others who could not obtain more land—
were soon squeezed from the ranks of the prominent community
members.

By the mid-1960s the minimum amount of grain land needed to
support a family had increased to about 2,000 acres (1,000 acres
harvested each year). The monetary value of such a farm—including
the value of land, equipment, livestock, and buildings—was well over
$200,000. The farmer now was the owner–manager of a heavily capital-
ized business.

The social implications of this change are illustrated by the new
relationship that developed between farmer and hired man. A widening
gap was separating the two, for the farmer had capital investments that
were completely beyond the reach of the hired man, who had no
prospect of ever owning his own farm or ranch—unless he was fortu-
nate enough to acquire one through marriage or inheritance. No longer
was the agricultural ladder a continuous series of steps from hired
employee to independent owner, for there were now two strata separated by an unbridgeable gulf.

The farmer and the farm hand were also separated by different attitudes and identities. In the past the farmer had identified with labor and the plight of the working man, but now he viewed himself more as a businessman–employer whose goals were at odds with those of labor. Not only did the farmer have something the farm worker could never achieve; the two no longer felt that they had the same interests.[5]

This shows that a two-tiered pattern of stratification had emerged in Starkey, and the distinction between the two strata was expressed linguistically in a number of ways. Some people distinguished between the "ranchers" and the "working guys," for example, others between the "haves" and the "have-nots." This division was a major feature of the social landscape not only of Starkey but of most of the inland portion of the county.

By local definition, a "have" was someone whose holdings were sufficient to support a family: this meant at least 2,000 acres of grain land or 4,000 acres of rangeland or some combination of both. Those who fell into this category I will refer to as the major landholders, who represented 16 percent of the households in Starkey, or 26 families.

The major landholders were the local well-to-do, and as such they were clearly set apart in local thought. But most of them also had close ties to the community, in part because the majority bore family names that stretched far back into Starkey's past: the inheritance of family property helped to bind at least certain members of each succeeding generation to the locality. The local roots of the major landholders had an important aspect. These were people who had been quite poor during the Depression, when their children looked with envy on the families of teachers and oil facility employees who had regular incomes and could occasionally afford to buy new shoes and overalls for their youngsters. The present success of the major landholders was sufficiently recent so that their humble roots were still part of their local image.

Agricultural profits surely were no longer very substantial after the war was over, for a mild form of depression had been an agricultural fact of life since the late 1940s. In the mid-1960s the landholders could justifiably complain that their incomes were hardly commensurate with the value of their investments. But certainly the local ranches were more often in the black than in the red, and the steadily increasing worth of real property increased the potential well-being of anyone holding title to land.

The evidence of the landholders' relative wealth was unmistakable. A few new, modern homes had appeared in and around Starkey by the mid-1960s, and almost all of them had been built by ranch families. An even clearer indication is that the major landholders could afford to own well-bred, well-trained horses. It is true that they also needed them for handling their cattle, but it was not only the rancher himself who owned a horse and became a proficient horseman. Riding and roping had become a fashionable pastime among wives and children as well. Riding and roping contests were held periodically throughout the county and beyond, and it was normally the youthful members of ranch-owning families who went: their parents could afford the horses and the necessary equipment, from cowboy boots to horse trailers.

The major landholders were hardly homogeneous, for some had more—and better—property than others, and one or two leased and did not own most of their farmland and thus occupied a precarious position among the well-to-do. In addition, some were strictly cattlemen while others raised grain. This was a very significant distinction, for it was thought to be grander to be a cattleman than to be a farmer. For example, a cattleman once commented to me that in all his life he had never been on a harvester—a remark that could only be taken as a boast. Similarly, in local usage the term *farmer* carried a somewhat negative connotation, and a man who raised grain was typically referred to as a rancher instead.

The line between cattleman and grain rancher was somewhat blurred, since the latter normally ran some cattle on his holdings—part of his property could normally be used more suitably as range land than as farmland, and cattle could be fed on the dry grain stubble left after the harvest. Most of the grain ranchers devoted much time to their herds and left routine farming operations like tractor driving to the hired help.

A group of six households were set apart from the other major landholders. These were what I call the wealthy elite. The holdings of each of these families were quite large, in several cases consisting of cattle ranches that had existed before the arrival of settlers. Most of the men in this category were cattlemen, and two were reputedly millionaires.

These people represented something very different from what Starkey was accustomed to. They had moved to the community almost at the same time, just before and after World War II, in order to manage the lands of their respective families, property that had formerly been run on an absentee basis. These people were distinguished from the other major landholders on several grounds. They were all relative newcomers, not members of old families, and they lacked kinship ties within the community. They or their families were also extremely well-to-do by local standards much before World War II began: they hardly shared the humble roots of the other cattlemen and grain ranchers. In addition, they had a different life style. Several of them built larger, more expensive houses than anyone else had even contemplated having—two of them had maid's quarters. They were generally better educated and sent their children to such universities as Stanford or Yale. The wealthy elite brought what one person called the "cocktail way of life" to Starkey. They frequently met for small dinner and cocktail parties, sometimes inviting a handful of other local ranchers.

Among the "have-nots" were what might be called the minor landholders: those who had sufficient agricultural holdings so that a substantial part of their earnings came from the sale of their own cattle and crops, but whose property was not enough to support a family. Nine households fell into this category. These were the people who had failed to increase their holdings when it had been possible to do so and therefore no longer enjoyed a place near the top of the social–economic hierarchy. Some of these people had once been among the wealthiest in Starkey.

To augment their incomes the minor landholders usually worked part time for others, often as farm hands on neighboring ranches, and if they did so they were said to "work out." It is significant that the term *working out* was never used in relation to the farm worker who had no property: he was strictly an employee, whereas the minor landholder was both independent rancher and part-time employee.

The minor landholder could also engage in what was called custom work, in which he was hired to use his own equipment to do specific jobs on other ranches. He might be hired to bring his harvester and help harvest another man's crop, or to use his tractor to plow the weeds that had sprouted in the summer fallow. A subtle shade of meaning colored the notion of custom work: the custom worker was conceived of as an independent businessman who contracted to do specific jobs, and not as an employee. In theory at least, it was more prideful to be the one than the other.

Custom work was not limited to minor landholders, for a few nonpropertied men were full-time custom operators. For example, one person owned both a harvester and a tractor and had enough work to keep him reasonably busy, whereas several others owned trucks for hauling hay. Although these men were said to own their own businesses, they were certainly not included among the "haves" in local thought, and they always appeared—both to me and to others—to border on bankruptcy. The full-time custom operator was invariably young, hardworking, and seemingly poverty stricken. He was also normally a newcomer: unlike the landholder, he did not have property to tie him to the locality.

A large category of "have-nots" in Starkey—represented in the mid-1960s by thirty men—was that of hired man or farm worker. These men drove the tractors or harvesters that could be seen day in and day out in the distant fields, and repaired fences, machinery, and the like when time allowed and weather dictated. Their hours were long and their pay, by urban standards, quite low. They did not have land to tie them to the community, and consequently they tended to be somewhat transient. Few of them were members of old families, and few had kin ties with others in the locality: of the 30 men, 22 had arrived during or since World War II, 2 were from families that had arrived during the Depression, and only 6 were members of or had married into families that had been in Starkey since before 1929.

The category of hired man was internally stratified in a hierarchy that was conceived of primarily as one of respectability. Those at the top were considered good, respectable people (at least by other respectables)—they were hardworking, dependable, stable, and competent. At the bottom were the unreliable and unsteady.

This distinction was expressed locally by the terms *foreman type* and *Okie type.* The foreman type did not necessarily have the title of foreman but was considered worthy of such a position: he was someone who "could run my own place and be successful," as one rancher put it. Those who were able to find jobs as foremen had the most coveted (and usually highest-paid) positions among hired men. They took over the routine management of the grain operation of a ranch while the land-holder devoted his time to bookkeeping, managing the cattle, and the like. This gave the foreman considerable independence and, usually, a good deal of authority over other workers at certain times, such as harvest. From the perspective of the landholder, men of this caliber were extremely rare, and indeed only seven men in Starkey unequivo-cally enjoyed the reputation of "foreman types" in the mid-1960s.

At the opposite pole from the "foreman types" were the "Okies"— who, people were quick to point out, were not necessarily from Okla-homa. One person gave the following description of this category:

There is a certain type of person in Starkey. Perhaps they're here for a couple of years and then move away, but might return several years later. Or maybe they stay here continuously but change jobs periodically. These people don't care for their children. They're like a bunch of rabbits—they don't care what their children do, like at school, so long as it doesn't put the parents out any. . . . Their children are usually filthy and run around all the time.

The "Okie types" were considered less competent and responsi-ble, more transient, and less respectable in their personal lives than the "foreman types." They wore tattered clothes, drove old, run-down cars or pickup trucks, and often rented the tiny, unsightly houses in a section of Starkey known as The Alley. Men in this category were often paid an hourly wage to do specific jobs, and the work—and thus the pay—was quite irregular. They were unlikely to remain in Starkey long enough to establish kin ties within the community, and few if any ever engaged in the community life. To borrow Vidich and Bensman's (1958) phrase, most of them were socially invisible. In the mid-1960s approximately ten men fell unequivocally into the "Okie" category.

Another type of employee was not bracketed with the farm worker in local thought, even though the two were quite similar in some respects. This was the cowboy.

The labor requirements of the large cattle ranches were filled in a variety of ways. For such odd jobs as mending fences a farm worker might be hired on a temporary basis and, for brandings and the gathering of cattle for shipment, friends and neighbors who had acquired the necessary skills were invited to help. But a few of the cattle ranches also needed a man either full or part time to help look after the herd.

The days of the bunkhouse full of cowboys had long passed, largely because of the pickup truck. The cowboy no longer spent a large portion of his time moving from one place to another on horseback, for he now carted his horse in a trailer to the field or corral where he was needed. He could now do the work that at one time had required several men. In the mid-1960s there were only four hired cowboys in Starkey, though several had retired and lived in the area.

The cowboy was one of the lowest-paid men in the locality, and yet he was looked upon with considerable respect. The job required roping and riding abilities that few people had, and so the cowboy was considered a highly skilled workman—highly skilled in accomplishments that were also fashionable. He also needed a good deal of knowledge about cattle (e.g., for diagnosing ailments). The cowboy was thought to be identifiable by such characteristics as his clothing and—so people claimed—his mannerisms. Supposedly, the knowledgeable individual would never mistake a cowboy for a farm worker, simply because of the way cowboys walk and perhaps because of the cowboy's cool reserve and dry humor.

In addition to dry-land grain crops and cattle, a third major type of agriculture in Starkey was irrigation farming (chiefly barley, alfalfa, and sugar beets). A few small parcels of land along the rivers had artesian wells and thus had been under irrigation since the turn of the century, and somewhat later the electric pump made it possible to bring water to other properties. But irrigation was severely limited by the generally uneven topography: only level land could be watered by a system of open ditches. Shortly after World War II the aluminum pipe and sprinkler made it possible to increase the acreage under irrigation, but the slope still had to be a very gentle one for this method to work, and in the mid-1960s irrigation farming had expanded only far enough to include most of Starkey Flat and portions of the relatively flat bottom lands leading to and from it. The rich, green, irrigated plots stopped just short of the hilly regions that stretched in all directions.

Irrigation farming represented a striking contrast with the predominant dry-land agriculture, and this was clearly expressed in local usage. The people who were engaged chiefly in raising irrigated crops were called farmers, never ranchers. And this distinction carried a heavy load of meaning, for the term *rancher* had a much more favorable connotation, as I have noted. One grain rancher (who leased much of his farmland) commented, "I would rather starve than make a buck in irrigation. I groan a little every time [my leasors] want to work up some more irrigated land."

As a category, the irrigation farmers were not very prosperous. None of them clearly rivaled the major landholders in social position, income, or capital investments, and indeed only two appeared to be financially secure. Most of them leased the land they farmed, and most had barely enough acreage to support their families (a minimum of about 200 to 300 acres was needed, depending on the soil). The turnover among irrigation farmers was fairly high, and consequently most of them were newcomers and were considered relatively transient. In the mid-1960s only two of the ten irrigation farmers in Starkey traced their descent from homesteaders.

The irrigated farms had seasonal labor requirements that were quite demanding. In particular, all summer the aluminum pipes had to be moved on a regular basis: each section had to be unlinked, carried by hand to a new spot, and rejoined. Sugar beets also needed hand weeding and thinning. Ideally, the farmer himself undertook the tasks that were mechanized—cultivating the soil, planting, and harvesting—and hired others to do more onerous jobs like moving pipes and weeding.

Part of the labor was supplied by local high-school boys looking for summer work, but most was provided by Mexican or Mexican-American migrant laborers. Seven to ten migrant laborers lived in Starkey during each summer season and occasionally were joined briefly by a busload of others recruited by labor contractors from the Central Valley. Two blacks living in Oak Flat also traveled to Starkey every day during the summer to work on irrigated farms.

These seasonal laborers were socially invisible. They took no part in local life, and since they were usually in the fields for most of the day few local people had a chance to learn their names, let alone speak to them. They were too marginal even to be included among the periphery.[6] By local usage they did not live in Starkey and were no more a part of it than the visitor who happened to stay at the motel.

The nonagriculturalists were another very large category of community members—about one-third of the households in Starkey in the mid-1960s. They also present an interesting contrast with the agricultural people. The agricultural occupations were classifiable in a fairly orderly fashion, and the various subcategories (such as wealthy elite, "foreman-type" farm hands, and migrant workers) fit together rather neatly. But there seems to have been no clear order or pattern of social subcategories among the nonagriculturalists.

One pattern that did emerge is that all the members of this category ranked below the "haves." Even the most successful and prosperous nonagriculturalists were not quite in the same league as the major landholders.

Another pattern is that the nonagriculturalists were ranked in a vague hierarchy of prestige—vague in the sense that the precise standing of individuals in relation to one another was not always very clear in people's minds. But the general form of the ranking was clear, and so was the way it was represented in local thought, which was as a scale of respectability not unlike that which applied to the farm workers. Those at the top were solid citizens—competent, industrious, and trustworthy, a credit to themselves and the community. Those at the bottom were thought to be somewhat disreputable, unreliable, underhanded, and shameless.

Near the top of the hierarchy of nonagriculturalists (some would say at the very top) was the couple who owned the more prosperous of the two stores (which was leased and run by another family), along with several rental houses in Starkey and other investments outside the community. The man was also the Starkey postmaster, and he had a reputation for honesty and aptitude. Another reasonably prosperous and high-ranking nonagriculturalist was the man who owned and (by himself) ran one of the two garages in town. He was thought to be a good mechanic, though somewhat slow and overpriced. The school superintendent was high on the list. He had been chosen from a field of applicants after extensive debate by the school board and had come to Starkey from a larger community elsewhere in the county, where he had served as an assistant school administrator. The teachers as a whole were among the high-ranking or "respectable" nonagriculturalists, and so were the employees on the state highway crew and the workers at the oil company facilities just outside of town. These people all had regular incomes, and their automobiles, houses, and clothing were reasonably fashionable and attractive. Perhaps a few of these nonagriculturalists ranked above the most respectable hired men—the "foreman types"; certainly the postmaster did so, and in some minds so did the school superintendent. But not the teachers. They and the state road crew and the oil facility employees, among others, were roughly equal in rank to the fully reputable farm employees. The teachers were even conceived of somewhat on the model of farm workers, for in a sense they were regarded as hired men (and women).

Other people were not quite solid citizens yet were not quite disrespectable either. The workers on the county road crew fell into this category. They were paid rather low wages, and unlike the state road crew (which was entirely separate) they did not seem to do a very commendable job. Their clothes were usually somewhat dirty and tattered, their houses run-down. The widow who eked out a living running the cafe (which she leased) was certainly careful in appearance. And she was hardworking. But she was quite poor and somewhat inflexible in the way she ran her business. She lived alone in a single tiny room just off the kitchen in which she spent most of her day. Another widow—very religious—lived in a small rented house in Starkey. Her main source of income was apparently her monthly welfare check. This woman was thought to be somewhat peculiar—if given the chance she talked endlessly about strange subjects, and she wandered about the park in the afternoons gathering dandelions, which she prepared for dinner.

At the bottom of the hierarchy of nonagriculturalists were the genuine disreputables. One was an elderly bachelor who lived alone in a shack near the church—which of course he had never been in. He was a derelict and an alcoholic. When he was able to he did gardening and odd jobs for a rancher whose house was located in town. One morning his employer realized that the man had not been seen for several days. He went to the man's small quarters and found him dead.

If it had not been for the rancher his absence probably would not have been noticed for another week or more. Another derelict alcoholic worked at whatever odd jobs he could find, but unlike the first he had a family, a wife and daughter. They lived in a small rented house in town and were barely able to survive. The young girl was a shy, seemingly friendless ragamuffin.

The social–economic hierarchy in Starkey was a system for ranking community members, yet it was also more than that, for it had a qualitative, ideational dimension. For example, to describe the wealthy elite it is important to mention their "old money," their relatively recent arrival, their "cocktail way of life," and so on. Again, merely to rank as higher or lower such categories as cattleman, cowboy, grain rancher, irrigation farmer, "Okie," and the like is to miss much of what it was that distinguished these social components from one another. The hierarchical ordering of both farm workers and nonagriculturalists was cast in the idiom of respectability.

But it is true that a useful way to organize these social categories and to summarize them is as a hierarchy of prestige. The "haves" were at the top of the system, divided into two groups: the wealthy elite and, below them, the other major landholders, who were mostly grain ranchers and old-family members. The "have-nots" were far more heterogeneous and much more difficult to summarize. They included such categories as minor landholder, irrigation farmer, farm worker, small-business owner, oil facility employee, county or state road crew worker, and teacher. But both agricultural and nonagricultural "have-nots" were internally ranked, and they exhibited roughly the same range of prestige from top to bottom. At or near the top of the hierarchy of agricultural "have-nots" were the minor landholders, the more successful irrigation farmers, and the "foreman types." They were roughly equivalent to such nonagriculturalists as the more prosperous small-business owners, the school superintendent and teachers, and the state road crew. At the bottom of the hierarchy were the somewhat transient and disrespectable "Okies," who in turn were roughly equivalent to the local derelicts among the nonagriculturalists. Outside the system entirely were the seasonal workers. Table 1 tabulates the household heads in Starkey by occupation and place of residence.

Table 1. Occupations of Household Heads (Excluding Bitter Valley and Pinefield)

	I	II	III	IV
Agricultural Occupations				
Major landholders				
grain ranchers	14	5	–	2
cattlemen	5	2	–	1
Marginal landholders	9	4	–	–
Irrigation farmers	9	–	–	1
Farm workers (excluding				
seasonal workers)	29	–	1	?
Cowboys	5	4	–	–
Miscellaneous	7	–	–	–
Total	77	15	1	4
Nonagricultural Occupations				
Teachers and superintendent	8	–	1	1
Other school personnel	3	–	–	1
Small-business owners	11	1	–	2
Employees of organizations				
with heads outside the				
community (e.g., oil facility				
workers, state and county				
road crews)	12	4	2	1
Other full-time employees	4	–	–	–
Total	38	5	3	5
Retired or Widowed (not listed				
elsewhere)	–	9	–	–
Work Outside Community (not				
listed elsewhere)	–	–	12	–
Unemployed	4	–	–	–
GRAND TOTAL	119	29	16	9

NOTE: The heads of 17 (9.8%) of the 173 households represented in this table were women.

Col. I. Live and work in Starkey. Col. II. Retired or widowed in Starkey. Col. III. Live in Starkey, work elsewhere. Col. IV. Live elsewhere, work in Starkey.

Starkey was far different in the mid-1960s than it had been in, say, 1920. The principle of individual economic achievement could not help but have a new complexion, since the family farm had become a heavily capitalized business and the social–economic hierarchy had become divided between the "haves" and the "have-nots." The signs of community deterioration—such as the increasingly run-down and old-fashioned appearance of the town and the feeling of malaise among the members of the community—must also mean that the principle of community participation and cohesion had changed.

If the community existed at all at this time, what had it become? What was the nature of local affairs, and how were they conducted? How did people divide on local issues—indeed, what kinds of issues could bring people into opposition? What had happened to the earlier folk theory of community? In brief, in what sense was Starkey something more than an aggregate of households?

Chapter 7 The Hierarchy of Communities

EVER SINCE STARKEY was founded it has been part of a larger network of communities, and it is important to discuss this geographic context. Several issues in particular need to be dealt with, including the extent to which Starkey was part of higher-order localities, the nature of the boundaries setting Starkey apart from its neighbors, and the nature of the smaller communities or subdivisions contained within Starkey's borders.

Rural sociologists have produced a sizable literature on the relations among rural populations and trade centers.[1] Questionnaires are sometimes used to discover where the inhabitants of a region shop, worship, bank, visit, and the like. The results are plotted on a map, which shows in graphic form the exent of a town's hinterland and the nature of its relations with other communities. This is a method with a long history, beginning with a classic study of a rural county in Wisconsin (Galpin 1915; see also Galpin 1911).

A drawback of this approach is that it does not reveal the way local inhabitants perceive intercommunity relations (see Haga and Folse 1971:42–44), which is what occupies me here. My focus is on patterns of thought and not on numerical tabulations of who goes where to do what, although a skeletal understanding of the latter should be a by-product of my account.

A basic principle behind the community's conception of its relations with others was that of community hierarchy, according to which the locality was conceived of as part of another community, which in turn was part of yet a larger one, and so on. Similarly, localities that were smaller than Starkey but attached to it were viewed as lower in the hierarchy and as "nesting" within the Starkey community.

The relationships between communities were conceived of somewhat differently at each level of the hierarchy. Not only did the sense of association diminish at each higher level, but the relationship took different forms as well.

Not all of the communities with which Starkey was associated were part of the hierarchy in the mid-1960s. In particular, most of the people in the small town had at least occasional economic ties with one of the large cities in the Central Valley, since, owing to its size, it had a greater range of goods and services than could be found in any of the nearby coastal cities. Small groups of women sometimes drove to the inland city to shop for Christmas presents or school clothes, and local farmers and ranchers occasionally dealt with the agricultural businesses there. But the relationship between Starkey and the Central Valley city—as it was viewed in Starkey—was missing the element of constituency, the idea that the smaller locality was a component of the larger one. The relationship was viewed in instrumental terms, for the interior city was seen chiefly as a place to go for certain needs.

This is understandable, since Starkey's eastern boundary (or, more accurately, the eastern boundary of Lorraine and Bitter Valley) was a major social watershed. The people living beyond it looked to the towns and cities of the Central Valley for most of their everyday needs and interests, and in Starkey they were considered to be of the interior and not of the coast. Starkey, however, was associated with the region bordering the Pacific. No issues arose during my research in which the town was identified with California's agricultural interior or with any of its localities.

Starkey's lack of association with the Central Valley was reinforced by the predominant mode of agriculture in the interior of the state. Starkey is part of a grazing and dry-crop region that runs along the coast, whereas much of the Central Valley is devoted to irrigated crops. The growers in the valley were referred to in Starkey as farmers, never as ranchers.

Yet Starkey was only vaguely oriented toward the general dry-crop and grazing region along the coast, for at the top of the hierarchy of communities—taking Starkey as the point of reference—was the county. Unlike some counties, which are administrative and jurisdictional units with little immediate social visibility or significance, the one in which Starkey is located was conceived of—in Starkey at least—as a major political, geographic, and social division, as is manifest in the fact that the local people were consciously aware of its boundaries and, therefore, of the localities it included. Community members could normally say whether another community, even a very small one some distance away, was or was not part of the county.

A few small localities just beyond the boundary line were included in the county in an equivocal sense if they were oriented toward the county seat, Saint Thomas, or toward some other trade center within the county, such as Oak Flat. The equivocal nature of these communities was held in mind, however. In discussions with people who had been in the community more than a few years I seldom detected any confusion over whether such a community was situated on one side of the county line or the other.

The significance of the county in local thought may have reflected the dominant role that Saint Thomas played in the region. This was the largest locality within the county—it was a small city—and the most important trade center, serving all the communities within the county and even a few beyond. The drive from Starkey's main street to downtown Saint Thomas took a little less than an hour, compared with at least two hours to the city in the Central Valley. Members of a Starkey household might travel to Saint Thomas several times a month; they might go to the interior city several times a year.

The political and administrative significance of Saint Thomas was illustrated by the readiness with which groups of Starkey residents went *en bloc* to meetings of the County Board of Supervisors to try to influence some decision on the community's behalf. This occurred every few years. What is more, the County Schools Office played a direct role in Starkey's school system, and at least a few county school administrators were known by name to Starkey school board members, teachers, and at least some parents.

As in the past, in the mid-1960s the county was divided in local thought into coastal and inland sections. The distinction between them was associated with the contrast between urban and rural life, or between city and country, a contrast that traditionally has carried a heavy load of meaning in American society. The "rural" category has come increasingly to imply inferiority, but not unequivocally so. Rural inferiority relates to such qualities as worldly sophistication and manners, but linked with urbanism are such characteristics as economic opportunism, moral indifference, and impersonality (see Johnstone 1940). So it was an ambivalent inferiority that Starkey felt toward the coastal section, since the latter was thought to exhibit—in moderate form—the usual urban imperfections.

Because of the greater population of the coastal section the balance of power in the county was tipped in its favor, a source of at least occasional irritation among inland residents. During my fieldwork the extent of this antagonism became manifest in a controversy over the location of a proposed junior college. The college officials had planned to establish the school close to Saint Thomas, where most of the county's population was concentrated, but a rancher whose holdings were in the inland section and close to the geographic center of the county donated land with the stipulation that the campus be built on that site. The officials rejected the gift on the ground that the coastal location was more suitable for a greater number of people.

The inland residents were incensed by this decision, and the matter quickly took the form of a controversy between the inland and coastal sections. A dominant view in Starkey was that the inland site was better because it was both free and central, and that the people of the coastal section wanted the college near Saint Thomas solely for economic reasons: the junior college would be a business boon to the merchants and property owners nearby.

The coastal site was finally selected, but a county bond election had to pass by a two-thirds majority to provide construction funds. When I left the community a common belief was that the residents of the inland region would sabotage the coastal promoters by voting against the bond.[2]

Early in the development of the controversy I asked a local rancher where he thought the college should be. He replied that not many people in Starkey would agree with him, but in his view the more reasonable site was the one near Saint Thomas. Two or three weeks later—when the issue had reached its peak—I overheard the same man heatedly attacking the "economic interests" that motivated the selection of the Saint Thomas site. The force of local opinion and solidarity had apparently changed his mind.

The localities in the inland portion of the county were differentiated on a number of grounds, including size, position with respect to one another and to Saint Thomas, and the like. One important element of this pattern of differentiation was the percentage of newcomers, whose local roots were thought to be rather shallow.

By the mid-1960s the population of Oak Flat had grown to about 7,000, and the town was thought to have attracted a fair number of newcomers. The appearance of several trailer parks was singled out as evidence of the influx of outsiders during the two decades following World War II. By contrast, Starkey and most of the other small, outlying communities were thought to have retained a larger percentage of old-timers. The greater number of newcomers in and around Oak Flat was thought of unfavorably as an index of the greater change that had taken place there.

While Oak Flat had a significant number of newcomers, the old-family members with a strong local focus were still very much in evidence. Until fairly recently the town's government and formal social life had been primarily in the hands of locals, but the latter appear to have abdicated their position to the newer community members. One reasonably informed Oak Flat resident remarked to me that the local merchants were "afraid to do anything controversial for fear of losing business, so the newer people are taking over."

The distinction between locals and newcomers had become crystallized in the town's shopping habits. Four grocery stores were operating in Oak Flat; two were owned and operated by old local families, whereas the other two were relatively new branches of national food store chains. The chain stores were under the management of personnel who had been transferred into the community by their firms. The chain stores did not seem to suffer from a scarcity of business, but it was not difficult to detect resistance to them. One person remarked to me, "I prefer shopping at [one of the locally owned stores]; I like to keep the money I spend in town." A similar pattern of resistance was evident toward other commercial firms. Two dry-goods stores were in business in Oak Flat, one locally owned and the other a branch of a national chain. Several Oak Flat residents stated to me that they preferred the locally owned store and would even pay higher prices there to avoid shopping at the other store. They felt uncomfortable being seen entering the chain store. The latter was also too impersonal for them. They could charge a purchase at the locally owned store simply by asking to do so, and they resented the "red tape" involved in charging an item at the chain store—it was an insult to them to have to produce identification and sign a sales slip.

The position of Oak Flat in the hierarchy of communities is manifest in that many of Starkey's residents shared the attitudes and felt the norms relating to the shopping habits of Oak Flat. A native-born Starkey resident remarked, "At the [chain stores in Oak Flat] they're aliens to me. They're outsiders as far as I'm concerned. I might do some buying there, but it's not like trading at [one of the locally owned and operated stores]."

These norms and attitudes were less manifest in the purchase of farm equipment and farm goods than in the sphere of domestic purcases. Oak Flat was an important outlet for farm equipment, but in recent years the firms in the Central Valley had begun to offer cheaper prices and better services, and as a result the Oak Flat businessmen were losing an increasing amount of farm trade. Their losses were minimized somewhat by the personal loyalty of at least a few of their customers. One Starkey rancher commented that he bought his machinery in Oak Flat "because we always have," but a more common view was that the Oak Flat stores were doing less for their customers than they should and that they did not deserve the loyalty they sometimes got.

Starkey's bond with Oak Flat was stronger than its ties with Saint Thomas, and far stronger than its link with the large city in the Central Valley. A community member summarized intercommunity relations and the hierarchy of communities in the following way:

There's the feeling [in Starkey] that "I would like to trade with them in Oak Flat rather than in the [Central] Valley if it's anywhere equal [i.e., if the prices were competitive and the range of selection adequate]." It's a feeling that you know this fellow pretty well and that if you can, you want to give him a break. But in the Valley cities the acquaintances are nil, it's like trading with Sears and Roebuck or Montgomery Ward. You don't know any of the people. But the acquaintances aren't as wide in Saint Thomas [as they are in Oak Flat]. It's the county seat, and that ties us to it. And the acquaintances are closer there than in the Valley.

The relationship between Oak Flat and Starkey was still marked by a degree of animosity and distrust, though perhaps less so than in the 1920s or 1930s. This animosity was evidenced by the common complaint that Oak Flat characteristically discriminated against Starkey people. During my fieldwork a Starkey youth was taken into custody by county law enforcement officers and had to appear before a justice-of-the-peace court in Oak Flat. Shortly after the boy's detention the Oak Flat newspaper carried the story in full, and one person from Starkey commented that it would not have done so if the youth had been from Oak Flat. Another suggested that the court was going to treat the boy more severely than it would if he were from Oak Flat. One influential Starkey rancher, unrelated to the boy, attended the hearing to see for himself that it was conducted fairly. I am unable to say whether the apprehensiveness in Starkey was justified, although I suspect that it was not.

The relationship between Oak Flat and the localities of its hinterland was still expressed in the annual Homestead Celebration. Interest in the event ran high: Probably a majority of the Starkey community members went to it. Until very recently both of Starkey's grocery stores were closed on that day, although, quite by accident, only one of them closed for the event in the mid-1960s.[3]

The nature of local involvement in the affair had changed in a significant way by the mid-1960s, for the men and women of Starkey now participated more as individuals than as members of a community. Starkey no longer entered a float in the parade, for example, although two of its satellite communities sometimes did so. Starkey's participation in the parade was restricted chiefly to people or families that entered on their own. A change that was uppermost in people's minds was that fewer families now ate the noon meal that was provided in the Oak Flat park. Apparently an increasing number were eating in the restaurants and at the homes of friends and relatives in Oak Flat instead of at the location in the park set a side for the community.

In the mid-1960s the Homestead Celebration was not the only annual event in Oak Flat that attracted large-scale interest in Starkey. Another was the county fair, held each summer since 1946 at the fairgrounds on the outskirts of the larger town. Nominally, it was county-wide in scope since it was run by a board of directors representing all parts of the county, but in fact interest in the event was limited chiefly to the rural inland section. The fair was viewed with great anticipation in Starkey, in part because of the carnival rides and professional entertainment, but in part too because local people entered into competition at the fair. Some of the women entered examples of their handiwork—mostly sewing, cooking, and art. The 4-H Club members entered their projects, usually a hog, sheep, or calf that had been cared for since the animal's birth, and all year the young club members looked forward to the ribbons they hoped to win. Farm workers, landowners, and others whose sons and daughters were among the contestants took time off from work at this busy time of year to witness the competition. A rodeo and gymkhana was held in which both children and adults displayed their skills at roping, horsemanship, and bulldogging, and some competed in novelty events like the women's nail-driving contest. The entrants in these matches were mostly local people from the Inland section, and most were known by name to the spectators. In some cases the winners were virtually predictable because of their performance in past years.

Starkey residents were unambiguous on the question of whether the community was part of Oak Flat or a distinct social entity. To most local people Starkey may have become less vigorous as a community, but it was not moribund. It was considered an independent community, and several features were singled out as evidence for this: the existence of an organized social life made up of such associations as the Women's Society; a town center with its stores, park, and the like; and most important, a distinct school system that provided a body of common affairs and a focus of local identity.

But the distinction between Oak Flat and Starkey and the integrity of the latter were less unambiguous than they may have seemed, and this became apparent when people were asked what would happen if the community were to dissolve. What would Starkey become if the school system were to close or be consolidated with another? If the organized social life were to come to a halt? And if the stores, park, and other concerns in the small town were to disappear? The view expressed was quite in accord with the principle of community hierarchy, for the opinion was that Starkey would be absorbed by Oak Flat. Starkey would become not simply a region located in the countryside beyond the outskirts of Oak Flat, but a neighborhood—a component—of the larger community.

I had expected some difficulty in establishing the boundaries of Starkey, which I assumed would be somewhat vague in people's minds. I acquired a detailed map showing every house in the region and asked a longstanding community member to tell me what he thought the outer limits were. I was surprised how easy it was for him to do this. He simply followed each road on the map with his finger until he came to the last household that was within the Starkey school district. I used the same tactic with several others and discovered that the local conception of community boundaries was both clear and consistent.

To say that the schools supplied the community boundaries is to oversimplify, for there were several schools in the local school system. Their articulation with one another provides the key to understanding both the outer borders and the internal spatial organization of Starkey.

In briefest terms, the widest limits of Starkey corresponded with the area covered by the Starkey high school. The school grounds were situated on the main street in the small town across from the park. The high school served about 100 students, who were taught by six teachers. The building also housed the office of the Starkey superintendent of schools, who oversaw the operation of the entire local school system. The support staff included a secretary; two maintenance men whose jobs included upkeep of the heavily-used school buses as well as the buildings and grounds of both elementary and high schools; and several part-time employees, some of whom drove buses, while others prepared and served hot lunches at the school cafeteria. The school board met one evening a month in one of the high-school classrooms to decide issues of policy and to handle personnel matters.

Three grade schools fed into the high school, so the high-school district was subdivided into three very unequal elementary districts. The largest was the district of Starkey proper, which served the children living on Starkey Flat and in the hills and valleys adjacent to it. The reason this was the largest is that it was the beneficiary of a long process of consolidation whereby the several one-room schools scattered throughout the farmlands outside the town were gradually absorbed by the one central school. As the population on the farmland declined[4] and the automobile (and the school bus) made travel easier, the school districts adjacent to the Flat closed their doors and sent their children to the Starkey school. The other two elementary districts that were operating in the mid-1960s were simply too remote from the town center to be consolidated and absorbed by the larger district, although one of them certainly would be eventually.

The Starkey elementary school, situated on a side street adjacent to the high school, had a teaching staff of four plus a secretary. By the mid-1960s it educated the children of what had once been five separate school districts, each of which at one time had been a relatively distinct community. But not all of these districts showed evidence of their earlier sense of identity, and most people could not remember the names of the schools that had closed before the turn of the century.

The most recent school but one to have undergone consolidation—the Alexander school—did so in the early 1940s, and by the mid-1960s its community life had entirely disappeared. And yet a hint of its earlier sense of community came to light during my research. Shortly before I moved to Starkey a local man purchased the old, one-room school building from the school officials and tore it down without warning—it had been unused for years and lay in total disrepair and apparent neglect. But the destruction of the former community symbol infuriated at least some people in what had been the Alexander district, and they reacted with bitter criticism. When I spoke to the man over a year later he was still quite sensitive about the matter.

The last one-room school to become consolidated with Starkey proper was the Howard school, which was forced to close in 1964 owing to the gradual slippage in its enrollments. Because this happened so recently it affords a close glimpse of the dissolution of a small district and of its absorption into the larger Starkey community.

Before its consolidation the district's only formal organization—apart from the board of trustees and the school itself—was the Howard Mothers Club, which was composed of most of the married women of the district, including those whose children had already graduated from the elementary school. The purpose of the club was to prvide services that were beyond the normal reach of the teacher and board members. For example, it led fund-raising drives for school equipment and supplied dinners and refreshments at school programs.

When I left the community in 1967, three years after the school had closed, the Mothers Club was still active. It held monthly meetings to consider the rather meager business that came up, after which the members turned to such activities as Bingo. Seven members attended almost without fail, and several others were more casual about going. Some of the women had graduated from the Howard school years ago, most had children who had been students there, and all had lived in the district for a major portion of their lives (though a few now lived in some other part of Starkey).

Two events—a Thanksgiving celebration and a Christmas party—enlivened the club's yearly calendar. Both festivities were intended for the entire family and centered on potluck suppers. The Christmas party is illustrative. Several days in advance the women decorated a Christmas tree in the school, and individually they prepared food for the supper. Each of them brought a few inexpensive gifts to be distributed by Santa Claus (played by a local man) after the meal was over. Before the school's closing the children presented Christmas music and a pageant, having been rehearsed for weeks by their teacher. But once the school had been consolidated there were no longer formal programs; instead, the evening was spent chatting. It is perhaps an index of the small district's gradual loss of identity and its absorption into Starkey that in 1966 the Christmas party was held not in the school but at the Starkey Community Hall.

The Howard Mothers Club had an uncertain future when I left Starkey. Even before the school closed no one considered Howard a very distinct community or felt that it had a strong sense of identity, for the locality was close enough to Starkey so that for many purposes its residents were incorporated into and identified with the larger town. When I left, the club was continued chiefly in deference to the feelings of several older members—one of whom had attended the Howard school as a girl, had seen her own children graduate from it, and had grandchildren attending it at the time the district was consolidated. The interest of most Mothers Club members was clearly flagging, and the group's demise was probably in sight.

After the school's closing the building was used only by the Mothers Club, and there were no prospects for a brighter future: There was not the slightest hope that Howard would ever be reactivated as a school. The larger unified school district owned the structure, which the school board now viewed as a minor liability—the old building required occasional maintenance, and gas for heating and electricity for lighting had to be continued for the occasional times when the building was used. And yet even the economy-minded board made no attempt to divest the district of its unwanted asset. An attempt to get rid of the schoolhouse would meet strong resistance, and the board mem-

bers knew it. They had no intention of getting entangled in a controversy of that kind.

Bitter Valley and Lorraine

Of the two one-room schools still operating in the mid-1960s, the first
served the children of Bitter Valley and Lorraine. These districts were
now far less independent from Starkey than they had been in the past—
in the mid-1960s one could describe them as satellites of the larger
community without fear of more than a token reproach. And now there
was only one small country school—the Bitter Valley school—serving
the region, which before had had two.

The first half of the 1940s was an active time for the Lorraine
community (which included Bitter Valley), just as it was for Starkey.
Lorraine maintained an around-the-clock air watch station during much
of World War II, and nearly every man and woman in the community
participated in the civilian defense program, the men drilling together
and preparing their rifles in anticipation of an enemy assault, the
women training in the basics of first aid.

But this flush of activity, like Starkey's, was deceptive. By the mid-
1940s the Community Club, equivalent to the Starkey Improvement
Club, was discontinued, primarily as a result of depopulation. For a
number of years the community had been dominated by Charles
Thomas, an extremely forceful man whose holdings far surpassed those
of any other member. He died in the late 1940s. At about the same time
the Lorraine school closed because of falling enrollments.

In the mid-1960s the small community center at Lorraine was
defunct. The school stood unused and empty; the old post office had
closed; and the community hall had been torn down years before. The
old dining hall was used solely as a polling place and was in disrepair.

But a few miles away the Bitter Valley school was still going, and
the Bitter Valley school district was still a distinguishable social entity.
Its hub was the schoolhouse, with a newly built teacherage standing
behind it. Next door, some fifty yards away, stood the old teacherage,
now rented to a farm worker. This small complex of buildings was
surrounded by open fields of grain and pasture.

The community life of Bitter Valley centered on its school, which provided a steady flow of local events such as the Christmas program and graduation ceremonies. These followed a common pattern. A program of songs and skits was presented by the children, led by their teacher; then cake, pie, and coffee were served by the Mothers Club. The events were attended not only by the parents of the schoolchildren but also by most other members of the community and even a few adults from Starkey proper.

The Mothers Club was an adjunct to the school and a civic group combined. An example of its role occurred in 1966, when it undertook to enter a community float in the Homestead Celebration parade in Oak Flat. The float was built on the bed of a truck by local men working in their off hours in a ranch building not far from the schoolhouse. The float portrayed a country school, and for the parade the children square-danced in an open spot on the truck bed. The Mothers Club regularly gave welcoming parties at the schoolhouse for newcomers and going-away parties for families that were leaving. During my research a young community member on leave from the army, a graduate of the Bitter Valley school, had a potluck supper given in his honor by the Mothers Club. After the tables were cleared he showed slides that he had taken while stationed in Vietnam.

Bitter Valley occupied a position subordinate to Starkey in the hierarchy of communities. The smaller locality manifested a clear sense of independence and community identity, and Starkey people looked on most of its affairs—such as interfamily quarrels—as outsiders do who do not identify with the issues. Yet the members of Bitter Valley considered themselves closely tied to Starkey. For example, if they were to describe where they lived to someone in Saint Thomas, they would say that they were from the area near Starkey. The larger community is about a half-hour by car from the Bitter Valley school, and until the highway was rerouted to bypass the small Starkey hub the Bitter Valley residents had to travel through its main street on their way to either Oak Flat or Saint Thomas. The Bitter Valley people traditionally did their grocery shopping in Starkey, although by the mid-1960s it is likely that a majority of them traded in Oak Flat. In the mid-1960s Starkey's organizations each had a few Bitter Valley people among its members, and we have seen that the children of the satellite district attended the Starkey high school after it opened in 1920.

During the period of my fieldwork fifteen households were considered to be part of the Bitter Valley community. The heads of six of these households were either major landholders or their married sons, who would soon inherit; the head of one was a property holder whose land was too small to support his family and who had to "work out" part time for others; two were hired men; one was the schoolteacher; and five lived with their families and worked at an oil company facility located a few miles from the Bitter Valley school.

Another six families lived within the Bitter Valley region but were not considered part of the community. By looking at these six cases it is possible to extract the chief principles behind community membership.

Two of the six families lived in the Bitter Valley district but had never taken part in the community's formal social life. They did not have children, and because they lacked close relatives in the community they did not have nieces or nephews in the local school. They had comparatively little contact with other people in the district, and what contact they did have involved such matters as returning stray cattle or borrowing equipment. When I asked one person whether these two households were part of the community, he answered that they "would be if they had children."

And yet another person who was regarded as a member of the community was a bachelor and had never taken an active part in local affairs. But he was closely related to others who had children in the school and who participated actively in community life; and although he did not normally attend social affairs he conscientiously donated money, materials, tools, equipment—even the labor of his hired man— when such contributions were needed. I asked one person whether this man was part of the community, and the reply was in the affirmative: "He doesn't go to things as much as some people, but whenever there is something like a cake sale or the need for assistance he is always willing to contribute."

Two of the households consisted of elderly couples who took little part in the community life of Bitter Valley but had once been active in Lorraine. Their houses were situated in the former Lorraine district, and they were considered the last remnants of that community.

The last two of the six households that were not considered part of the Bitter Valley community are particularly significant. Both families had school-age children in the mid-1960s, and both lived relatively close to the Bitter Valley school. But owing to a peculiarity in the way the boundary between the school districts was drawn, their homes happened to be just over the line in Lorraine, and technically they could send their children to the elementary school in Starkey if they chose. Shortly before I began my research they had been involved in a serious controversy with several Bitter Valley families; as a result they had transferred their children to the Starkey school and virtually severed all ties with their neighbors.[5] I asked one man from Bitter Valley whether these two families were part of the community, and he replied sarcastically, "Well, at least they *live* in the Bitter Valley area." Another remarked, "They are outsiders by choice. They essentially pulled themselves out of the community."

The main principle behind community membership was participation in local affairs, for to be part of the community was to be involved in some way in the events that took place there. Since the local affairs centered chiefly on the school, a family with school-age children was drawn into active involvement. If one lacked children of one's own, the children of close relatives served—a childless person was drawn through obligations of kinship to support local projects, attend graduation ceremonies for nieces and nephews, and the like.

Pinefield

The second one-room elementary school feeding into Starkey high school in the mid-1960s was in the small, out-of-the-way community of Pinefield, located southeast of Starkey proper. In the mid-1960s Pinefield included thirty-eight households that collectively were well known for their strong sense of community identity. Pinefield was thought to be one of the most distinct and independent small communities in the entire region. The farmland was devoted almost exclusively to dry crops and grazing, but the appearance of the surrounding countryside was unmistakably different from that of the Starkey area, in that Pinefield had greater rainfall and therefore more abundant vegetation. Whereas relatively barren hills typified the land around Starkey, Pinefield was surrounded by vigorous though relatively open forests of oak and pine.

Pinefield's hub was very small. It consisted of a fire station, a little-used church, a community hall, a combination bar, restaurant, and service station, and a small school staffed by one teacher. A few rickety houses crowded the community center, and the whole ensemble was bound together visually by a stand of splendid old trees that framed the small structures beneath.

The local organizations did not center exclusively on the school, for the groups that dominated local affairs were the Farm Bureau and the Community Club. The latter had responsibility for the community hall, and to raise money for its upkeep and repair it gave an annual dance similar to the ones held in Starkey and Lorraine years before. A Mothers Club met occasionally and undertook projects that benefited the Pinefield school, but unlike its analog in Bitter Valley it directed its attention exclusively toward the small school and its membership consisted only of the mothers of school-age children.

Pinefield's connection with Starkey was restricted almost entirely to school affairs, and even that link was somewhat tenuous. From the time the region was settled in the late 1800s until the Starkey unified school district was created in 1964—an event to be discussed shortly—the Pinefield school was an independent entity with its own elected governing board. Even after unification and the dissolution of the Pinefield Board of Trustees, the Pinefield school tended to operate independently of the larger Starkey system, as we will see.

This tiny community never had a secondary school of its own, and before 1936 its children went to Oak Flat if they wanted a high-school diploma. But in that year Pinefield formally became part of the Starkey high-school district and its children began attending the Starkey high school. If it had not been for that link (which eventually led to the incorporation of the small elementary-school district into the unified system), Pinefield would not have been any more closely tied to Starkey than it was to other small communities nearby.

Pinefield never had significant economic relations with Starkey. The road from Pinefield to Oak Flat did not pass through Starkey, and it took about as long—approximately forty minutes in the mid-1960s—to drive to either trade center. Since the range of merchandise and services was greater in Oak Flat than in Starkey, the people of Pinefield almost never had cause to do business in the smaller town. It was also quite unusual for a Pinefield man or woman to take part in the formal social life of Starkey proper. The relationship between the two communities was summarized by one person with the remark, "We're only *school* oriented toward Starkey."

Pinefield regarded itself as wholly autonomous from Starkey, and a Pinefield resident would deny that his or her community was part of the larger community. I asked one Pinefield resident what he thought most of his neighbors would say if I asked them whether they were part of Starkey. He replied, with emphasis, "They would resent it." Pinefield's sense of independence was fortified by a measure of antagonism toward the larger community. For example, Pinefield residents commonly complained to me—and to the school board—that the high school reserved its most worn-out bus to serve the students of their community. This hostility had not broken out into open conflict, but it could have, and the new unified school board was quite circumspect in its decisions affecting the small community.

It is now possible to understand the intricacies of Starkey's boundaries and also the relationships among the geographic units making up the larger Starkey system. The area served by the Starkey elementary school—the region of Starkey proper—once consisted of five independent districts, each with its own social life; but in the mid-1960s they had coalesced into a single community. Only two of these districts, Alexander and Howard, still exhibited even a trace of their earlier social identity, and that was rapidly disappearing. Starkey proper had become virtually a single community without major geographic subdivisions.[6]

Two other small districts were associated with Starkey. By the mid-1960s Bitter Valley had become directly subordinate to Starkey in the community hierarchy, for it was dependent on the larger community economically, socially, and educationally—its families shopped at the Starkey center and joined the Starkey organizations, and its children attended the Starkey high school. Bitter Valley was distinct but not independent, and eventually its school would be consolidated and closed and it would be absorbed into Starkey proper.

Pinefield was a different matter altogether, for it did not consider itself subordinate to Starkey. Instead, this small, out-of-the-way locality looked to Oak Flat as its superordinate in the hierarchy of communities. It regarded Starkey as little more than a compeer—albeit a larger one—whose high-school facilities it shared. Whereas Bitter Valley was a satellite of the larger community, Pinefield looked upon the latter as a rival.

It is possible to throw further light on the relations among these communities by describing the events leading to school unification. Before unification—the meaning of the term will become clear in a moment—each elementary school was headed by a separate board of three trustees, the high school by a board of five. The trustees were elected from among the voters of the respective districts. When unification took place these separate entities would be reorganized into one unified system under the trusteeship of a single board of five members.

The impetus for unification came from the state legislature, which hoped to streamline school systems throughout California by consolidating them into larger and more efficient units in which both the high schools and the elementary schools in a region were brought together within a single structure. The plan was considered an enlightened one and generally received the support of professional educators, but it often met strong opposition from the voters. The laws setting up procedures for unification made resistance difficult, however, and in the 1960s school districts all over California were merging into unified systems.

Early in the 1960s the Starkey high-school board decided that unification was unavoidable, but its members were afraid that when the change came it would mean combining with the Oak Flat school system. This was patently unacceptable, so a plan was devised to prevent it. The plan was to unify the several schools within the Starkey high-school district—including Starkey high school and the three elementary schools—before they were forced to join with Oak Flat. There was a catch to the plan, however. The proposed unified district would have fewer students than the law permitted, so an influential and articulate community member went before a panel of state authorities to argue for an exception to the law. His argument was that the Starkey region was sufficiently remote geographically to warrant its own unified school system. The argument was accepted and Starkey was allowed to go ahead with its plan.

The electorate had to be won over, for the proposed district had to be approved by a majority of the voters of the region. To achieve this a series of meetings was held in each district, ostensibly to explain the proposal but in fact to win its acceptance. The measure was indeed approved by the voters, and in the summer of 1966 the Starkey Unified School District came into being.

The voting pattern was quite significant (see Table 2). Nearly all the voters of Starkey proper approved the plan (99 percent), and a substantial majority of those in Bitter Valley did so (83 percent). But only a minority of the Pinefield electorate voted in favor (39 percent). The Bitter Valley vote reflected a degree of concern over combining with Starkey, as well as a sense of community independence. The Pinefield vote reflected even greater concern and independence.

Limiting our attention for the moment to the majority vote in Starkey proper, nearly all the voters apparently were opposed to unification and would have preferred to vote against it. They saw no educational advantages to the change, which in their view was foisted on the community by distant state officials. But it was clear that unification would eventually come, so the issue before them, as they saw it, was whether to be part of a future Oak Flat system or to set up their own. The overwhelming majority chose the latter as the less objectionable option.

If the majority vote in Starkey proper reflected a desire not to merge with Oak Flat, what was the basis for that desire? For reasons that need not concern us here, unification with Oak Flat would have meant a substantial school tax increase in the Starkey region, easily double the original tax rate. This was a powerful force behind unification in Starkey. Another factor—impossible to evaluate precisely but certainly important—was the animosity that was felt toward Oak Flat and the desire to remain independent of the larger trade center.

The people in Bitter Valley and Pinefield who voted in favor of unification did so for the same reasons: they feared a substantial tax increase, and they were wary of being under the thumb of a school

Table 2. Vote on School Unification

Voting Area	Percent Yes	Percent No	Number of Votes Cast
Pinefield	39	61	44
Bitter Valley	83	17	23
Starkey proper	99	1	154

board dominated by Oak Flat. One Bitter Valley resident summarized the alternatives open to him, and the basis for his vote, when he said: "My wife and I voted for unification because it was either being unified with Starkey or ultimately being unified with Oak Flat."

Those in Bitter Valley and Pinefield who decided to vote against unification with Starkey felt that the price they had to pay to avoid combining with Oak Flat was simply too dear. They preferred opposing unification with Starkey now and opposing unification with Oak Flat when the time came. It may also be that some of them were convinced that unification with Starkey would pass regardless of their vote, which they therefore used as a form of protest.

Several objections to unification with Starkey were expressed in Bitter Valley and Pinefield, even by those who decided to vote in favor of the measure. One argument was that school taxes would go up if the measure passed. Although there was some basis for this concern, the increase would not be great, not nearly as much as would be the case in the event of unification with Oak Flat. Another source of concern was summed up by the term *local control,* which entailed two arguments. First, it was thought that by compelling unification the state legislature was trying to wrest control of the schools from the hands of local people in order to give it to professional educators. Unification meant fewer school boards, the argument went, and consequently less influence by laymen on school affairs. Second, people in Bitter Valley and Pinefield expressed the fear that a unified board dominated by Starkey proper would not be as responsive to the needs of their communities as their own school boards. In particular, it was feared that a unified school board would not take adequate measures to keep the outlying schools open. This apparently was the principal reason for opposition in both Bitter Valley and Pinefield, and it was a major concern even of those who voted for the measure.

Why did the people in the outlying districts not want their schools to close? For one reason, the parents thought their small children would have to spend too much time on the school bus each day if they attended classes in Starkey. This fear was clearly justified, since the high school students living in the remote areas spent about two hours a day riding to and from Starkey on the bus. Second, community identity was involved. When I asked one Bitter Valley resident to explain the resistance to unification, he said, "The first thought that came to people's minds over unification was that the Bitter Valley School would close, and that it was too long a trip to Starkey for their children." When asked whether there was a feeling that the community itself would be affected, he said,

Yes, a big argument against unification was that Bitter Valley would lose its community identity if it went through. Before unification the school was taken for granted. If it wasn't here the community wouldn't exist, there wouldn't be anything to get the people together—there are no community dances and so on.

Another Bitter Valley resident commented, "That's why people have opposed unification throughout the county. They know that when the school closes the community is gone." When I asked him whether community identity was the principal reason for the opposition, he replied, "It's one of the reasons."

A correlate of community identity in Bitter Valley and Pinefield was antagonism toward Starkey, and this was another factor behind the concern over unification that was felt in the two small localities. Before unification one Bitter Valley resident said, "As it is, Starkey tells Bitter Valley what to do." After unification another Bitter Valley resident commented, "I was surprised that the school hasn't had any big flare-ups since unification. I was sure there were going to be all sorts of problems."

The arguments against unification were much the same in Pinefield as in Bitter Valley, although the opposition was expressed with more force in the former community—as can be inferred from the vote. This greater resistance is explained by Pinefield's stronger feeling of dissociation from Starkey. Having their school governed by a board dominated by a rival was a greater concession than most people in the little community could make.

The sense of local identity and independence in the small school districts was formally recognized in the way the unified school system was set up. The basis of the organization was the principle of confederacy, and the constituent units of the confederacy were the elementary-school districts that had traditioally been the community units of the region. The new board was made up of five members, and in the legal documents establishing the system it was specified—by local choice, not state law—that they were to be elected from the original districts. Three board members were elected from Starkey proper: one each from the former Alexander and Howard districts and one from what had been the Starkey district before its consolidation with the other two. A fourth trustee was elected from Bitter Valley and a fifth from Pinefield.

The way the unified board operated is instructive, for the trustees representing Bitter Valley and Pinefield were given wide latitude in matters concerning their schools. On one occasion the well at the Bitter Valley school needed major repairs. The school superintendent and the trustee from that district were called, and they alone decided how to deal with the problem. When a matter arose that concerned only one of the outlying schools but required the formal action of the entire board— such as salary negotiations for the teacher at one of the outlying schools—the other board members deferred to the wishes of the trustee from that district if possible. When parents in Bitter Valley or Pinefield had questions or complaints about their local school they normally addressed themselves to their own trustee, who therefore was intimately involved in the everyday affairs of the elementary school in his region.

The teachers at the Bitter Valley and Pinefield schools operated somewhat autonomously with respect to the larger unified system. This was especially true of the teacher in Pinefield. Each year the schools held an open house to allow the public to see the children's work. The 1967 open house was planned by the school superintendent, and the date and time of the event were entered on the school calendar. It was to take place in the evening. That afternoon, several hours before the open house was scheduled to begin, the superintendent telephoned the teacher at Pinefield to see what he had planned and ask if he needed help. The teacher replied, "Come on up, I'm having [the open house] right now." In recounting the story to me the superintendent remarked that this "would make a lot of [school] administrators pretty upset" and that the Pinefield teacher was not really "a part of the larger system."

Both the opposition to unification in Bitter Valley and Pinefield and the way in which the unified system was organized illustrate the sense of community identity in these small localities. Mixed with—and perhaps underlying—the purely practical fears about higher taxes and long bus rides, for example, was a desire to maintain the community, to keep it alive. And the continuation of the local school was a way of achieving this end.

The motivational roots of this sense of identity are beyond the scope of this study, but the issue is worth comment, speculative as it may be, in order to tie the present discussion to the earlier one about reputations and reference groups. The men and women of Bitter Valley and Pinefield (and of Starkey as well) had personal investments in their communities in the sense that the local group was an important source of social identity and a significant arena for the achievement of social position. Most of these people had acquired—or cultivated—personal reputations for industriousness, neighborliness, community minded-ness, and the like. If their communities lapsed, their good (or bad) names no longer mattered very much.

It might seem that the adult members of Pinefield and Bitter Valley had little to lose from being incorporated into Starkey, for most of them already had identities within the larger community. But the identities they enjoyed there were those of distant neighbors rather than fellow townsmen. The people of the outlying communities were regarded by Starkey residents as members of somewhat different social systems, and as such they were outside the local classifications of periphery and core, establishment and nonestablishment, and the like. So if the outlying communities were to lapse, these people would have to rene-gotiate their social identities.

If this was true of the well-entrenched members of Pinefield and Bitter Valley in relation to Starkey, it was even more true of Starkey in relation to Oak Flat. Surely the members of Starkey proper would have opposed unification with Oak Flat even if a tax increase were not at issue. If the local social system were to dissolve, they would find themselves absorbed into a larger, more diversified one that included not only ranchers, farm hands, country schoolteachers, and the like but also lawyers, doctors, barbers, washing-machine repairmen, bank and chain store managers, bartenders, plumbers, and so on.

A striking feature of intercommunity relations at all levels of the hierarchy is the pattern of hostility toward higher-order units. Starkey had exhibited a degree of hostility toward Saint Thomas and Oak Flat almost since its founding, and it continued to do so in the mid-1960s. Similarly, both Bitter Valley and Pinefield assumed a strongly contrary position with respect to Starkey. This pattern obtained even when there were no apparent grounds for ill will. For example, the Starkey Unified School Board—which clearly was dominated by Starkey proper—went to unusual lengths to avoid alienating the smaller communities of Bitter Valley and Pinefield, which nevertheless were unrelenting in their mistrust and feelings of abuse. This brings to mind the way the Starkey high school became independent of the Oak Flat school system years earlier. The movement to dissolve the tie came from within Starkey and manifested a deep-seated feeling of mistreatment, and yet Oak Flat seemed willing enough to accede to the change when it was proposed. The implication is clear: the suspiciousness and ill will sprang as much from anticipated or even imaginary wrongs as from real ones.

These negative feelings seem to be related to the sense of community identity, for hostility and mistrust are greatest in the communities with the strongest sense of identity and are at their peak when the local identity is threatened. For example, when the people of Bitter Valley and Pinefield were faced with the prospect of having their schools placed under the jurisdiction of a school board dominated by Starkey, the autonomy of their own localities became insecure and their resentment toward the larger community grew. And this resentment was stronger in the community with the greater sense of local identity.

This pattern is reminiscent of what has become a standard theme in the literature on rural communities in America. The farm families living in the open countryside have traditionally exhibited hostility and mistrust toward the towns and townspeople with which they were associated. According to Thorstein Veblen (1923a, b), this was due largely to a conflict of business interests. The local businessmen extracted as much as they possibly could from the farm population, which therefore became alienated from the town. Even earlier, Galpin (1915) proposed a somewhat less cynical interpretation in which the farmer had to share some of the blame. According to Galpin, the farmer neither was responsible for nor had any control over the institutions and services of the town, and yet he traded there and felt that he deserved a voice in its affairs. The townspeople felt that the farmer contributed so little to the village that his claims were empty. The animosity between the two groups was inevitable.

The most extensive treatment of this problem is provided by Brunner, Hughes, and Patten (1927:96ff.), who conducted a study of 140 rural villages in the 1920s. According to their study, the farmer's antagonism toward the trade center was due chiefly to inadvertent acts on the part of the townsmen. Conflicts of economic interest were clearly a major factor in town–country relations, but even when economic matters were involved a simple misunderstanding was usually at the heart of the problem. The writers cite a case in which the merchants in one trade center decided to remove the hitching posts from the main part of town on the ground that the automobile had almost completely replaced the horse. The farmers interpreted this as an unfriendly act directed toward them, and they protested. But the townsmen did not take their complaints seriously and failed to return the hitching posts. The farmers took their trade to other nearby centers, and only then were their feelings understood and the hitching posts put back.

It is tempting to interpret this incident according to the principles at work in the Starkey region. It is possible to suggest that the trade center was surrounded not merely by independent farmsteads but by small neighborhood communities. These stood in an asymmetric relationship with the town, for they were part of its hinterland and were therefore subordinate in the hierarchy of community relations. It was this subordination, I suggest, that was behind the farmers' ill will. When an issue arose that seemed to the farm people to express the subordination of neighborhood to town, the members of the outlying communities responded with mistrust if not anger.

This interpretation holds that intercommunity relations are to be viewed, at least in part, at the level of symbol and metaphor. For example, when a campus for the county-wide junior college was to be acquired, the proposal that it be located in Saint Thomas stimulated the rancor of the inland communities not simply for the practical reason that they wanted the site closer to home. They were predisposed against the Saint Thomas site regardless of its objective merits, and the hostility they felt sprang largely from the way in which this matter dramatized the subordination of their communities to Saint Thomas. Similarly, the claim that the Starkey school board assigned the most worn-out bus to the Pinefield route may or may not have had any basis in fact, for the hostility in Pinefield was a response to the symbolic aspect of the issue. Accordingly, it is not sufficient to point to the objective content of actions or events, or to single out the likelihood of conflicting interests, to explain the pattern of hostility between town and country or between two communities of unequal size.[7]

A historical pattern of a somewhat different order emerges from the discussion of community relations. This is the growing importance of the schools and the declining importance of trade, a pattern that is evident in various parts of rural America. According to J. H. Kolb, for example, high-school attendance has become a key factor behind community boundaries in rural Wisconsin, whereas in the past the main factor was trade (Kolb 1959:9, 120–30).

In Starkey, shortly after settlement a variety of small communities formed around the small one-room schools that were distributed across the countryside, but by the turn of the century all of these communities—or neighborhoods—looked toward the small trade center on Starkey Flat that provided most of their everyday needs. The families that traded in Starkey came to identify with it and to have a stake in its social affairs. In particular, their local reputations were bound up with the roles they played in the emerging community. To some extent, trade was the agent that brought the community into being, and the organized social life that appeared was a reflection of the social system that had formed around the commercial center.

But the situation had changed by the mid-1960s. Chiefly because of the automobile, Starkey people were able to travel far greater distances than before, and they could do so on a routine basis. Their trading habits shifted to larger and less limited trade centers, including Oak Flat, Saint Thomas, and even the large city in the Central Valley. The stores in Starkey played an increasingly minor role.

As this was taking place, standards of education were changing and a high-school diploma was becoming a near-necessity for most young people. As a result of both consolidation and unification, the school system also became more centralized. The Starkey schools now emerged as a major factor in the community. The school and school affairs were a chief focus of community interest, and as we will see, school events played a major role in the locality's organized social life. Starkey had changed from a trade-centered community—trade serving as the nodal point for a number of small school district communities— to a school-centered one.

Chapter 8 The Pattern of Community Affairs

THE STATEMENT THAT the schools had become the center of the community expresses a crucial point about the historical development of the locality. But it is also an oversimplification: even the most extensive account of school matters can hardly exhaust the body of material that belongs under the heading of community affairs. A wide variety of undertakings, events, organizations, and issues were to be found in Starkey, and these need to be explored in order to understand the sense in which Starkey was a community and the form that community displayed.

I have remarked that at one time one of the most notable and distinctive features of Starkey was the importance, real or supposed, of the Methodist church. Everyone who commented on this matter agreed that the church's importance had declined. A typical comment was made by a rancher who said that at one time "it was difficult to live in Starkey unless you were a member of the Methodist church" but that this was no longer true. Another remarked, "Fifteen years ago or so [in the early 1950s] the community was divided between those who went to the Methodist church and those who didn't. The people who were the in-people went to the church. This situation doesn't exist today."

According to a man who had served at different times on the boards of trustees of both the elementary school and the high school, a Catholic teacher would not have been hired in Starkey until about the 1950s. Before that time Catholics would have been discouraged from applying by being told that they probably would not be happy in the community. But in the mid-1960s a Catholic teacher was employed at the high school. His religion was not taken into account when he was hired, and there was no evidence of open opposition to him, although it is probable that his beliefs stimulated some covert rancor.

Consonant with local thought about the church's decline as a social force in Starkey, the Methodists were believed to be less capable of maintaining standards of conduct than they had been in the past. A common view was that the level of local morality had declined because the number of churchgoers had become too small to fight effectively, the stalwarts too old, or both.

What was the state of local moral norms in the mid-1960s? Moral censure was attached to a variety of things, including sexual impropriety, and perhaps even more to public displays of obscenity and rowdy behavior in general. But Starkey was not unusual in its emphasis on these standards, even though it was commonly believed that in these respects the community was morally superior to neighboring towns (and certainly to the urban centers somewhat farther away). Nor were sex, obscenity, and rowdyism controversial issues at home. Aside from a few "young toughs" in the community, and perhaps a few other scandalous individuals, no one would have opposed the Methodist stalwarts on these issues.

The moral norms that stood out in Starkey during the mid-1960s, as before—in part because they were controversial matters in the community and in part because they served to distinguish Starkey from its neighbors—were those involving alcohol. It was as if all moral questions came into focus in relation to this matter. And as a rule the change that was pointed to by local people when discussing the declining influence of the church was the change in drinking patterns.

The division in the community between drinkers and nondrinkers was still manifest. One person remarked to me, "There are two clans [in Starkey], the wets and the drys." Another said, "I have always felt that drinking is the way the community divides."

This division was illustrated graphically a few months after I had arrived in the locality by a woman who had read James West's *Plainville* and for some time had hoped "to write a book on Starkey." She had worked out her own account of the community and wanted to describe it to me. When we sat down to talk the woman took out a sheet of paper and drew on it a large diamond (see West 1945:117). She then divided the diamond with several horizontal lines which, she said, represented class divisions: the highest class was at the top, the lowest at the bottom.[1] Next she bisected the diamond with a single vertical line: the community, she said, is divided between those who are moral and those who "have some moral blemish." She took out a second sheet of paper and wrote on it the names of all the families that came to mind, assigning each one a number. Then she entered the number for each family at the appropriate place on the diagram: the higher the socioeconomic position of the family, the higher it was in the diamond; the more moral the family, the farther it was to the right.

Drinking patterns were the chief principle behind an individual's placement to the left or the right of the vertical line. It was not the only one, to be sure. For example, a very proper, middle-aged, churchgoing nondrinker—a widow—was placed to the left of the line because of her involvement with a somewhat disreputable bachelor. But in the overwhelming number of cases the deciding factor was the family's adherence to the local drinking norms.

What, then, was the basis for classifying a person as a drinker or a nondrinker? Whether or not the person drank had little to do with his or her classification, for a number of people who were nondrinkers by local definition—who fell to the right on the diagram and who others would agree ought to be placed among the nondrinkers—were known to drink. The nondrinkers were people who adhered to the norm that one did not allow evidence of drinking to come into public view. Nondrinkers did not go to the Starkey bar, did not buy alcohol at the one store in the community where beer and wine were sold, and did not drink openly in the community or in contexts in which outspoken teetotalers were present. Nor did they even leave beer or wine in their refrigerators to be seen by anyone who might come to their homes. The nondrinkers therefore included both drinking nondrinkers—those who drank but adhered to the local norms in doing so—and genuine nondrinkers.

The fact that a drinking nondrinker drank was typically common knowledge in Starkey, so his (or her) efforts to avoid the open display of drinking did not usually fool anyone, nor were they necessarily intended to. Elsewhere (Hatch 1973) I have suggested that the drinking nondrinkers kept their drinking from public view in order to minimize disagreement and disharmony. They wanted to avoid offending the genuine nondrinkers and, hence, to avoid injecting a potentially disruptive issue into their relations with others with whom they had close social ties.

This interpretation may be extended to encompass the principle that Starkey was a reference group. People adhered to the norms of the nondrinker not only to avoid the ire of the genuine teetotalers but to avoid losing their esteem as well. Whatever the drinking nondrinkers may have done in their private lives, publicly they wanted to be known as upstanding citizens by local standards (or at least by the establishment's standards). And possibly above all, they wanted to avoid the appearance of siding with the drinkers.

Those who were considered drinkers in Starkey made little or no effort to keep the evidence of their drinking habits from emerging publicly. They openly acknowledged that they drank, engaged in discussions of drinking with nondrinkers present, and even drank beer in the park on such occasions as the annual Starkey Barbecue. However reputably they may have conducted their lives in all other respects, the openness—or flagrancy—of their drinking gave them an image of disreputability in the eyes of both drinking nondrinkers and genuine nondrinkers. What is more, the drinkers were not indifferent to the opinions of the more "reputable" members of the community. By virtue of their drinking they signaled their disrespect for the churchgoers and all that they represented.

A set of events that I observed at a branding in 1966 illustrates the drinking norms and the way they relate to the division between drinkers and nondrinkers. The incidents occurred at a branding that was held at the main corrals of one of the large cattle ranches outside of Starkey; this branding was larger than most and was attended by several local ranchers.

One of the ranchers was Bill Donelson, who was among the strongest advocates of abstinence in Starkey. Another was Ed Walters, a 50-year-old drinking nondrinker. Walters had a milk carton filled with whiskey and ice hidden in his pickup truck, which was parked out of sight of the corrals. Throughout the branding Walters quietly offered drinks to those he knew would accept, and two or three at a time they walked to his truck to imbibe. Shortly after the work was finished Walters told one of the cowboys to expect another drink once Donelson left, since "Bill is against that sort of thing." At one point during the branding Walters was recounting a drinking experience when Donelson walked up to the group. Walters immediately—and conspicuously—discontinued his story.

In a sense drinking was appropriate on this occasion. Cattle branding is traditionally considered a masculine sport in which the participants have the chance to practice and demonstrate their riding and roping skills. What is more, there were no women or children at this particular affair, and this heightened the sense of masculine independence. Donelson could not help knowing that Walters and others normally drank at events of this kind, and sooner or later he would hear that some of them were drinking at this one, if indeed he did not already know that they were. What Walters' behavior did was to keep the issue of alcohol from becoming openly acknowledged in his relationship with Donelson and to keep Walters on the nondrinkers' side of the drinking line even though he drank.

A more extensive set of events involving the Starkey Women's Society is also illustrative. The Women's Society, to be discussed at greater length shortly, should not be confused with the earlier Women's Club, for the two organizations were nearly opposites. Unlike the older Women's Club, the Women's Society soon began to play a leading role in community affairs and included some of the most respectable members of Starkey. It was begun in 1946 by the wife of the Methodist minister, which perhaps ensured that the most outspoken of Starkey's nondrinkers would join. The Society grew quickly, and by the end of the first year the women of the wealthy elite and a few other ranchers' wives had begun to assume a leading role in its affairs.

The wealthy elite (varying in number between five and seven households at different times) consisted mostly of young married couples who were comparatively new to Starkey when the Women's Society was founded. During the late 1940s and early 1950s they made little attempt to adhere to the local drinking norms, and one man in particular was especially open about drinking. According to one account, this man

enjoyed going against the [community] —for example, he loved the bar, and he took people in there who would never have gone in had they not been with him. One night his wife, with her usual flair, decided to go to the bar and see what was so great about it, so she and some other women went there and walked around inside to see what it was like.

The parties that were occasionally held in the homes of the wealthy elite apparently stimulated considerable comment in the community. One person remarked that "wild stories began to be told about this group." Another stated that the actions of the wealthy elite were probably "a real dilemma to the nondrinkers, since it was the first time that someone with position and power came into the community and drank."

The women of the wealthy elite injected their drinking habits directly into the Women's Society. During the late 1940s and early 1950s the Society held public dances to raise money, and some of those who went, including at least some of the wealthy elite, brought bottles of liquor and drank openly. At one of the Women's Society meetings it was also suggested that the organization begin selling drinks at the dances, but according to one of the members the group "decided not to because of the disruption it would have caused in the Society." The organization also held at least one social event for members and husbands at which alcohol was served. A strict non-drinker had originally suggested the party, and (according to one of those involved) "the drinkers thought it would be terribly dull and wanted drinking. They compromised and served beer." Finally, on one occasion the Society held a meeting at the home of the wealthy elite woman who had visited the bar, and she served drinks to the group. When the drinks were served, a young woman, a nondrinker who drinks, glanced at her aunt, a rancher's wife who was a drinking nondrinker. The niece saw her aunt accept the drink, so she did too.

In the mid-1960s the issue of drinking simply did not arise in the Women's Society. The dances had been discontinued years before; couples parties for club members had ceased; and the idea of serving drinks at the organization's monthly meetings now seemed inconceivable. One change that helps explain this situation is that for the most part the wealthy elite had come to restrict their drinking to private contexts. They now adhered to the norms of the drinking nondrinker. But it also appears that alcohol was tactfully excluded from Women's Society affairs because drinking was too difficult an issue for the group to cope with. It was not one of the hard-core nondrinkers who led the movement to eliminate drinking, however, for the prime mover seems to have been the aunt who had accepted a drink at the meeting mentioned earlier. This is significant inasmuch as she was one of those who was most affected by the predicament that drinking had created.

It is remarkable that the movement to eliminate alcohol from the affairs of the Women's Society was so circumspect that the wealthy elite were unaware that it was taking place. When the women of the wealthy elite were asked in the mid-1960s why the dances had been discontinued, their explanation was that local interest and support for the events had begun to flag; when asked about the problems created by drinking, they stated that these did not play a significant role in bringing an end to the affairs. A very different response came from other members of the Society, however, as the following comments indicate:

The Society has no social events because of the drinking issue. You'll notice they don't have any social events at all any more. They used to; for example, they had dances. But they were wild.

[I asked an outspoken nondrinker why the Women's Society stopped giving dances:] Drinking. People were passing out at the dances, and were potted out of their minds. People felt it wasn't good to have this going on with high-school children right there to see it. [One woman of the wealthy elite] passed out at one of the dances.

I think that the reason there are no couples' organizations [in Starkey] is because of the drinking issue. This is the reason they haven't tried to sponsor dances, for example—they would create problems which would be almost insoluble. If the Women's Society sponsored dances there would be battles within the group at every meeting.

This case contains a number of interesting facets, including the gradual adherence of the wealthy elite to the local drinking norms. But most significant is the reaction of the women who were not among the wealthy elite—longstanding community members who were drinking nondrinkers. They were being threatened with "exposure." Even if they did not drink at parties or public dances given by the Society, their attendance alone was enough to count as a tacit endorsement of drinking. Their response was clear. As discreetly as possible—so discreetly in fact that the wealthy elite did not even know it was happening—they eliminated the situations in which they would be forced to violate the norms.

If the drinking–nondrinking division was still so clearly manifest in the mid-1960s, in what sense had the drinking norms declined? In brief, they had become more relaxed without becoming less precise. The drinkers apparently were allowing their drinking to take place more openly. Perhaps the most obvious manifestation of this change is that drinkers were now drinking beer at the annual barbecue in the park (Hatch 1973:247–48). Another was the behavior of at least some of the schoolteachers. Teachers were particularly subject to the norms regulating the use of alcohol, but by the mid-1960s some of them served liquor in their homes, drank at the community events at which liquor was appropriate, and bought beer and wine at the local store that sold them.

Nevertheless, the drinkers' tippling was not completely unfettered. For example, the drinking in the park was limited to beer and was restricted to men; what is more, none but the most disreputable members of the community—the "alcoholics" and derelicts—allowed the effects of alcohol to show in public.

One relative newcomer told me that he had felt free to drink openly in Starkey only since the early 1960s, even though he had never had any direct ties with the church and had never pretended to be dry. Another person summarized the current state of affairs with the comment, "The nondrinkers don't ostracize the drinkers like they used to."

It is also possible that the drinking nondrinkers were less guarded in their drinking habits than before and that there were more contexts in which they would drink. An example, perhaps, is Ed Walters, the man who provided whiskey at the branding described earlier. It seems likely that in the 1930s, say, he (or his equivalent at that time) would not have imbibed in a context of that kind and would not have recounted drinking experiences even with others who drank. A drinker might have done so, but not a drinking nondrinker.

The belief that the moral influence of the Starkey Methodist church had declined was one part of the changing image of that organization, but there was another. Long-time residents assert that although the institution had once been a community church this was no longer true. And they point to the 1950s as the period in which the change came about. What, then, was meant by the term community church?

This issue was pointedly raised for me—without my asking—by the man who served as pastor of the congregation in the early to-mid-1950s, when the Methodists' position in the community was declining but before the change was fully realizd. He had been quite struck by the community (having just graduated from seminary, this being his first pastorate) and by the place of the church within it. To illustrate his impressions he remarked that he had been asked to perform all weddings and funerals in the community, regardless of the relationship that the people involved may have had with the church. To further illustrate, he told an anecdote about a stranger who had come to see him one afternoon. The man, it seems, was a door-to-door Bible salesman. He had tried selling his wares at about four houses, and each time he was asked by the householder whether the minister approved of what he was doing. So the stranger decided to go to the parsonage, introduce himself, and explain his business. The minister was unimpressed with what the man had to sell and told him so, and the man promptly left town. In brief, the minister's view was that he had been cast in the nondenominational role of community ecclesiastic. In his words, he was placed "in charge of all things pertaining to religion in Starkey."

The question of what it took for a group to count as a community organization was touched upon earlier, when the Women's Club of the 1930s was discussed. The Women's Club never enjoyed the status of a community organization and was never thought of as a legitimate instrument for conducting local affairs. It is likely that one reason for this was the comparative disrepute of its members, some of whom were drinkers. By contrast, the church was the bastion of respectability.

But the church was more respectable in a different sense as well, for among the Methodists and their supporters were the most notable contributors to Starkey. At least some of the opinion leaders in the community, the very ones who had proved themselves capable of carrying out community affairs and were willing to do so, were associated with the church and gave it the stamp of legitimacy. If the church undertook an activity, at least some of the established leaders could be counted on to support and promote it, and as a result the support of other community members could be won. It is true that the Women's Club was also drawn into community activities; for example, it played a major role in acquiring the park. And yet its members had not acquired reputations of true devotion to the betterment of the locality—and they could not count on acceptance of their undertakings by nonmembers.

What was meant when it was said that the church was a community church is that the organization was engaged in activities that were thought to benefit not only churchgoers and their supporters but also the members of Starkey generally. The Methodists' antagonists could attend without feeling alienated or uncomfortable. They had a stake in the Community Christmas Program, say, or the Ladies Aid Bazaar—

both church-run events. By contrast, nearly all the activities of the Women's Club were looked upon as serving the interests of the Women's Club itself, and attendance at its affairs was construed as a matter concerning the women's group and not the community as a whole.

It seems that before the church's decline virtually everyone in the locality would have said that religion *ought* to play a major role in small-town life. Even the church's main opponents would probably have agreed with this view in principle, even though they would have found fault with the stalwarts in the Starkey congregation. In short, to a broad cross-section of Starkey the ideal image of a small town reserved a special place for the local church.

But the situation had changed by the mid-1960s, for now the church did little more than serve the devotional and social interests of its members and supporters. This change can be seen in local funeral patterns. In the mid-1960s virtually all funerals were held in a mortuary in Oak Flat, unless the deceased happened to have been a regular churchgoer. And attendance was normally limited primarily to family members, friends, and neighbors. It is true that the services were often announced on the bulletin boards at the two stores, but even so funerals were not widely attended.[2]

It would seem that this change reflected something more than the mere appearance of a mortuary nearby, for I suspect that during the earlier period a mortuary would have been considered an inappropriate place to hold a funeral—the services should ideally have been conducted in a church, and especially in the local church with the customary church people taking part. What apparently occurred was a partial secularization of the burial process, with the result that the church's importance in local life—and thought—was diminished.

Another issue that shows that the church had lost ground both in the image of the ideal community and in local affairs is the split that occurred among the Methodists in the late 1940s. The minister at that time was liberal in his religious views, and he became concerned about the dominance of fundamentalists in the congregation. He attempted to restrain some of the conservatives from presenting their own beliefs to the Sunday School classes, and eventually he replaced some of the Sunday School teachers with church members whose beliefs were closer to his own. The fundamentalists regarded his behavior as insulting, and they grew increasingly alienated.

Around 1950 the strain reached the breaking point. A few of the most conservative members withdrew from the Methodist organization altogether and formed a separate Pentecostal congregation. A majority of the conservatives could not bring themselves to leave, however; they quietly but unhappily submitted to the changes.

Two families spearheaded the founding of the Pentecostal group. Before the split occurred, they had been among the leading members of the Methodist congregation, in that they occupied lay offices in the church and devoted a great deal of time to it. One of these families was also especially active in community affairs. Several other people with conservative beliefs began attending the Pentecostal services once the church had been established. These included a few who had previously been members of the Methodist congregation but were not among its leading members.[3]

It is hard to imagine this split taking place earlier than it did—say, in the 1920s or 1930s. Important as religious belefs may have been to the congregation at that time, something else as well was at stake in a person's association with the Methodists. The church occupied a special place in the community. It was not only a major community organization but the bastion of respectability and a symbol of the establishment. It would have been very difficult for a person to leave it, especially someone active in local affairs and concerned about his or her reputation as a cooperative and community-minded person. It seems likely that the pressure of public opinion would have prevailed on the dissidents—and the minister as well—to maintain the integrity of the congregation. But by 1950 the community's focus had already begun to shift away from the church, and its leading members now had less at stake in continued association with it.

The Ladies Aid—now called the WSCS (Women's Society of Christian Service)—had also deteriorated. Once a key element in such community undertakings as the May Day festivities and the sponsor of a major community event of its own, the annual Bazaar, by the mid-1960s it had become a minor church-affiliated organization. Only about fifteen women regularly attended meetings, and they were all regular churchgoers. The Bazaar consisted almost solely of a dinner given for the purpose of raising money. There were few homemade articles for sale, and plays were no longer presented. About 125 to 150 people, including children, usually attended—fewer by far than in the past.

One of the clearest indications of the shifting position of the church in the community was the Community Christmas Program. Local interest and involvement in the event reached a peak during the late 1930s and early 1940s, when the production was carried out almost entirely by the church. In the mid-1960s some people still attended the event on the ground that it was a "community affair," but they were becoming fewer. One person summarized her view of the changes with the comment, "I don't think of [it] as a community thing any more. I think of it as a school program now."

During the 1940s the event was transfered from the Community Hall to the high-school gymnasium, thereby increasing the school's involvement, and the high-school board, having responsibility for the gym, assumed an official interest in the program. In the late 1940s the high-school principal also began to play an important role in the event. He now handled the bookkeeping that was required, which suggests that he may have been a key figure in the overall supervision and direction of the program. By the late 1940s several community organizations besides the church had come to play a role in the production, and each paid an equal portion of the costs. Finally, an increasing share of the program was presented by the schoolchildren under the direction of the school faculty instead of the church.

By the late 1940s mounting pressure was put on the school board to have the church completely sever its relations with the program. The main argument was that the school should not be involved in a sectarian event, although local sentiment against the Starkey Methodists may also have played a role. The agitation was effective, and at the urging of the school board the church withdrew from the production.[4]

In the mid-1960s the Christmas Program was organized almost wholly by the Starkey elementary and high schools, the children providing most of the entertainment and the faculty providing most of the direction. But this had not become exclusively a school affair by any means. The Starkey Women's Chorus presented several selections, and other community organizations were involved in various ways. The Parent Teachers Organization (PTO) decorated the gym and made popcorn balls to give to the children; the Women's Society donated $20 to the PTO to cover its costs; and the Lions Club enlisted one of its members to play Santa Claus at the affair.

In the mid-1960s services at the Pentecostal Church in Starkey were usually attended by fewer than fifteen people. The congregation was so small that it could support only a part-time minister who earned his living at a secular job elsewhere in the county, where he lived. The Pentecostals had virtually no impact on Starkey, and the only time they became visible in the community was when they combined with the Methodists on such occasions as Easter sunrise services. Even the small church building—converted from an old house—was not highly visible, for it was located on a rather out-of-the-way side street.

Attendance at Methodist services was not much greater than attendance at Pentecostal services, for it ranged from about 20 to 40 people on most Sundays.[5] But average attendance is a poor indicator of the church's position in the community, for unlike the Pentecostals, the Methodists had a large pool of supporters—people who seldom if ever attended on Sunday mornings but still identified with the local church. For example, about 100 to 150 people normally attended services on the Sabbath preceding Christmas, and at least that many attended the WSCS Bazaar. Although the Methodists had retreated in their role in the community and were far less conspicuous than in the past, they had hardly disappeared. This was evident in the hostility that they could engender among some people—the Methodist Church still symbolized the establishment, even though the symbolic association between the two was far less perfect than it had been at one time.

The process of secularization that had caused the Methodist Church to recede both in community life and in the local self-image was parallel to the decline of trade. Just as religion had come to play an increasingly smaller role in the community, the local business establishments had lost a growing percentage of their retail sales to other trade centers. What is more, as both trade and church declined, yet a third element, the schools, moved forward in importance. Virtually every family in Starkey was involved in the school system by virtue of the state requirement—and their own expectation—that all children must receive an education. The role of the schools is suggested by their importance in defining community boundaries and also in the way school-related topics tended to dominate conversations. Discussions—and often bitter feelings—developed over such issues as the firing of a teacher in mid-year; the proposal to hire a controversial member of the community to teach in one of the schools; the need to build a new school building, increase school taxes, or add another teacher to the staff; the expulsion of a child of one of Starkey's respectable families; and stories about the sexual promiscuity of some of the high school children—and teachers—and about evidence of drinking at high school dances.

Several cases of community involvement in school affairs will be described at length in the following pages. A school issue usually began as a topic of discussion among a few parents who were directly concerned, and one or more of them would eventually speak to a member of the school board or, more rarely, the superintendent about the matter. If the issue was an important one, each member of the board would receive a number of phone calls and visits from people who wanted to express an opinion or urge a particular course of action. If the issue was especially volatile, the board called a community meeting to discuss the matter—and usually to legitimize the decision it would eventually have to make.

Some school events enjoyed the status of community events, in that attendance was not limited to the families and friends of schoolchildren but included a mixed assortment of ranchers, farm workers, store employees, and so on. Attendance at, say, a baseball game in which the Starkey team played a rival high-school team was considered a show of support for the players as well as a sign of community spirit. The reputation of the community itself was implicated in the size of the crowd.

A person's attendance at such events was validated for the next several days in conversations with others. At the cafe talk might turn to the high-school girl, a member of a wealthy elite family, who was injured by a line drive foul while sitting on the sidelines watching a league game. Or a person might mention the unexpected and comical appearance at a basketball game of a derelict community member dressed in sweatshirt, ill-fitting slacks, and new white tennis shoes—and hardly able to conceal his pride in his new footwear.

A community organization had been created to serve the schools. It was modeled on the national Parent Teachers Association (PTA), but its members chose to remain an independent body on the ground that they preferred local autonomy to subservience to a nationwide institution. To emphasize their autonomy they adopted the title of PTO (Parent Teachers Organization).

The PTO was begun in 1954, when the school was experiencing considerable turmoil. Some members of the community had become bitterly antagonistic toward both the school board and the principal for their emphasis on academic as opposed to vocational and athletic subjects. The controversy came to a head with the board's decision to expel a student who was considered to be a very disruptive troublemaker—a case I will discuss in another chapter.

It was apparently as a result of this controversy that the Women's Society decided to propose the formation of a parent–teacher group. Explicitly, the organization was to assist the schools in whatever way it could and to provide better communication between faculty and community. Implicitly, it appears, its purpose was to lend support to the beleaguered principal and school board. Three members of the Women's Society were appointed to meet with the principal to discuss formation of the group with him, and his support was easily won. A public meeting was then called and the PTO was born.

By the mid-1960s the controversy that had spawned the organization was only a memory and the PTO was hardly a vital force in Starkey. Its primary purpose was to raise money to purchase supplemental school equipment and materials—for example, it bought trees to be planted on the school grounds and a typewriter for the elementary school—and it held raffles, community dinners, and the like for this purpose. The organization also engaged in two small-scale annual undertakings: it gave a reception at the beginning of each school year to welcome the new teachers, and as noted earlier, it assisted in the Christmas Program.

In spite of the prominence of the schools in Starkey, they were narrowly confined in their activities, seldom if ever venturing into areas of community life that were not directly concerned with education. But it seems that in local thought an active, meritorious locality needed something more than school affairs. At the very least, Starkey needed a program of occasional community gatherings, and beyond that it needed a series of undertakings for the general improvement of the locality.

What, then, was the structure or framework by which community affairs were carried out? One organization existed for the express purpose of attending to the common affairs of Starkey. This was the leading community organization, the contemporary equivalent of the earlier Improvement Club and Farm Bureau. It spearheaded improvement projects and was the chief vehicle for stimulating and coordinating local undertakings. But it seldom worked alone in these matters. Other local organizations—special-interest groups that were not devoted expressly to the general interests of the community but had been formed for more limited reasons—were occasionally drawn into community-wide affairs. The spirit of improvement was still manifest.

Each local organization had a distinct image, and by conveying these images it is possible to throw light on the roles the groups played in the community and on the way in which community affairs were conducted. In particular, each had an image that was composed in part of negative elements, and each had its antagonists, if not enemies, who generally agreed in their assessment of its imperfections. As a rule, one of the leading imperfections pointed to—and one of the major handicaps to be overcome in engaging in community affairs—was that the group was associated with a particular segment or faction in Starkey. No group was thought to be fully representative and truly disinterested.

In the mid-1960s the leading community organization was the Women's Society, which, as mentioned earlier, was begun shortly after World War II by the Methodist minister's wife. Her plan initially was quite modest, for she envisioned an organization that would be devoted chiefly to charitable activities and handicrafts. She invited some friends—churchgoers—to her home to discuss the idea, and they decided to invite all the young women in the community to join and mailed out invitations for the first meeting, to be held at the Clubhouse in the park. Membership expanded beyond churchgoers almost immediately, for the group quickly became somewhat fashionable, attracting most of the wealthiest women in the community.

The earliest projects were indeed for charity, but the Society was soon diverted toward local ends, and particularly toward park improvements that would benefit the Starkey children. Eventually, however, the organization became the principal instrument for conducting local affairs. To understand this development it is necessary to describe the conditions that underlay it.

The most important condition was the vacuum that had been created by the decline of the Farm Bureau, which was already failing by the late 1940s and was completely moribund a decade later.

Another organization, the Hunting and Conservation Club (or Conservation Club for short), partially filled the void, but it could not do so completely. As we will see, the Conservation Club was started in the mid-1940s for the purpose of promoting game conservation, and later it provided hunting privileges for its members on local ranchlands. Its main interest was hardly the improvement of Starkey as a community. What is more, the organization was riddled with conflict, and perhaps most important, its membership included a substantial number of people from outside the locality whose principal reason for joining was simply the desire to hunt.

And yet the Conservation Club was pulled ineluctably into community affairs during the 1950s. Between 1951 and 1961 the club and the Women's Society together staged the Starkey Barbecue, which quickly became the leading annual community event. The Barbecue was a money-making affair, the profits going in part to finance local conservation measures and in part to help pay for community improvements. Each year the club's members were required to attend work days in order to remain in good standing; as originally planned, the work days were to be for conservation measures such as building guzzlers (watering places) and laying out sanctuaries for quail. But throughout the 1950s the work was frequently devoted to improvements in the park instead. In 1953, for example, the organization enlarged the swimming pool, donating both the labor and the materials for the project. Later, in cooperation with the Women's Society, it constructed tennis courts in the park and improved the restrooms. A letter from the club to the county board of supervisors in 1953 stated that "the Conservation and Hunting Club, in addition to its work in game preservation, is also concerned with the other recreational facilities in the community."

The reason the goal of community improvement could become

even a subsidiary focus of such an unlikely organization was probably that, except for the schools, the Conservation Club was the largest and most viable group in Starkey during the 1950s. A large percentage of the men belonged, so the group was widely representative of the local population. But in addition, little else was available, so the Conservation Club acted as a lightning rod for the booster spirit.

The organization suffered its own problems, to be discussed later, and did not last long. By the early 1960s it was all but defunct.

It was in this context that the Women's Society came to play the role it did in Starkey's community life. The women's group had been closely allied with the Conservation Club, in part because the most active and influential members of the one were married to the leading members of the other. The Women's Society was at one time thought of, in a sense, as the women's auxiliary to the Conservation Club, and relations between the two groups took place largely over the breakfast table. The Women's Society itself, then, was easily drawn into community affairs through its collaboration with the men's group, and it often took the lead in community undertakings and thus stimulated the men in their role. As the Conservation Club declined and finally dissolved as an effective organization, the Women's Society assumed the lightning rod function on its own, for now it was the principal organization in Starkey.

What, then, were the undertakings of the Women's Society? The organization needed, first of all, to raise money to pay for the improvements it sought to achieve. During the 1940s and into the 1950s it held dinners and dances in the Community Hall, but these, as we have seen, had been discontinued by the mid-1960s. The continual and longstanding money raiser was the Starkey Barbecue, to be discussed shortly.

The Society also provided community contributions of a sort that did not make money. Each year until 1960 it entered a float in the Homestead Celebration parade, and until about the same year it gave a reception in the park each fall for the new teachers, an undertaking that had been taken over by the PTO by the mid-1960s. The women formerly decorated the gym and provided popcorn balls for the children at the Community Christmas Program, although this too had recently been turned over to the PTO.[6] Other miscellaneous projects included the sponsorship of swimming lessons for the children each summer and the presentation of a small scholarship to a Starkey High School graduate each spring. One recent and controversial project was a drive to improve the physical appearance of the town.

The park in particular had been a major focus of interest for the Society. The women purchased playground equipment and contributed money toward the construction of the tennis courts. Throughout the 1950s they spearheaded the annual park work day in conjunction with the Conservation Club. In 1954, for instance, the Conservation Club and the Women's Society together held a cleanup day at the park; built a barbecue pit, a horseshoe court, and a sandbox; painted; and installed a septic tank for the new restroom.

A particularly significant undertaking was conducted in the late 1940s and early 1950s. The Society had been holding dinners and dances in the Community Hall, but the old building had become quite run-down and the women wanted to initiate a project to repair the structure. Improvement Club trustees (who held title to the Hall) resented the Society's intrusion into their bailiwick, so the Society helped reconstitute the Improvement Club in order to effect the repairs. Only a few meetings of the newly revived Improvement Club were held and attendance was quite small, but donations were solicited in the name of that organization. One person commented, "They even went into Lorraine [for contributions], and very few people refused to pay." Under the formal sponsorship of the Improvement Club, a large supper and program were held in the Hall to raise money, and the proceeds from one of the Starkey Barbecues were donated to the fund by the Women's Society. As a result, the building was painted and reroofed, a new toilet was added, and the basement was repaired. Much of the labor was donated. The high school boys' club, for example, did most of the painting. When the repairs had been completed, the Improvement Club became defunct once again.

An account of the activities undertaken by the Society is hardly sufficient to elucidate the organization's position in the community and its role in local affairs, for the question of its local image must also be dealt with. Community members' opinions about the Women's Society ranged from open support to open resentment and opposition. At least one of the Society's programs fomented considerable disagreement and heated argument. One person summarized a view that was com-

mon: "The Society is a necessary group. It puts on the Starkey Barbecue, which wouldn't be if it wasn't for the Society. But I think you have to
watch out for extremes from groups like that, because they wield the
power and sometimes they misuse it." Its antagonists also claimed that
the Society was concerned more with publicity than with benefiting
Starkey: "What I have against the Society is that they seem to be glory
seekers. It always seems that when something is done it's the Society
that gets the credit, even when other people have had a lot to do with
the thing."

Perhaps most important, the Society was thought by some to be
snobbish:

I don't have much in common with those people. It seems like they get together
to dress up and so on.

The Society are the snobbish people in Starkey. They always have thought they
were better than other people.

Some are opposed to the Society. They say it's primarily for dressing up and for
snobs, but that isn't true.

The aspect of snobbishness in the Society's local image reflected
the fact that the group had become somewhat fashionable. In the mid-
1960s, as before, the women of the wealthy elite and of other well-to-do
households were quite prominent in the organization. But in their view
at least, this was only because other people—the Society's critics—
were unwilling to endure the drudgery of working for the community.
The Society explicitly attempted to maintain a socially diverse membership and to overcome its image of snobbishness and exclusiveness,
and indeed its members represented a broad range of the social
hierarchy in Starkey—although the well-to-do were in the clear
majority.[7]

Associated with the claim that the Women's Society was snobbish
was the fact that it was aligned with the nondrinking component of
Starkey and, thus, with the establishment. This is a complex issue that
will be dealt with later.

Another local organization, a men's group, was associated in a
way with the Women's Society. This was the Starkey Lions Club.[8] The
Lions Club presents a striking contrast with both the Conservation Club
and the Women's Society, for even though it was established with civic

goals in mind, the Starkey chapter never distinguished itself as a community organization as I use the term here. It never acquired the lightning rod function that characterized the other two organizations.

The Lions Club was begun shortly before American involvement in World War II, was discontinued at the height of the conflict, and resumed again in the 1950s. Membership was never extensive: twenty-five men were on the rolls when it re-formed, and the number declined steadily from that point. By the mid-1960s only eight people regularly attended the biweekly meetings.

Unlike the Women's Society, the Lions Club was not associated with the establishment or the nondrinkers in local thought. Drinking was a normal part of the club's affairs, in that parties for members and their wives were occasionally held at the Clubhouse in the park at which liquor was served. In the mid-1960s the membership was about equally divided between drinkers and drinking nondrinkers. The organization was always careful to keep its drinking from becoming too obvious, however. For example, the drinking nondrinkers saw to it that empty liquor bottles did not find their way into the trash at the Clubhouse, inasmuch as the members of the Women's Society—which superintended the building—would probably come across them there. Instead, the bottles were taken home.

Perhaps the leading component of the local image of the Lions Club was its supposed ineffectuality. It had carried off a few relatively minor events and projects in the past, but nothing significant. It had sponsored a few dances to raise money, for example, which it used to finance a children's baseball team in Starkey. It had laid out the baseball diamond in the park, and each year it appointed one of its members to play Santa Claus at the Community Christmas Program. By the mid-1960s it had begun collaborating with the Women's Society in the Starkey Barbecue. But probably the achievement with the most telling—and unfortunate—effect on the group's local image had to do with the Community Hall.

In the 1950s, shortly after the Lions Club had re-formed, the aging trustees of the Improvement Club decided to turn the Community Hall over to the newly revived organization—which, they reasoned, would be a relatively permanent body and therefore a suitable one to assume directorship of the building. The Lions Club, in a flush of self-assurance, set out to make improvements shortly after acquiring the structure. It began by demolishing the rickety stage that occupied one end of the Hall. The plan was to replace it with a small dining or conference room. But the project foundered almost from the start. The new room was never finished and the scars left by the removal of the stage were never repaired.

It is in this context that we understand the organization's local reputation, which is summed up in the following statements:

There is the feeling that to some extent the Lions Club is ineffective. It tore down the stage in the Community Hall and never replaced it. People said, "See, just like always, they were going to do big things but didn't finish." That caused a lot of comment. It's not so much bad feelings toward the Lions Club as it is a lack of support. People feel it is ineffective, that it can't get things done.

The Lions Club started with big guns in Starkey. For example, they built the ball diamond in the park for the youth baseball team. But they got too many projects, and they started folding up. . . . People lost interest because they couldn't finish anything.

By the mid-1960s at least, the relationship between the Lions Club and the Women's Society was not entirely amicable. The one tended to look upon the other as a censorious instrument of the establishment, whereas the other tended to view the first as a somewhat bootless group with nonestablishment leanings. The two engaged in several cooperative undertakings—most notably the Starkey Barbecue—and their exchanges were the picture of studied cordiality. But hostility broke forth occasionally in a variety of ways. For example, in the mid-1960s a minor dispute developed when the Women's Society accused the men's group of failing to clean the Clubhouse adequately after one of its social affairs.

The Starkey Barbecue was presented jointly by the Lions Club and the Women's Society in the mid-1960s, and it was the single most important community event at that time. It is instructive in that it provides a clear glimpse of the operation of community affairs.

Eighty households in Starkey—nearly 50 percent—included one or more members who assisted in some way in the affair, and several people from Bitter Valley did so as well. Adding to this the number of local people who attended but did not assist, about 70 to 80 percent of the community participated. Not everyone who attended was from Star-key, however, for the Barbecue attracted a number of outsiders, includ-ing some who had lived in Starkey in the past. One of the main attractions of the Barbecue was the chance to renew friendships and visit with relatives who had moved away. The number of meals served had been recorded since 1955, so a reasonably accurate estimate of crowd size is possible (see Table 3).

The main focus of activity was the noon meal, which was eaten at picnic tables under the large shade trees in the park. A brief opening ceremony was presented shortly before the food was served. This included the entrance of an honor guard composed of 4-H Club mem-bers on horseback, the raising of the American flag, and a prayer given by the Methodist or Pentecostal minister. If it was an election year, candidates for county, state, and national office made speeches after the meal was over. Later in the day a rodeo was held in the corrals of one of the ranches just outside of town, and swimming races were held at the pool. Two additions were introduced in 1967: a square dance in the Community Hall, and an art show for local exhibitors in a corner of the park near the picnic tables.

The effort needed to feed such large crowds was considerable, and preparations began a month or two in advance when both the Lions Club and the Women's Society began assigning jobs to their members.

Table 3. Number of Dinners Served at Starkey Barbecues, 1955–1967

Year	Adults	Children	Total
1955	605	190	795
1956	640	219	859
1957	637	221	858
1958	629	202	831
1959	599	209	808
1960	764	302	1066
1961	680	193	873
1962	807	206	1013
1963	638	177	815
1964	644	211	855
1965	799	256	1055
1966	817	222	1039
1967	633	199	832

Many nonmembers were also assigned tasks. Of the approximately 100 adults who contributed their efforts to the 1967 Barbecue, only 37 were members of either the Women's Society or the Lions Club.

A characteristic of the way the affair was carried out is that very little formal direction or leadership was needed. Most of the people who helped had done so before, so they knew what to do and how to do it. Indeed, even the assignment of jobs was routinized, since the participants usually assumed the same roles year after year. For example, I was at the Lions Club meeting at which plans were made for the 1966 Barbecue. Someone asked whether a particular individual—a nonmember—should be asked to participate in his usual capacity as a meat server. Another commented that there was no choice, for the person involved would feel slighted if he were not asked. Later the meat server told me privately that he was tired of working at the Barbecue every year and that he wished he could avoid doing so.

Each year a member of the Women's Society was assigned the overall directorship of the Barbecue. This was one job that was not held by the same person twice, for it was enormously demanding. And it entailed very little authority, in that the person in charge served as a sort of technical adviser and coordinator, making sure all the participants were carrying out their roles and urging them on if they lagged, finding answers to the myriad questions that arose, and serving as the communications link among the various work groups.

Soon after the assignments had been made the designated people began ordering food—meat, bread, beans, and lettuce. A week or two before the event the Lions Club members and a few friends drove into the hills with pickup trucks to collect firewood. The day before the Barbecue the Lions Club gathered at one of the stores to cut the meat, while a group of women cut bread at the school cafeteria and other people hauled large collapsible tables from a nearby ranch and set them up in the park to be used for serving food. Early the next day fires were started in the barbecue pits where the meat would soon be cooked; the salad was made in the Clubhouse; beans were prepared in the school cafeteria; and about seventy women brought cupcakes that they had made at home. Others brought sauce, butter, bread; coffee, and so on. A public-address system was set up. Soon the meat was put over the fire to cook, the food was arranged on tables, and the servers prepared to dish up the food.

The explicit purpose of the Barbecue was to raise money. It was begun in 1947 by the Women's Society, and the profit from that year's event was used to buy playground equipment for the park. The next year's Barbecue was given for "Community Hall improvements," according to the records, and the next was advertised as a "benefit for the Starkey community" and the Improvement Club. In 1951 the Women's Society and the Conservation Club began collaborating in the event, the Conservation Club receiving two-thirds of the profits and the remainder going to the Society. The Barbecue advertisements during those years state that the events were "to benefit conservation and Starkey Park." The Conservation Club participated in its last Starkey Barbecue in 1961 and the Women's Society ran the affair alone until 1964, when the Lions Club was invited to assist. The Lions Club received one-third of the profits and the Women's Society received the rest. The proceeds from the 1966 Barbecue were used to pay for "community improvements" and "youth activities."

The Barbecue was a money-making venture—a reasonably successful one—and it was viewed in that light. It was thought of as a way of raising cash to sandblast and repaint the swimming pool, to hire a swimming instructor for the children, to landscape the small space between the post office and the store, to maintain the tennis courts, to finance the Christmas Program, and so on—all small but important items that helped make Starkey a better community.

There was another dimension to the local image of the Barbecue. It was considered evidence of Starkey's community spirit, and indeed it was regarded with some pride. It was also conceived of as intensifying that spirit. For example, one person remarked to me that the Barbecue had a "unifying effect on Starkey."

Two other organizations were active in the mid-1960s. The first was the Starkey Square Dance Club, which began in 1965 and had about 35 members. It met once a week in the Community Hall to dance, and occasionally its members attended dances held by other clubs in nearby towns.

Its membership was socially heterogeneous, and the organization was not clearly associated in local thought with any particular segment of the community. They included farm workers and major landholders (though not the wealthy elite), members of the establishment and the nonestablishment, some churchgoers and some people who were hostile toward the church. Drinking played no role in the club's activities and therefore did not become an issue in club affairs.

The Square Dance Club was not conceived of as a community organization in the strict sense; rather, it was viewed as a special-interest group. In particular, it was not regarded as a legitimate instrument for conducting local affairs. This became evident in the context of an issue that I will discuss at length in another chapter. For several reasons general agreement had grown in Starkey that the Lions Club should no longer hold title to the Community Hall, and since the square dancers made more use of the building at this time than any other organization they wanted to assume ownership of the structure and responsibility for it. But few people agreed with them. Eventually a superintending committee was formed, made up of representatives from each of the major organizations—including the Square Dance Club. It was felt that the square dancers had an interest in the building and therefore deserved a formal role in its supervision; but since the group was not clearly community oriented in its focus and had an uncertain future, it should not be given full authority.

Another special-interest group was the Starkey Women's Chorus, which had been formed by a rather crusty schoolteacher in 1959—she was quite vocal in her criticism both of specific individuals and of Starkey in general—and disbanded when she left in 1966. This too lacked the reputation of a community organization, even though it offered an annual concert in the high-school gym and sang at the Christmas Program each year. It was occasionally drawn into community affairs, however. For example, it was asked to contribute to the acquisition of a community public-address system, which it had no reason to think it would use, and it responded by voting to give $100 from its treasury. It is not quite clear how the decision to contribute came about, but the general outlines of what occurred are revealing. The chorus members initially decided in favor of the contribution, but the director—presumably as a display of opposition to the community—wanted to donate to charity instead, and she apparently managed to reverse the original decision on her own authority. Another vote was taken at the group's next meeting and the contribution to the public-address system was restored. The second vote was construed as both a rebuke to the director and a sign of community support.

Two other special-interest groups were organized for children and therefore were not directly involved in adult affairs. One was the local Boy Scout troop, which barely surfaced at the level of everyday life in the community and about which most community members knew virtually nothing. Second was the 4-H Club, which was somewhat more visible. One reason for its visibility is that it sometimes performed community services such as cleaning up vacant lots, and another is that by its nature the group stimulated rivalry and resentment, which spilled over into the adult population. The organization was founded on the principle of competition, each child having his or her own project, such as the raising of a calf or hog. The rivalry reached its peak every summer, when most of the projects were entered into competition at the County Fair.

All the local organizations were occasionally drawn into community affairs when it was felt that an issue needed a wide base of support. A common pattern was for the Women's Society to decide that a program was called for and to appoint one of its members (sometimes more) to be in charge. This person was instructed to solicit representatives from the other organizations to serve as a steering committee.

An example of this pattern was a box social given while I was in the community. The event was discussed at a Women's Society meeting as a means to raise money for the community public-address system. One of the people who suggested the box social urged that representatives from various organizations be in charge of it so that it would be a community event and not a Women's Society affair. This was agreed upon, and representatives were solicited from the Lions Club, the Women's Chorus, the WSCS, the PTO, and the 4-H Club—each to serve along with the Women's Society representative, who was tacitly recognized as the person in charge once the steering committee convened. The inclusion of the 4-H Club is suggestive, inasmuch as it is a children's group. Its representative was the adult leader of the organization, and the rationale for incorporating the group into the affair was that some of the 4-H children were from families that were not usually involved in community life.

On another occasion the Women's Society decided to hold a meeting with Starkey's elected representative to the county board of supervisors to discuss the future of the Community Hall. It was decided that delegates from the following groups should be officially invited to attend: Women's Society, Lions Club, Square Dance Club, WSCS, PTO, 4-H Club, and Boy Scouts.

The reason given for this pattern of collaboration—to increase the number of people who would support the undertaking—can be seen at two levels. On the one hand, it can be viewed in quantitative terms: Collaboration with other organizations was sought in order to draw their members into the affair. If the Women's Society invited the Women's Chorus, say, to participate in an undertaking, then the number of people involved included the combined membership of both. On the other hand, the pattern of collaboration can be seen as a means of establishing legitimacy for an affair. Each community organization—including (or especially) the Women's Society—had its critics, who were prone to oppose or criticize virtually any program that might be proposed. If other groups were drawn into the undertaking, the affair could be construed as not merely a special event of that particular organization but a legitimate community affair. Both interpretations were given expressly by community members, but the second received greater emphasis. The main purpose of the steering committee in charge of the box social, for example, was to establish the principle that it was truly a community undertaking and not a Women's Society affair.[9]

A common theme in the literature on rural America (e.g., Warren 1972:59–62) is a distinction between two forms of organization. On the one hand are the special-interest groups and on the other the genuine community organizations (including both formal voluntary asociations and less formalized structural patterns) that are devoted to the common affairs of the locality and are representative of the community as a whole. By all accounts the special-interest group is winning out. The historical trend is away from what Alexander and Kraenzel (1953:78; see also pp. 86, 88) call "the true community way" of doing things. At one time a single social body with its own common affairs, the farm community is becoming—or has become—a heterogeneous agglomeration of people going their separate ways.

In Starkey during the mid-1960s a similar distinction was apparent in local thought, as is manifest in the contrast between the images of the Square Dance Club and the Women's Society. What is more, in that community at least, the special-interest group had not clearly replaced the true community organization by any means. A body of common affairs was in evidence, as was a spirit of boosterism in the way they were attended to. One principal community organization was the focus and springboard for community undertakings. It was the Women's Society that led the drive to create the PTO, spearheaded the project to buy the community public-address system, and the like.

And yet the Women's Society had its detractors—people who questioned its credentials. In a sense they tended to assimilate it to the status of a special-interest group. To them it was a creature of the establishment, and its programs often reflected nothing more than what a certain clique of women took upon themselves to define as community affairs and goals. The same dilemma had been encountered earlier by the Women's Club when it set out to construct the Clubhouse in the park. The problem is that whether a given issue "counts" as a genuine community affair cannot always be answered unequivocally. But now the question is applied not to a set of issues but to a community organization.

This leads back to the question of whether Starkey was still a community. Its boosters could point to a variety of successful accomplishments—such as the acquisition of a public-address system—that indicated that community spirit and cohesion were still alive. The detractors, however, could stress just the opposite by suggesting that these accomplishments were little more than the pet projects of a somewhat snobbish and unrepresentative special-interest group.

Certainly the Women's Society went to great pains to overcome its reputation for snobbishness and exclusiveness and to establish its credentials as a genuine community organization. Attempts were made to enlist new members from throughout the community, and one regular member began wearing blue jeans to meetings to help combat the group's image as a group of high-society women. And to thwart and disarm its critics it usually created a steering committee composed of representatives from the other community organizations whenever it sought to undertake a project that needed widespread support. What is more, the Women's Society could claim that it was reasonably successful in accomplishing its goals and in generating support for its programs among nonmembers.

But the question remains: was it or was it not a special-interest group? And the answer, it seems, cannot be given, for the issue is not resolvable by pointing to specific facts that are independent of local opinion. Whether the Women's Society was attending to genuine community affairs or merely carrying out its own pet projects depends on the perspective of the individual in the community.

It seems reasonable to suppose that the same ambiguity surrounded both the undertakings and the status of the major community organizations of the past, the Improvement Club and the Farm Bureau. The problem may be less clear in relation to them only because time has blurred the division of opinion over their programs and policies. On the other hand, it seems reasonable that their status as true community organizations was more secure than that of the Women's Society of the mid-1960s, if only because both of the earlier organizations were often used by the established community leaders as vehicles for conducting local affairs. Dissensus seems to have been less pervasive then.

The historical pattern according to which the basis for participation in local affairs shifts from locality to interest—to use Warren's (1972:59) phrase—cannot be conceived of as a clearly definable event to be pinpointed by the disappearance of a specific type of structure or local organization. Nor is it possible to say whether the process has already occurred in a locality by making a quick check of the local organizations. The case of Starkey suggests how the transition does occur. It comes about slowly as the legitimacy of community undertakings and organizations becomes increasingly difficult to achieve. The ideal of an active community with a vigorous community life continues to find expression in community undertakings, and community organizations that are oriented toward strictly local affairs continue to exist, but acceptance of these undertakings and organizations is less and less easily won.

One last issue concerning the form of community affairs needs comment. It is very significant that the leading organization in Starkey in the mid-1960s was exclusively for women. By contrast, its earlier counterparts, the Improvement Club and the Farm Bureau, were intended for the entire family, and in truth they were dominated by men. Indeed, local affairs were once largely in the hands of men—the community leaders—operating through these community groups.

This development was no small matter. It signified a drastic change in the nature of the community, for no longer was it considered a worthy undertaking for a man to occupy himself with local affairs. Better that he devote himself to what counted most, his occupational role, and leave these other matters to the wives and mothers who had time for them. I will return to this issue in another chapter.

Chapter 9 Public Amiability, Private Disharmony

THE QUESTION SURROUNDING the status of the Women's Society—was it a genuine community organization or a special-interest group?—leads directly to one of the most important and pervasive features of community life: the establishment–nonestablishment division.

The problem of factionalism and divisiveness was uppermost in my mind when I first entered the community, for one objective of my research was to look into local mechanisms of social control. The goal was to discover how social pressure and other forms of sanction were employed by community members against one another and to discover whether the operation of those sanctions was somehow associated with local factions or interest groups. But the investigation proved completely unrewarding at first: the application of sanctions in the community virtually never occurred in an open and straightforward way, and—or so it seemed at first—there was almost no pattern to local factionalism.

What did emerge immediately was a pattern of public amiability. Instead of individuals or blocs of individuals engaging in open dispute, taking sides publicly and openly manipulating social resources in relation to opponents, the local people—even enemies—nearly always displayed an attitude of friendliness and good humor when they came into contact. For example, when two men (whom everyone knew to be bitter enemies) met on the street outside the post office or while entering the gym to watch a high-school basketball game, they were likely to exchange polite greetings. At most they might simply avoid speaking, ostensibly taking no notice of each other. The outsider who happened to observe this chance meeting would be unaware that an "event" had just occurred—although to the local insider the occasion would merit careful (but discreet) attention and perhaps a comment to friends later. Similarly, if a volatile subject was raised in a public context—in the restaurant during a busy time of day or in a conversation among a heterogeneous group of people at a community affair— virtually no evidence would appear that deep-seated feelings were involved. The issue would be discussed as casually as the weather, and perhaps even more superficially. About the only tip-off to the observer might be an awkward silence at some point.

This pattern of public amiability assumed objective form in the proceedings of the school board, for during the two years of my field research only one split vote occurred among the board members, even though they often disagreed on matters of policy. Disagreements were expressed politely and tentatively, and when votes were cast the minority inevitably deferred to the majority. The one split vote that did occur is revealing. On this occasion a particular board member could not bring himself to vote with his colleagues, but instead of openly breaking with them he abstained.

The observer's impression of amiability would not last long, however, because he or she would soon hear the insider's account of events—for example, as the cluster of people talking together at a community affair was reduced to two or three friends. For attitudes and opinions were very different when expressed in private, and there was little concerted effort to deceive the outsider about such matters. The people may have wanted to portray their community as a friendly place to live, but this motivation was seldom strong enough to keep them from mentioning a choice piece of gossip or scandal if the occasion arose.[1]

The impetus behind the public display of amiability was not the desire to deceive the outsider but the need to avoid a direct confrontation with opponents. Open disagreements and arguments are especially difficult in small communities, in which a person's enemies and adversaries can hardly be avoided in everyday life and in which a dispute with one person ramifies throughout the local social system.

The pattern of public amiability occurred against a backdrop of almost incessant disagreement, recrimination, disapprobation, and counterreaction. This surely was not unique to Starkey. Perhaps one of the most common traits of small communities throughout the world is the theme of local disharmony, which must spring almost inexorably from the demands of living together on a daily basis in a face-to-face group.

In Starkey, then, there were two countervailing patterns, one toward disharmony and another toward amiability, and these corresponded to two different levels of community life, the public and the private. The distinction between the two levels is fundamental to understanding a wide variety of small communities, including, for example, the Welsh village studied by Ronald Frankenberg in the 1950s. In Frankenberg's analysis an essential feature of the public–private dichotomy also becomes especially clear: conflict within the local group was forestalled by removing disagreement from the public sphere and confining it to the private sphere:

The fact that villagers would not underline the Church–Chapel division does not mean that they were unconscious of it. We have seen that they expressed it freely in private. . . . As long as the split in the village is not openly revealed and made public, life can be carried on as if the split was not there. (1957:97)

Gossip plays a major role in local systems of public amiability and private disharmony, in that it is the primary vehicle for the expression of private animosity. To investigate the fractiousness of a small community like Starkey is to focus largely on gossip and scandal.

The issue now is to inquire whether there were regularities or consistencies—enduring cleavages—evident in the disagreements at the private level in Starkey. Was there a thread of continuity linking apparently distinct issues and supposedly unrelated instances of dispute?

It is possible that there was not, of course, for the animosities and disagreements may conceivably have varied from one issue to the next. Each case of social cleavage would then be little more than a transient and isolated illustration of the quarrelsomeness of small-town life.[2] This was the picture that some community members themselves presented when asked about these matters. For example, when I asked one person why some Starkey families were so hostile toward one another, he replied, "Primarily it's personalities, personalities which don't get along. This is even the case within families. . . . The bitterness toward the Donelsons is mostly a result of conflict over hunting rights." I asked him to name some of the factions in the community, and he said,

There might be a pattern, but I can't see it very clearly. For example, if an issue comes up before the school board you'd expect those with certain interests to take the side that would benefit them. If there was an issue over higher taxes those with land would be against it and those without land would be in favor. There are some patterns, though. If Bill Donelson took a stand on an issue you would probably find that his brothers would take the same stand, and Bradford would back him. And you would expect to find that the Whitmans would tend to oppose him, moderately or strongly. But on the whole factions aren't very clear-cut, nor is the power wielded by certain individuals very clear-cut.

On the other hand, some people did perceive community divisions of a pervasive and enduring nature, but on the surface at least their views showed little consistency. Some felt that the community was divided between the drinkers and the nondrinkers, others emphasized a division between landholders and nonlandholders. A few suggested that the community was divided between those who were willing to contribute to the betterment of Starkey and those who were not, whereas still others stressed a division between those who controlled local affairs and those who were excluded from control. Several persons remarked on a longstanding and acrimonious rift between two groups of families, the Donelsons and the Falconers. The phrases used to distinguish these opposing segments of the community were equally varied: the "contributors" versus the "detractors," the "haves" versus the "have-nots," the "ranchers" versus the "working guys," the "land-owners" versus the "nonlandowners," and those who "put on airs" versus those who do not.

It turned out that these statements about community-wide divisions and the contrasting terms used to label them were not inconsistent or unrelated, for in each case the same set of people tended to reappear as opponents. Each of the preceding statements and terms may be conceived of as an attempt to represent the same social cleavage, but by reference to only one of its several aspects. This cleavage, of course, was the establishment–nonestablishment division.

The crux of the division,[3] as we have seen, was a disagreement of an ideological nature. There were two contradictory conceptions or folk theories of how the community was organized and run. In the final analysis, a person's alignment in the community was a matter of which of the two ideologies he or she expressed in interpreting local events.

In the mid-1960s these folk theories closely resembled those that I have described for the earlier period, although the emphasis seems to have shifted somewhat—an issue to which I will return later. The folk theory that characterized and defined the nonestablishment was the view that the community was run by a vaguely defined nucleus of people, notably the Donelsons, but more generally the major landholders and others associated with the Methodist church. The people who dominated Starkey's social life, it was thought, were petty and censorious, and self-seeking in the activities in which they engaged, which ostensibly were for the community's benefit. Their community endeavors were not truly oriented toward the goal of bettering Starkey, for their actions were motivated by a desire for self-display and public adulation.

According to the folk theory that characterized and defined the establishment, on the other hand, Starkey had for years exhibited remarkable resourcefulness and cohesion for a small town. The reason it had done so was the selfless devotion of some of its members, who had contributed enormous amounts of time and energy to such projects as the construction of the Community Hall, the park, and the swimming pool. What is more, throughout its history the community had included a number of people who had impeded constructive efforts by their constant sniping and complaining. These people tended to be hostile toward the church and what it stood for, and the Falconers were prominent among them.

When events took place in the community they were interpreted differently according to the folk theory to which the individual subscribed, and as a result divisions of opinion on local issues were not random. In case after case, public opinion at the private level tended to divide along the same lines.

Three kinds of data were used to flesh out the opposing ideologies. The first was material elicited in interviews. In private conversations I remarked that it seemed to me that one could divide the community between those who tended to side with the Donelsons and those who were aligned with the Falconers. This usually actuated a lively discussion not only about where different individuals stood in relation to the cleavage but also about why they were classified on one side or the other. By this means it was possible to obtain a rich corpus of material from which the competing images of local affairs could be extracted.

The second kind of data was case material. Privately, community members manifested very strong feelings about a number of recent events in the community. The details of some of these were reconstructed as carefully as possible, and then different interpretations of the events were gathered in order to locate divisions of opinion about them.

The third kind of data was the flow of everyday gossip that normally began whenever a few people came together. Here too, differences in point of view on local issues were sought and folk theories of community extracted.

The interview technique hinged on the unique place occupied in the community by two sets of families, the Donelsons and the Falconers. The six Donelson families constituted the core of the establishment and were perhaps the most controversial people in Starkey. One person commented: "The people who have been in Starkey for years are not neutral about the Donelsons. They either like them or they don't."

The contemporary Donelsons were the descendants of Arnold Donelson, the community leader who had died bedridden and broke in 1935. His sons were quite industrious, and all but one became economically successful by local standards. Five of the six Donelson families living in Starkey in the mid-1960s were major landholders. One person summarized a common attitude toward the Donelsons' success as follows:

The Donelsons, when they lost their land, somehow decided to get as much back as they could, any way they could. The Holdens [another cluster of families who were descended from homesteaders] aren't that way; they're happy as long as they can make the mortgage payment.

Four of the Donelson families living in Starkey in the mid-1960s were those of Arnold Donelson's sons; the other two were those of grandchildren who were now married and had children of their own.

The Donelsons tended to be outspoken in their opinions, which were often controversial. They were also considered to be "contributors" to community affairs. Most of the men had served on the school boards at one time, most of the women had been active in community organizations, especially the Women's Society and the Methodist Church, and Bill Donelson had been a community leader of some note during the 1940s and 1950s. One person commented, "The biggest objection all along the line is that the Donelsons are into everything. People resent the fact that if anything goes on to amount to anything the Donelsons are in on it—and unless they can make some kind of a show they're not in on it."

Most of the Donelsons were said to have been wild in their youth, but in the mid-1960s all of them were considered quite respectable. All now were nondrinkers. Several were outspokenly opposed to alcohol, while others drank moderately in private. Bill Donelson was a leader in the Methodist church before the Pentecostal congregation broke away, and so was his wife—in fact she was one of the two stalwarts who founded the Starkey Pentecostals.

The four Falconer households constituted the core of the nonestablishment. Two of these families were partners in a beekeeping business; the head of the third had a small irrigation farm on Starkey Flat; and the head of the fourth was a wage earner. Unlike the Donelsons, they were not among the well-to-do landholders, the "haves," but they were not among the unfortunate or shiftless members of the community either. They had respectable occupations and by local standards were comfortable, though not prosperous.

The Falconers came to Starkey in the early 1930s. They were then a single household supported by the father's beekeeping business. From the very beginning they did not find the locality congenial. The Falconer children often fought with their peers, and the mother "thought people were against her boys." She may have been right. One woman commented, "I suppose [my parents] wouldn't have let us marry a Falconer. But the girls chased them, they were the darlingest of kids. Still, I couldn't have asked one of them into the house."

Even as children the Falconers were avid hunters, and soon the boys became known as poachers. On one well-remembered occasion they were chased from a duck pond by an irate owner who fired shotgun pellets over their heads as they ran. The Falconers were frequently compared with Indians. It was said that they were quiet, independent people and excellent hunters:

They have Indian blood, they're pretty quiet if you don't know them; but they're pretty nice people. They'll do anything to hunt. And they're crack shots, too. If they shoot at a deer they'll kill it. They're just like Indians.

The Falconers are nearly outlaws. They're fiercely independent.

They were also described as hard to get along with. They were said to have a "chip on their shoulder" and to "feel they're discriminated against"; one person remarked that there was "an important negative phase to their personalities."

The Falconers were drinkers and "anti-church"; they were "detractors" in that they had not taken an active part in community affairs and were openly critical of the major community institutions, especially the Women's Society. They refused to attend (let alone assist at) the Starkey Barbecue.

The interview technique I employed—remarking that it seemed to me that the community could be divided between those who tended to side with the Donelsons and those who tended to stand with the Falconers—was used primarily to discover the grounds for assigning people to one side or the other. The following was the most perceptive (or illuminating) response to my introductory comment:

You mean [the division] between the landowners and the rest of the people. It's also the difference between those who, you might say, put on airs and those who don't. On the one hand they drink and don't care if people know, and on the other hand they drink where people won't see them doing it. You can also say it's the difference between those who do things for the community and those who don't do a thing for it.

From these conversations about the Donelsons and the Falconers there emerged three principal criteria for assigning people to either side. These constituted differentiae by which the social categories of establishment and nonestablishment were defined and distinguished from each other. The criteria were wealth, or relative standing in the social–economic hierarchy, moral respectability, and participation in community affairs. In brief, the establishment was thought to consist of the wealthier members of the community, the church goers (or church supporters) and nondrinkers, and the active contributors. The nonestablishment had the opposite characteristics.

Each of these criteria is to be seen in a context of past issues, events, and controversaries, and each needs to be discussed in turn, beginning with participation in community affairs.

A person's contributions to the community—or lack thereof—were frequently cited as grounds for placing that individual on one side or the other of the establishment–nonestablishment division. The following statements are illustrative:

My family would be on the Donelson side as opposed to the Falconer side; for example, my mother and grandmother were all active in things.

Betty is a good person, and she has done a marvelous job raising her family. But she's with the outsiders [i.e., the nonestablishment]. Maybe it's because she's too busy supporting her children to join things. Maybe it's because of [a moral indiscretion committed in the past].

Barbara is that way, too [i.e., associated with the nonestablishment], maybe because she never belonged to anything. She was never in the church, hasn't done too much for the community.

Equally significant is the fact that establishment and nonestablishment people offered different evaluations of what was meant by contributing. To the establishment, the contributors were exemplary and the noncontributors selfish. But the nonestablishment presented a strikingly different picture. The following comments illustrate the establishment viewpoint:

The good things in Starkey today are due to the people you can count on when the chips are down. If there was a dance tonight and they needed someone to decorate, they would be there. These are the ones who would do the nasty, unpleasant things when they had to be done. [The person then named nine establishment people, as well as one woman who was nonestablishment but frequently contributed.]

Some people have raised families here but did very little work. . . . As far as contributing to the community is concerned, they haven't done anything. Wilson, the old man, and his wife. They never entered into anything in the community, they lived off by themselves. If they had trouble with the kids or with taxes then you'd hear something from them. I wouldn't say that of Bill Wilson [a son]. He might go in and help you. Frank [another son] would fall in with the opposition.

The Falconers won't do anything for the PTO or 4-H. They won't be on the school board. It's always said that they have a chip on their shoulder.

[Speaking of several nonestablishment people]: They take everything out and put nothing in. By contrast take me—I support things. I take a part in the Starkey Barbecue, for example. But I do this in a background sort of way, I'm happy to serve but not as a leader.

The Jensens have never given to the community, they've always taken. There is not a single thing Mrs. Jensen has ever done for the community.

On the other hand, the following illustrate the nonestablishment view:

[I asked one nonestablishment person why one of the Donelson families is not disliked as much as some of the others.] They don't get their names in the papers as much as the rest of them. It seems that whenever something is done the Donelsons do it. The kids at school feel the same way about the Donelson children. The Donelson kids are out front, they're the wheels. . . . Maybe it's just that there will always be leaders and that those who are not leaders will resent them.

The "haves" are the contributors, but they aren't contributing for the community, but for how it looks. Besides, some of the people on the other side have contributed a great deal.

Around Starkey the working guys outnumber the ranchers. Still, the ranchers control what is going on here. It's the same way all through this area—Saint George, Pinefield.

It is understandable that the establishment often referred to the Donelson–Falconer division as a division between the "contributors"—those who were "for the community"—and the "detractors," "do-nothings," and "agin'ers"; and that the nonestablishment often referred to the establishment as the "controllers," those who tried to "run the community."

The local image of the Women's Society illustrates the differences in the way people evaluated community participation. That organization was clearly associated with the establishment in local thought, and a person's opinions about it reflected his or her alignment with respect to the factional split. In the preceding chapter I noted that three common criticisms of the Women's Society were that its members sometimes misused their power, that they were snobbish, and that they were glory seekers. These were simply manifestations of the nonestablishment's views on the general role of the establishment in the community. On the other hand, some typical establishment comments on the Society reflect its perspective on community participation:

The Society is important in Starkey, because it is the organization that gets things done. I feel that those people who don't attend are selfish, they aren't doing what they should for the community. I look down on those people who don't belong to the Society.

Some people won't have anything to do with the Society. The Falconers, to start with. Betty Falconer complains that they all go to the Society just to show off their clothes . . . [but] that isn't so. [The person then named six other people, all nonestablishment, who were against the Society.]

The second criterion distinguishing the two sides of the division was morality, for the establishment was considered more upright, straitlaced, or prudish than the nonestablishment. The following are some of the replies of one establishment person to my request that he locate several community members in terms of the Donelson–Falconer split:

Kenneth is with the Donelsons, and his brother, also; they're good, moral people.

I think that if Ed and Mary were together [they were divorced] and leading a good life [each drank publicly, sometimes heavily, and each was regarded as sexually promiscuous] they would definitely be on the upper side.

John is difficult to place. His wife isn't accepted by the community because of her background. And since he has had trouble with his home life and everything . . . He has had money but has spent it. Sometimes he hasn't paid his bills. He's lost the feeling in the community of an upstanding person. But he doesn't have the Falconers' chip on his shoulder.

Once again, the two sides of the division evaluated this criterion differently. From the establishment point of view their moral uprightness was a worthy attribute, whereas to the nonestablishment it was sanctimonious and insincere. The Donelsons especially—at least some of them—were considered self-righteous and censorious, qualities that were thought to be rather unsuitable for them since they had been as wild as anyone in the community during their youth. The efforts of the drinking nondrinkers to conceal their tippling was also considered sheer hypocrisy.

I asked one member of the establishment to describe for me how a newcomer to Starkey would view the "established group." She gave what could pass as the nonestablishment's image as well:

The "haves," the established group, are goody-goodies, everybody's conscience. You have to abide by their rules. The older families accept you if you accept their moral views, which are of the older generation: clean living—for example, no drinking, or if you drink you do it privately and do not argue in favor of drinking; exhibiting attributes such as hard work, frugality, cleanliness, polite children. The newcomer would look on the established group as good members of the community, and highly judgmental. . . . And they are harsh in their judgments. The other side feels they are just as good but that the established group doesn't think so. They see the established group as being a judgmental, domineering group.

The Methodist church was still associated with the establishment in local thought. Those who were classified with the Donelsons were considered church supporters, even if they never attended church affairs, and those who were classified with the Falconers were thought of as anti-church. An establishment person who did not attend a single Methodist service while I lived in Starkey, and whose wife occasionally worshiped with the Pentecostals, stated reproachfully that "There are some people who would make a dig at the [Methodist] church any chance they get. [He named several nonestablishment people.] One time John said that if you ever need help you should go to the bar, not the church." Another person, whose father was nonestablishment, stated that "My father has a chip on his shoulder about a lot of people, and I don't agree with his feelings about most of them. . . . He won't have anything to do with the church—he doesn't think much at all of the church people."

The third criterion was wealth, and in this respect the establishment–nonestablishment division resembled a class distinction. The following statements were made by a member of the establishment:

[Referring to an old-family member who was near the bottom of the social hierarchy:] He's on the Falconer side, he's never done anything with himself.

[Referring to yet another community member:] He's with the Donelson side; he came to Statkey with nothing and made something here. He's a go-getter, made a good living, has bought some property.

People associated the major landholders in particular with the establishment. I asked one nonestablishment person to name Starkey's leaders, and he replied,

You mean the controllers? . . . The school, community, and everything else, it's the ranchers who control things. . . . Most of them I get along with to speak to, but they're not in the same company as . . . [here the person named several Starkey schoolteachers and seven other community members, including the Falconers, all of whom were nonestablishment]. The Whitmans [who were major landholders] are on the different [i.e., the Donelson] side, although I've never had any run-ins with them. Bill Donelson and I will speak, but Bill's brothers just look down at the ground when we meet.

It is easy to understand why the establishment–nonestablishment division was sometimes referred to as the distinction between the "haves" and the "have-nots."

The wealth and life style of the "haves" frequently attracted the envy and enmity of the "have-nots." For example,

The "haves" are more social conscious, they have different criteria for judging people. . . . The Lawrences [who were "have-nots"] don't try to impress people, they make no pretenses—look at their house, for example.

The feeling toward the Donelsons today comes from the fact that they think they're important. They used to be poor, but now they have money.

Two recent issues in particular have exacerbated the division between the major landholders and the nonlandholders. The first involves military service in World War II. Nearly thirty local men served in the armed forces during the war, but not all of those who were physically qualified to serve did so. A number of eligible men received deferments because their labor was needed at home, and nearly all of them were the sons of major landholders. In at least two cases land was acquired for men of draft age so that they would not be called up. As a result, most of those who went to war were from families that had no land whatever or were the sons of farmers whose holdings were comparatively small. Those who stayed home not only avoided the hardships of military service but were able to enjoy the agricultural profits of the war years and were in a position to enlarge their holdings if land became avaiable. Going to war turned out to be an enormous economic handicap.

A Starkey rancher had served on the local draft board during the war, and it was widely believed that he had used his position to keep close relatives—all of whom were major landholders during the period of my research—from serving. On one occasion two community members were naming for me those who did and did not serve in World War II. One of them turned to me and said, "You see the connection, don't you? The ones who didn't go are all related to [the rancher who served on the draft board]. The ones that did go weren't related to him. . . . Don't think it doesn't bother him when he goes to bed at night." In another conversation a member of the establishment commented,

When you stop to think of it, none of the [here she named several major landholder families, including the Donelsons] went to war. It was the [she now named several nonestablishment nonlandholders, including the Falconers] who went. You don't know how bitter people were over that.

The second issue that aggravated the division between landholders and nonlandholders was hunting. From the time Starkey was founded most of the local farmers and ranchers permitted nearly unrestricted hunting on their lands. But after World War II increasing numbers of people wanted to hunt, including many outsiders who were willing to travel long distances to do so. Simultaneously, the deer population in the Starkey region increased markedly. During the late 1940s large numbers of uninvited sportsmen began roaming the ranches and farmlands in search of game, sometimes failing to close gates behind them and enabling the cattle to feed in the grain fields or become mixed with other herds. Water tanks were occasionally shot at, leaving the tanks empty and the cattle dry. The danger of grass fires and accidental shootings was severe. As a result, by 1950 nearly all the landholders of the region had begun to restrict hunting on their property.

The case of the Winters' ranch illustrates the problems this caused. For years the Winters had granted unlimited hunting privileges to their harvest crews, who usually carried rifles with them at work. Upon sighting a deer, the men dropped what they were doing to chase the animal, even if it meant crossing into an adjacent ranch. But by the late 1940s the neighboring ranchers had begun to restrict hunting on their lands and to complain to the Winters about their harvest crew. The Winters at first merely cautioned the workers not to cross the boundary lines, but the trespassing continued, and as a result it was decided that the hired men could no longer hunt on the ranch at all. Most of them were infuriated by the new policy. One in particular reportedly became "pretty mad about it" and tried to talk a young and rather bellicose relative into picking a fight with one of the ranch owners.

The following statement was made by a nonestablishment person and illustrates the antagonism created by the hunting restrictions:

Some went into the service during the war and others didn't. Some didn't go in because their father was on the draft board. After the war, Glenn [Falconer] and I were driving [on a public road] through one of the ranches, and we came across the owner [one of the sons who had not gone to war]. He was mad and said, "Just because you went to war you think you can hunt wherever you want." And we weren't even hunting! Glenn, John, and Joe [all of whom were nonestablishment] were the first in the service. Glenn got shot up pretty bad, and still they begrudge him hunting.

The controversy over hunting leads beyond the matter of wealth to another set of issues altogether. These are the issues concerning the Conservation and Hunting Club, and they throw light on both the establishment–nonestablishment division and the place of the Donelsons and the Falconers within it.

In 1945 twenty-three men met in the high school to inaugurate this organization, which was to have as its primary aim a program of game conservation. Although the area of membership extended somewhat beyond Starkey's borders, the club at first consisted almost exclusively of people from Starkey, and its main organizers and leaders were Donelsons.

The first activities were devoted to experiments intended to increase the quail population. The members fenced in small game preserves in which they constructed guzzlers and allowed the brush to grow as cover for the birds.

The club received an unexpected boost as a result of the problems landholders began to experience with trespassers after the war. In the late 1940s hunting rights on several of the largest ranches in the Starkey region were turned over to the club, which in return was to regulate and police hunting on those lands. Approximately 120,000 acres eventually fell within the club's jurisdiction. Each club member was assigned by lot to hunt on certain days and in certain areas, whereas nonmembers could not hunt at all within the club's jurisdiction unless the landholder himself gave permission.

The two requirements for membership were a small annual dues payment and the donation of one day's labor per year. Both were used to establish game preserves within the club's area of jurisdiction, although as noted earlier, community improvements also benefited from both the treasury and the work days.

The acquisition of hunting rights by the organization had dramatic effects, one of which was a sudden increase in membership. Virtually the only way a landless community member could hunt—legally—was to join. Throughout the 1950s the membership was about 150 people, of which only 55 percent or so were Starkey residents; those from outside the community came mostly from other parts of the county, primarily the inland region, although a few lived as far away as San Francisco and Los Angeles.

Another effect was to stimulate conflict over the organization's goals. At first the focus of interest had been game conservation, a topic dear to sportsmen, but the Donelsons who founded the club were ardent conservationists. Their interests extended to the preservation of flora and fauna of all kinds and included such ecological problems as overgrazing and erosion. They were a tiny minority in the organization, the majority consisting of those whose sole reason for joining was the desire to hunt. Among them were the Falconers. But in spite of the majority interest in hunting, the Donelsons occupied most of the formal offices in the club and had far more influence on its affairs than their small number would indicate.

Animosities were always close to the surface, as is suggested by the minutes of a club meeting in 1951 in which a discussion was reported about "the problem of members who joined the Club for purely hunting privileges." The Donelsons sometimes used the club as a platform to argue conservation measures, and this stimulated dissension. One particularly controversial issue was a charge raised by a Donelson that a local rancher was allowing his land to be overgrazed, to the detriment of the natural fauna. A man who had been a member at the time commented, "I didn't want to be associated with the club when it got to doing that sort of thing."

The club had to regulate hunting in order to retain its hunting privileges, and this led to continual dispute. One ex-member said, "There were too many people in the club, so you couldn't hunt more than several times a year. And they even told you where to hunt." Another remarked, "I was in for about a year. They put in guzzlers and so on, and then they started telling you when and where to hunt."

Grievances like these were perhaps inevitable given the degree of interest in hunting, but it seems likely that the general ill will that the nonestablishment felt toward the Donelsons contributed to the feelings of mistrust and hostility within the club. A theme that pervaded the affairs of the organization was that the Donelsons were in control—which was not altogether inaccurate, since they occupied the major offices and performed the routine tasks that made the club work. But beyond that, the motivations and fairness of the leaders were called into question, for it was believed by many rank-and-file members that the organization was not democratic in its operation and that the Donelsons were using their influence to give themselves breaks that others did not enjoy. The opinions that were expressed on this subject more or less reflected the nonestablishment's image of the establishment:

The Conservation Club was dominated by a few people and they had to run it their own way. I suppose they have been used to running things for years.

The reason the Conservation Club broke up was that the Donelsons ran it and gave the benefits to themselves. They put up the list in one of the service stations showing who could hunt, where, and when, and everyone could see what was happening.

The reason [the Club disbanded] was that the Donelsons were running it and got all the good hunting.

By contrast, the Donelsons' interpretation was that their own actions were exemplary and that it was their critics who were to blame for the Club's failings. This opinion reflected the establishment's view that the nonestablishment were selfish and quarrelsome. The following statements were made by two of the Donelsons involved:

Everyone had something to complain about. People wanted to hunt without paying their dues or working. They would join but fail to meet the requirements, and yet they would show up to hunt. Primarily Starkey people did this, not outsiders. Things didn't go well after a while.

> The Club started out in conservation, for quail. . . . They found they could increase the game supply considerably by means of wildlife sanctuaries. . . . Everyone squawked, but it worked all right. If someone violated the rules their privileges were taken away, for a year, maybe. Pretty quick, though, the rules began breaking down. The hunters went after more game. So the club got to be a farce.

For reasons that are unclear to me, the landholders began removing their property from the club's jurisdiction in the late 1950s—probably because the organization had become ineffective in controlling trespassers. By 1961 virtually all the land had been withdrawn and the club no longer offered a hunting program. This produced a sharp decline in membership and by 1963 only twenty names remained on the rolls. It also produced a refocusing of interest away from hunting and toward game conservation; in the mid-1960s one of the organization's main goals was to oppose federal and state legislation that was thought to be opposed to sound principles of conservation. As a local group it had virtually become defunct. In the mid-1960s most Starkey people would have been surprised to find that the club still existed at all.

The Bradford ranch was one of the largest single holdings in the inland section of the county, and its entire acreage had been under the jurisdiction of the Conservation Club during the 1950s. Many club members had spent time on the ranch building guzzlers and fencing and posting game preserves. After the Bradfords had terminated their agreement with the club they entered into a new one exclusively with the Donelsons and a few of the Donelsons' relatives. In return for hunting privileges the Donelsons would control trespassing on the ranch.

Many former club members—including the Falconers—were enraged, for the Donelsons now enjoyed the benefits of the game preserves that had been built by others. Within a short time several acts of vandalism occurred. Paint was smeared on some of the no-hunting signs that the Donelsons had erected, and clear evidence of trespassing was left on the Bradford property. The Falconers were suspected. In the mid-1960s another incident occurred that was blamed on the Falconers. By law, deer could be hunted only during a certain portion of the summer, and then only bucks were to be shot. In the spring of 1966—out of season—the skin of a recently killed doe was draped over one of the Donelsons' no-hunting signs. This was met with anger from some and cheers from others as an act of defiance by the Falconers against the Donelsons. A few months later about 30 dead jackrabbits were dropped some 50 or 60 feet apart down the center of a county road leading through the Bradford ranch. This was interpreted in similar fashion, for it was assumed that the animals had been shot by Falconers while trespassing on the Bradfords' property.

The anger toward the Donelsons was exacerbated by their persistence in pressing charges against people who were caught hunting ilegally. The most notorious such instance occurred in the early 1960s and involved a Starkey schoolteacher, Mr. Steadman. Steadman was new to the community and was not fully aware of the local restrictions on hunting or of the sensitive nature of the matter. One afternoon he was driving on the county road leading through the Bradford ranch and spotted a deer. He had his rifle with him—it was the peak of the hunting season—so he got out of the car and shot the animal from the side of the road, wounding him. At about that moment Frank Donelson drove by and stopped. Steadman asked him if he thought anyone would mind if he pursued the animal. Donelson brusquely told him that someone would mind, and drove on. Steadman then went home.

A private meeting was called at which Frank informed the other Donelsons about the shooting. Although not all of them agreed, the majority decided that legal action had to be taken as a warning to others.

That evening a part-time deputy sheriff—and a nonestablishment community member—informed Steadman that a charge of illegal hunting had been filed against him. About a week later the deputy called again, saying that the Donelsons had "thrown the book" at Steadman and that he should prepare to be taken to jail in Oak Flat. The deputy would return shortly to make the actual arrest. The teacher waited nervously until late evening for the officer to come, and when he finally arrived he apologized for the delay. It seems that he had been detained by other matters. The Donelsons had just caught two other people hunting illegally, and they had to be taken to jail first. One of them was a Falconer.

Several nonestablishment people tried to persuade Steadman to falsify his story to avoid conviction, but he refused to do so, and as a result he was convicted, fined, and given a suspended jail sentence.[4]

The following statements give some idea of the feelings in Starkey about these arrests:

The anti-Donelson forces went into operation and really blew the whole thing up. . . . Steadman's poaching could have been handled more discreetly, but the Donelsons wouldn't think of treating him any more lightly than anyone else.

The Donelsons acted more like policemen than neighbors, and a lot of people got quite worked up.

But the Donelsons felt that their unyielding approach was both legitimate and necessary. One of them said,

When we took over and patrolled the Bradford land people tried to see if we were going to enforce the rules. This caused a lot of ill feeling, because we couldn't be lax. If we gave in to someone the others would feel they had a right to favors, so we agreed not to just run off the people we caught hunting. Instead we decided to take them to court, and we did this with eight or ten people, including several local people. Even when the district attorney's man said there wasn't much of a chance for conviction we pushed the case and made the man sweat it out. Usually the guy changed his plea to guilty on the day before the trial and paid his fine. As a result, hunting is now under control on the Bradford ranch.

The significance of hunting disputes can hardly be overestimated. One person who was discussing the Donelson–Falconer division commented, reflectively, that "The hunting situation is the basis for the whole thing, in a way." But then he qualified his remark: "The Falconers didn't contribute to community functions. Maybe it would have been different if they had." It seems that hunting disputes were as much an expression of the cleavage as a cause, for I doubt that the Donelsons would have been so resolute in the prosecution of wrongdoers if the acts of wrongdoing had not been colored by factional distrust and misunderstanding.

How was it possible for a cleavage so clear in general outline and so fundamental to remain so ill defined in local thought? Why was it usually perceived, if at all, in terms of only one of its aspects? This question takes us to the heart of the establishment–nonestablishment division.

What was *not* vague in people's minds was the folk theory by which they represented the community to themselves—whether it happened to be the establishment version of that theory or the nonestablishment version. Although a person might be quite clear about the merit of the contributors and the disrepute of the detractors, for example—or about the cheap self-adulation and censoriousness of the controllers—he or she could become quite uncertain when assigning specific individuals to either side. In this sense the folk theories were clearer at the level of thought than at the level of application.

There were at least two reasons for this difficulty of application. The first is that the three differentiae by which people were assigned a position on one side or the other were not absolute standards. For example, one woman in particular was hard to place. She was a drinker by local norms, since she openly bought beer and wine in Starkey and gave parties at which drinks were served. And yet she regularly attended the Methodist church. By the criterion of morality she fell on both sides of the division. What is more, she was simultaneously a contributor and a detractor, for she was regarded as a person who could be counted on to work for the community and was a member of the Women's Society. But she and her husband, a teacher, were both bitter toward the Donelsons and other major landholders because of the way they tried to run the community. Her husband was strongly distrustful of the Women's Society and she was moderately so—in spite of her membership in the organization.

A person could also be classified as establishment by one of the three differentiae and as nonestablishment by another. For example, one man was a major landholder and *ipso facto* a member of the establishment. But he was considered an alcoholic, and it was said that if he did not have a capable and conscientious foreman to run his ranch for him he could not continue farming.

In short, the criteria for determining where a person stood in the system were so imprecise that instead of clarifying the establishment–nonestablishment division they often helped blur it.

A second reason for the indeterminacy of the division in actual application is that most people avoided revealing their alignments. For example, one woman whose parents were unequivocally nonestablishment tended to share her parents' nonestablishment views, but publicly she tried to avoid being classified with the "agin'ers." She was asked to help with the Starkey Barbecue each year, and for her to refuse would have been not only an embarrassment in itself but also a clear sign that she was aligned with her parents after all. Her desire to avoid such an interpretation was one reason she consented to help.

Publicly, most people in Starkey avoided aligning themselvs openly with one side or the other and were therefore "neutral," so that distinct, solidary factions did not appear. Only about twelve families, including the Falconers and a number of their close friends, were openly and unequivocally nonestablishment. Some fifteen families, including the Donelsons and their close friends, were openly and unequivocally establishment. Most of those who were openly associated with either side were manifestly hostile toward those who were openly associated with the other, whereas the "neutrals" could move easily with both sides. One "neutral" remarked, "I am comfortable with either [the Falconers or Donelsons], but they couldn't get along with each other." Some Donelsons and Falconers did not speak to one another when they happened to meet.

In view of this characteristic of indeterminacy and of the sizable number of "neutrals" in the system, how is it possible to speak of a genuine cleavage in Starkey, or of two opposing alignments? The problem is resolved by setting aside the somewhat deceptive way in which the people represented the establishment–nonestablishment division to themselves—which is to say, by reference to the criteria of wealth, morality, and community participation—and to look beneath the public facade of neutrality that many people exhibited. A person's true alignment could be established by determining which of the two folk ideologies he or she exhibited in interpreting events. Privately— "beneath the surface," as one person expressed it—virtually no one who took any interest in community life was neutral. Almost everyone was privately aligned with either the Donelsons or the Falconers. And in almost all cases those who were privately aligned with the Falconers confidentially exhibited the attributes of the nonestablishment: they were anti-Donelson, anti-church, and anti-Women's Society, and they were opposed to the ranchers' putative control over community affairs. Similarly, those who privately sided with the Donelsons confidentially manifested the opinions of the establishment.

Not everyone gave total allegiance to either side, of course. Criticisms of the Donelsons and Falconers, for example, were expressed not only by their opponents but by their friends as well. A person who was aligned with one side or the other did not necessarily dispute the opponents' evaluations, but a person who sided with the Falconers, say, regarded the criticisms of the Donelsons as more grievous, whereas a person aligned with the Donelsons felt the opposite way.

The manner in which I determined the private alignment of one community member illustrates how a person's leanings were assessed. I had spoken to Larry Krebs on several occasions in the cafe, but each time other people were present. Krebs had been careful to avoid disagreement and to appear neutral whenever controversial issues were raised. Eventually he and I found ourselves alone, and when the topic of Donelsons versus Falconers was broached he said,

The Falconers are a lot better people than the Donelsons. The Falconers aren't going to backbite like the Donelsons; if they have something to say they'll say it to your face. The Falconers have a lot more friends than the Donelsons. There are just a few who are friends of the Donelsons. . . . But a lot of people like the Falconers. The Donelsons are against everybody. They're even against themselves—if one wants to go hunting they have to call all the rest and tell them they're going to. They've done a lot of things to hurt people. For example, one person was collecting some wood to burn on the land the Donelsons police, and one of the Donelsons gave him a bad time about it.

I eventually determined that Krebs was also moderately anti-church, critical of the Women's Society, and strongly opposed to the way the ranchers tried to run the community.

Since I had been misled about Krebs' alignment, I wondered whether others might be too, so I asked one establishment person whom I knew quite well whether he could say which side of the division the man was on. Without hesitation he said it was the Falconer side.

In spite of the public stance of neutrality that most community members assumed, others were usually aware of their actual, private alignment, so even though a person may have regarded another as neutral in one sense, he or she could often say which side that individual would belong to "if it came down to choosing sides." But there were not many situations in which community members had to choose sides, and as a result there was usually little cause to take deliberate account of people's private alignments. It normally took a moment's reflection for a person to identify another person's actual position with respect to the cleavage.

If a person was reasonably careful about the open expression of views that might betray his or her alignment, what was the tip-off to others that enabled them to guess that person's private leanings? In part it must have been that comments made in private were repeated by others, and in part that those whom the individual chose to associate with gave strong hints about his or her private inclinations. And perhaps there were occasions on which the person's private views broke forth publicly: during the height of the controversy over the arrest of Steadman, for example.

There were also several actions that manifested a person's leanings in an even more subtle fashion. One of these was drinking (see Hatch 1973). Those whose behavior caused them to be categorized as drinkers signaled that they did not have sufficient regard for the establishment to abide by the rules that it sanctioned. By contrast, those who drank discreetly enough to be considered nondrinkers signaled just the opposite. Drinking habits were a very sensitive index of a person's alignment. Indeed, the purchase of a bottle of wine in Starkey, or the drinking of beer in the park, could even be a form of defiance and opposition—a mild version perhaps of the doe skin draped over the Donelsons' no-hunting sign.

This throws further light on the drinking norms in Starkey and on the division between drinkers and nondrinkers. If a nondrinker were to drink openly it would betray something more than willingness to engage in behavior that some people found offensive. It would also express opposition and defiance toward them. The drinking nondrinker wanted to avoid not only offending or being thought badly of but also being classified as an "agin'er" or opposer, with all that this meant in the community.

Another action that symbolized a person's leanings was grocery shopping. Much of the shopping was done outside the community, but most Starkey people shopped at least occasionally at one of the two local stores. One of them was run by a newcomer who was almost completely outside the community life, whereas the other was owned by a member of the establishment and run by a Donelson. The clienteles of the two stores conformed fairly closely to the establishment–nonestablishment division. An establishment person with whom I had spoken at length about the division saw my car parked in front of the nonestablishment store one morning and commented playfully, "I see you've gone over to the other side." On a different occasion someone else remarked, "The people who trade at [the newcomer's] store would dang sure go to town [Oak Flat] before they'd go to the other store."

I have remarked that the two competing ideologies of the establishment and the nonestablishment were cultural idioms for interpreting local events. It follows that people tended to express different interpretations of those events according to whether they were members of the establishment or of the nonestablishment. Several cases illustrate these differences. I will discuss three here, all of them involving the schools.

The events I describe occurred before unification took place, so each school had its own board of trustees. What is more, the school boards tended to be composed mostly of establishment people and to be associated with the establishment in local thought. For example, one nonestablishment person commented, "The school board has been run by ranchers; they've had the board dangling on a string." By contrast, the following comments represent the establishment's view of the school boards:

The property owners tend to go along with the board as long as it's being reasonable, and so do the other people that are active in things. Then there are some others who would try to lead some opposition to something now and then.

The out-crowd [the nonestablishment] wouldn't back [the school board], but the in-crowd would.

The first case involves Mr. Larsen, who was principal of the Starkey high school during the mid-1950s, a high school-student named Frank, and the high-school board.

Larsen placed heavier emphasis on academic courses than on either athletics or vocational programs, and the more affluent members of the community—those who wanted a college education for their children—supported him in this. The major landholders and the establishment generally (as well as the school board) held him in high regard. But the less affluent, and especially some members of the nonestablishment, would have preferred greater stress on vocational training and athletic achievements; these people were Larsen's primary critics.

Several students were disrupting the high school at the time, and Frank was the worst offender. He was a very large, strong boy and quite unruly, although much of his rebelliousness was playful and not malevolent, so that those who were close to him could disapprove but still tolerate his actions. Frank's family was clearly associated with the nonestablishment.

Frank was repeatedly in trouble at school. On one occasion he and several others smeared paint on the outside of the school building. On another occasion he apparently threw a rock through a window of Larsen's home—although Frank was not observed hurling the rock, his car was seen driving away afterward. Larsen's baby was sleeping near the window at the time and the prank could conceivably have taken the child's life.

The school board felt that the school's authority was seriously damaged by these pranks and decided to seek legal action against the boy. The sheriff was notified, charges were filed, and Frank was soon ordered to appear in court at Saint Thomas.

Community sentiment was not unanimously behind the board, for some people felt that the trustees were being too harsh. George Donelson, who was one of the trustees, asked several of his friends and relatives to attend the court hearing as a show of support for the school board, which suggests that the controversy was fairly heated.

After listening to the details of the case the judge proposed to treat the boy lightly and even offered to pay for damages out of his own pocket. But Donelson rose to speak against leniency. The case, he said, involved something more than a broken window; the life of an innocent child had been endangered. The judge was not swayed and punishment was not served.

Even though Frank had been expelled from school shortly before the rock-throwing incident, he often loitered on the school grounds, looking into classroom windows and disrupting classes. He was as much a problem after his expulsion as before. In response, the board now drafted a regulation giving itself the right to exclude undersirables from school grounds and school events; it had copies placed in the two stores, and community members were urged to sign an accompanying petition. Apparently a large proportion did sign, but the fact that the trustees submitted the rule to public approval indicates how intense they felt the issue had become. Once the board thought it had enough signatures it proceeded to bar Frank from school property. On one occasion Frank attempted to attend a high-school basketball game but was stopped and escorted out of the gym by George Donelson—in front of a watching crowd.

Both the board members and the principal were being baited by Frank and some of his friends throughout this period. For instance, George Donelson, who lived several miles outside of Starkey, occasionally found the boys parked by the side of the little-used road leading to his home, "daring him to stop." According to one account, "The bar group was egging the boys on."

Larsen resigned the following year and left Starkey. It is not clear what role the disruptions played in his decision to do so.

It is difficult to reconstruct people's alignments on these issues, since most of them tried to appear neutral. But considering only those who were openly involved, it is clear that nonestablishment people were on one side and establishment people on the other. One member of the establishment described those who sided with Frank as "those people who feel they're discriminated against. . . . They're bad hombres, agin'ers. . . . These people don't support things in the community—church, school, and so on."

People on the two sides of the division presented strikingly different—but characteristic—interpretations of these matters. Taking people's views about Larsen first, one establishment person commented,

People were divided over Larsen. The "have-nots"—the nonparticipants, the ones lacking in community spirit or orientation—were against him. Certainly no one was against him on academic issues, because he was very good academically. I think that some of the people felt he shortchanged athletics. . . . Larsen had trouble with the kids who were in agriculture and weren't interested in things. The people who were against him were those whose kids were in shop or wanted to play football or basketball.

On the other hand, a nonestablishment person said, "Larsen was a 'yes-man.' There were a lot of hens and roosters [disapproving people] around town then, and every time a kid went down the street they phoned Larsen up and told him."

The following statements illustrate opinions about the actions taken against Frank; first, the establishment viewpoint:

I'm sure Larsen left Starkey because of what happened to him, he left for his own peace of mind and the safety of his family. One kid had a hearing at Juvenile Court. Larsen had disciplined him or something, anyway he had tried to enforce some of the school rules and the kid went afoul of him. The kid was just a bum, and he drove by Larsen's house one night and hurled a rock through the window. . . . [Some] people castigated the school board for getting mean with the kid, they condoned the kid's little acts of violence against Larsen, they didn't like Larsen. It was felt that they [the school board] had to take the kid to court, because they had to make it felt that the board and the school would support its rules.

The kid should have been punished. It was more serious than a broken window, because of the baby.

[The following statement was made by a person who was on the school board at the time.] Problems were arising [at the school]; for example, kids were throwing paint, fighting. Life was being made miserable for Larsen, the principal—they were throwing rotten eggs at him, to take an example. I felt we should take the bull by the horns, get a campaign going. . . . They finally ran Larsen out [of the community].

On the other hand, the following represent the views of the nonestablishment toward the actions taken against Frank:

They were picking on Frank. Others were getting him into trouble, picking him out to blame him. Instead of denying the things he was accused of, Frank would accept the blame. He wanted to be a big shot, that's why he took the blame. He was just a big kid. He didn't do one-tenth of what he was blamed for—although he asked for a lot of it. One time he and his girl friend were near the high school, it must have been Hallowe'en night. Some other kids were painting the school, and somebody saw them. Every one of the kids that was doing the painting left, but Frank and his girl stayed; they had been watching, but weren't doing anything. He got accused, and never denied doing it. They [Larsen and the school board] wouldn't let those kids on the school grounds. One night there was a basketball game in the gym, and Frank went in to see it. Donelson was on the school board, and he saw him and escorted him out of the gym in front of all those people. Can you imagine that?

[The following was made by a relative newcomer, a nonestablishment person:] I heard that several years ago when Donelson was on the school board a boy in the community had gotten in trouble, and Donelson tried to hang the kid at a hearing.

The nonestablishment saw this as just another case in which the establishment had tried to impose its will on the community. Opposition to such highhanded tactics was called for. In the opinion of the establishment, drastic measures were needed and the school board was not acting in a highhanded manner at all. But the bitter opposition that came from the nonestablishment was typical of those people, who were "agin'ers" and always felt that they were discriminated against.

The second case involves Mr. Warwick, who replaced Larsen. Warwick was a firm disciplinarian, a quality that was welcomed by the board at this point, but it soon became apparent that he was suffering from a mental disorder. For example, he attended a school Hallowe'en party in what was regarded as a ridiculous costume, and throughout the event he behaved erratically. His relations with the board quickly soured, and the trustees began to fear that he might become violent if provoked. One board member began barricading the doors to his home at night out of fear of what Warwick might try to do to him and his family. The trustees met secretly on several occasions to discuss the matter, and by early winter they decided that Warwick had to be replaced at once. As required by law, the board summonsed a state official to investigate and determine whether the dismissal was justified, and he concurred. Throughout these proceedings Warwick's impending ouster was kept completely secret—from both the community and the principal.

Warwick's behavior became increasingly bizarre, and on the day of his dismissal—the day before Christmas vacation—at least one trustee was with him in his office at all times and refused to allow him even to see any of the students, none of whom knew what was taking place. At the end of the day Warwick was driven away from school and out of Starkey. It was not until then that the community learned that he had been dismissed, and to avoid embarrassing the man further the board never offered a public explanation of the dismissal.

There seems to have been little reason for a division of opinion over Warwick, and yet traces of such a division are apparent. In particular, at least some members of the nonestablishment suspected that the board might have been acting out of spite. For example, one nonestablishment person commented,

Maybe Warwick was all right. My wife and I never knew him, but there was some feeling that Warwick treated [the children of two establishment board members, one of them a Donelson] like everyone else's, and that was why he was let go. Apparently Warwick told one board member's boy that he [Warwick] knew who he was but that it didn't make any difference. This got back to the board member and didn't sit too well. Warwick told all the kids that he would treat them alike. The board would never tell why they dismissed him.

Because of the board's secretiveness about the matter—and the comparatively short exposure that most people had to Warwick's behavior—the firing took place in a near-vacuum. People did not have sufficient information to assess the board's actions, and the nonestablishment ideology helped supply the missing motivations.

The third case occurred the year before I entered the community, and the issues were still quite fresh.

The case centered on an instructor, Mr. Winthrop, who started teaching in the Starkey elementary school in September 1964. Within a short time several parents began to complain privately to one another about the strict discipline he maintained in the classroom. One mother in particular, Mrs. Harner (whose husband was a ranch foreman), became concerned about the effects he was having on one of her children.

Barbara Donelson had a child in Winthrop's class,[5] and at first she thought little of the complaints. But in January 1965 her boy was sternly reprimanded by the teacher, and because the child became so upset the principal called her up and asked her to come to school and discuss the problem with both him and Winthrop. The meeting convinced her that the teacher was indeed a very severe disciplinarian. She was also surprised when she asked to see some of the child's schoolwork to see how he was doing; she said to me,

They had hardly done anything in that class. . . . Winthrop's class was unbelievably behind. In spelling, for example, my boy had only done about three weeks' worth of work [school had been in session for about four months]. Apparently the class was behind because Winthrop spent his time talking, and teaching such things as how to hold a pencil. He wasn't teaching them the material.

Mrs. Donelson was now quite concerned. She began discussing her views with other people whose children were in Winthrop's class. In

February or March 1965, an informal parents' meeting was held in one of the homes to discuss the issue, and shortly thereafter several mothers decided to hold a more formal meeting at the school and to invite Winthrop and the principal to attend. Mrs. Donelson was not the only person behind this meeting by any means, although she handled the arrangements for it. In particular, it was she who informed all the parents that the gathering would take place. The other instigators did not want it known that they had a part in this affair, and as a result nearly everyone in the community mistakenly assumed that Barbara Donelson was solely responsible for the meeting.

From the point of view of its instigators, the formal meeting was intended as a means to determine what the parents could do to help their children catch up in their schoolwork. According to Mrs. Donelson, it was not supposed to be a "personal attack" against Winthrop: "I tried not to make it a personal attack, and in fact I did a lot of soul searching before I got involved. I felt bad about what I had to do, but I felt I had to do it. I was concerned about the children—not only mine, but all of them."

The teachers strongly opposed the parents' criticisms of Winthrop, for they felt that only professional school staff should judge his performance in the classroom. They thought the primary reason for the opposition to him was that he had "crossed" the children of some influential people, especially Barbara Donelson. The following statements were made by two of the teachers who were openly involved in the issue:

Winthrop had crossed [the parents who were against him]. He had disciplined their children, and they didn't like it, so they tried to get him fired. But I don't accept the idea that a man should be fired for those reasons, so I backed Winthrop.

The people who were against Winthrop might have had a legitimate gripe, but they didn't care what means they used in trying to get rid of him. . . . Mrs. Donelson's kids are bullies, from what I can gather. . . . Her boy had talked back to the teacher or had done one thing or another. So it looked pretty ridiculous for her to call a meeting blaming the teacher.

The teachers also felt that some of the opposition to Winthrop was stimulated by certain features of his private life:

This is the thing with Winthrop. In a small community people are clannish, they accept those who are like them and reject those who are different. Winthrop is

English. Some women feel it's almost indecent how young his wife is. She was a junior in high school when she first came here. Everybody thought the trailer he lives in is a junk heap. . . . He's different, there are all those things against him.

The teachers' view of the formal gathering was that it was a "witch hunt meeting." Before it took place the elementary and high-school teachers met privately, and with one exception all decided to do what they could to support Winthrop. They began by contacting people who they thought would be sympathetic to them, including one of the five elementary school board members and the parents of several of Winthrop's pupils.

The formal meeting was held in the school cafeteria with the principal officiating. The principal, Winthrop, and an official from the office of the county superintendent of schools sat at a table at the front of the room; most of the teachers, the elementary school board, and most if not all of the parents of Winthrop's pupils were in the audience.

The meeting took a different course from what had been formally planned, for there was little discussion of how the parents could help their children catch up. What developed was an open debate over Winthrop's teaching methods, several parents and teachers speaking forcibly in his favor, several others speaking just as forcibly against him. Winthrop was called upon to discuss his methods and to demonstrate some of his techniques. By the end the majority were clearly on his side; after the meeting was over the teachers were ebullient, his critics humiliated. One of those opposed to Winthrop said, "After the meeting it was clear that some of the people had been swayed to Winthrop's side. The teachers were overjoyed, they were laughing and joking about it outside. They boasted that they really put 'those people' down."

The meeting was thoroughly discussed in the community afterward, and the criticisms of Winthrop's opponents, especially Barbara Donelson, were stinging. The recriminations against her were severe enough so that she withdrew entirely from the dispute, refusing to discuss the matter with anyone but close relatives or friends. Mr. Harner was outspokenly opposed to Winthrop at the meeting, and although he was criticized too, the gossip against him was not as severe as the gossip against Mrs. Donelson.

The school board hesitated to ask Winthrop to resign, but in 1966 it did so. By law the board could not discuss personnel matters publicly, and it is impossible to say what happened at the meeting at which it was decided to dismiss him, but it was clear from private conversations that one trustee supported him and four were against him.

Not everyone agreed that people's alignments on this issue coincided with the establishment–nonestablishment division, perhaps because only a few of those who had been involved were willing to commit themselves openly. Nevertheless, the establishment–nonestablishment division and the division of opinion over Winthrop coincided fairly closely.

Barbara Donelson was unqualifiedly with the establishment; Mr. and Mrs. Harner were publicly neutral with respect to the establishment–nonestablishment division, but privately they were aligned with the establishment. These three people were the leaders of Winthrop's opposition, and they drew most of their support—both public and private—from establishment people. There were two exceptions: two nonestablishment mothers were strongly opposed to Winthrop from the beginning of the controversy, and throughout the dispute they remained the only nonestablishment people to side publicly with those who were against him.

The teachers were either members of the periphery and, thus, uninvolved in community life, or with the nonestablishment. All but one rallied to the support of Winthrop. The one who refused was a member of the periphery and had been at odds with his colleagues for some time. The people whom the teachers contacted for support before the meeting were all nonestablishment men. The wives of three or four of these supporters disapproved of the teacher, but because of their husbands' involvement in the affair they were so guarded about their feelings that few people found out about them; in one case the husband did not know.

Only one of the five elementary-school trustees sided with Winthrop, and he was the one who had been contacted by the teachers before the formal meeting took place. He was the only nonestablishment board member.

The people who spoke in favor of Winthrop at the formal meeting were members either of the nonestablishment or of the periphery, while those who were vocal in opposition were all members of the establishment—except for the two nonestablishment women noted earlier. At the beginning of the meeting a number of people were uncommitted to either side; most if not all were either members of the nonestablishment or of the periphery, and most sided with the pro-Winthrop contingent by the time the meeting was over. One nonestablishment person explained why he thought this had happened:

Probably a lot of the parents didn't know if they were for or against Winthrop until they went to the meeting in the cafeteria. I think they were anti-Donelson more than anything else. I think they took sides after they saw how the lines were drawn, between the "haves" and the "have-nots."

Not only did people's alignments on this issue correspond with the establishment–nonestablishment division, but their interpretations of these events reflected the folk theories of the two sides.

The criticisms of Mrs. Donelson are enlightening in this regard. She was criticized far more severely than Mr. Harner, even though he was equally outspoken against Winthrop; for example, Harner excoriated the teacher at the formal meeting. What is more, the nonestablishment people felt that Harner's criticisms of Winthrop were sincere but that Donelson's were not. One of the teachers remarked, "I'm sure that Harner believes Winthrop was wrong, but I'm not convinced that's true of the Donelsons." In this person's view, Donelson became involved in the issue out of spite. The differences in people's reactions to Donelson and Harner may have reflected the different positions the two people occupied in the establishment–nonestablishment division. Donelson was unqualifiedly a member of the establishment, whereas Harner was publicly neutral.

Considering the differences in interpreation of the whole affair, the following comments represent the nonestablishment's viewpoint:

So their kids [i.e., the children of those who openly opposed Winthrop] crossed Winthrop, or Winthrop crossed their kids, whichever way you want to look at it. The stories got back to the parents, and Barbara [Donelson] being kind of a leader and so on. . . .

The problem was that Winthrop was just strict. The whole thing was that he stepped on the wrong kids' toes. I would like to see [those who were vocal against Winthrop] kept from running the school.

On the other hand, the following represent the establishment's interpretation of the controversy:

Before the meeting in the cafeteria the teachers all got together. Their meeting was entirely mercenary; the feeling was that if this can happen to one of us it can happen to any of us. So they decided to fight the thing. The cafeteria meeting was not supposed to be a personal attack against Winthrop. . . . But it was made to appear that Winthrop was being persecuted, that he had been doing a superior teaching job. Winthrop said he would no longer use this superior teaching method, implying that the people who were persecuting him were now depriving all the children.

The teachers had made it look like a wrong was done to a fellow teacher, made it look like the thing developed because Winthrop had either disciplined the wrong children or had given bad grades to the wrong children. They did this to safeguard their own position. [One of the teachers] went to [the nonestablishment board member], [the teacher] said he was going over as a friend and not as a teacher, and he convinced [the board member] for the teachers. [The teacher] is apparently a real con artist. I don't see how he could have kept a straight face talking to [the board member] about this.

Having developed friendships with people on both sides of the dispute, I tried to mediate between them by showing that their opponents were sincere in the opinions they expressed and that their motivations were neither self-serving nor spiteful. I was utterly unsuccessful. My friends on both sides thought that I had been "gotten to" by their adversaries and became angry and suspicious.

This division in Starkey was not new by any means, for clear evidence that the community was mentally divided by its members between the establishment and the nonestablishment goes back at least to the 1920s. But the way the two sides were distinguished from each other in local thought had changed.

What had not been significantly modified was the attribute of community participation. Both before and after World War II, the members of the establishment were conceived of as the "contributors"—or the "controllers." It was believed that this was the portion of the community that was concerned enough to attend local affairs—or the portion that insisted on running things. It seems likely, however, that the criterion of morality had become somewhat less important, consonant with the decline of the church's importance (real or supposed) in local life. The Methodists probably were not as closely associated with the "contributors" (or "controllers") as before and probably did not generate the degree of hostility that they had in the past.

But the most significant change seems to have been the appearance of wealth as a criterion in distinguishing between the establishment and the nonestablishment. I have no evidence that this factor entered into the division before World War II.

There is much danger in relying on oral history to reconstruct a matter as subtle as this, but the matter may be stated in a somewhat less objectionable form without altering the basic point. Both the principle of community participation and the issue of morality *were* clearly evident in people's discussions of the pre-World War II community. So even though it cannot be said unequivocally that wealth played no role at that time, it is reasonable to suggest that if it did so then, it was not as important as the other two criteria. Wealth—or more accurately, the local social–economic hierarchy—seems to have become more prominent over time as an organizational factor in Starkey.

The literature on rural America devotes very little space to the study of factionalism and conflict. This topic has been virtually ignored, apparently because it is generally assumed that factional strife is not significant in the rural community in this country. For example, Walter L. Slocum (1962:365) suggests that factionalism is relatively unimportant because "the energies of American farmers are focused on economic competition in an impersonal market rather than upon personal strife."[6]

Factionalism may not be as striking a phenomenon in Starkey as it is in some parts of the world, such as the small communities of Malta (Boissevain 1965). But the subtle should not be confused with the unimportant. It seems that a large portion of the social life of the community is not fully comprehensible outside the context of the establishment–nonestablishment division. First, the two competing folk theories served to guide local people in interpreting local events and thus to influence how they responded to those events. In particular, the two ideologies guided the local person in assessing the motivations of others who were involved in community affairs. The case of Winthrop is illustrative. Depending on the folk theory to which one subscribed, he was either the victim of a spiteful and influential member of the establishment who was accustomed to running the community according to her own pleasure, or he was the focus of a concerned parent and community member who was seeking to correct a serious problem in the school. Second, a variety of features in the community symbolized the establishment–nonestablishment division, and the way people responded to those features reflected this symbolic aspect. For example, the Women's Society and the Methodist Church both symbolized the establishment, as did the norms adhered to by the drinking non-drinker. To appreciate the place of an organization like the Women's Society in Starkey it has to be seen in relation to this symbolic dimension, and the same is true of such matters as drinking.

It is very unlikely that these principles concerning folk ideologies and symbolism, along with their implications for community dynamics, are unique to Starkey. The specific forms taken by factional ideologies may vary from one community to the next, as may the symbols associated with community divisions; but surely the general pattern described here is one that occurs in small towns throughout the country.

Chapter 10 Conducting Local Affairs

THE QUARRELSOMENESS OF Starkey's community life was pervasive—it was a continuous theme in activities of all kinds and helped shape (or at least give texture to) virtually all issues and events. For one thing, it made people hesitant to assume roles of leadership and responsibility. Starkey exhibited a conservative social milieu, for whatever positive rewards may have flowed from active participation in local affairs, innovativeness or assertiveness were likely to arouse criticism and, thus, to offer strongly negative rewards as well.

This pattern was not unique to Starkey, for it has been reported in studies from various parts of the world. For example, Michael Kenny (1966:25), writing about a rural village in Spain, describes "an underlying resentment towards any innovation for good or evil and an indefinable pleasure in the misfortune of others." As a result, few attempted to assert themselves or to attract notice.

Ronald Frankenberg's research in a Welsh border village (1957; see also 1966) uncovered a very distinctive adjustment to the conservatism of the local social milieu, for in Glynceiriog the local community members avoided leadership roles. Positions of authority were thrust onto "strangers," newcomers and other outsiders who lived in the community but were not fully part of it. Glynceiriog lacked clear-cut leaders largely because the social cost of leadership was too high.

But Starkey was not like Glyceiriog in this respect, for in the California community distinct leaders did emerge, which may seem to contradict the principle of social conservatism. But the contradiction is not real, for by all accounts the Starkey leaders received almost constant criticism for the roles they performed, and part of their task was to rise above these attacks—the leader had to accept the brickbats good-naturedly and to avoid responding in kind. These were even-tempered men who could get along with others in spite of malice—and if they could not, they were not considered genuine communty leaders.

The crucial difference between Starkey and Glyceiriog was not that the social milieu of the one was more conservative than that of the other, but that there was a strong positive inducement for the talented and willing person in Starey to overlook the criticism that leadership entailed. Effective performance as a leader carried a great deal of prestige.

It is important that the inducement in Starkey was not material advantage, a point related to one mentioned earlier, that the Starkey leader had no material power to buttress his authority. Both of these characteristics are to be seen in the context of the fact that the local community was not the arena for major political decisions—decisions involving financial gain, personal livelihood, or physical well-being. For example, Starkey was not the place where zoning laws were made and modified, with all that this might mean for the making and breaking of individual fortunes, for zoning regulations were created, altered, and annulled at the county seat. One would not expect to find, say, bribery of Starkey's leaders, for there was simply nothing worth bribing them for.

The conservative social milieu made the innovative and assertive leader a vulnerable target, and the absence of truly significant decisions at the local level meant that there was little profit in thrusting oneself into the role of decision maker. Together these two principles elucidate a striking feature of local affairs: the absence of hierarchical patterns of authority. The notion of superordinates setting policy that was binding on others is wholly inappropriate; nor was it a critical attribute of the leader that he have the capacity or authority to make decisions. The way policy was arrived at, rather, was by a pattern of diffuse decision making (see Barnes 1954) according to which the individual—even the genuine leader—avoided responsibility for decisions as much as possible. Events normally were engineered in such a way that a large number of people were involved in arriving at a course of action and responsbility was diffused throughout the community.[1] The critical attribute of the leader was not the authorily to decide policy (although his opinions may have had more impact than other people's) but the capacity to accomplish local goals once policy had been decided: he was a doer or pusher, a person who could mobilize the collective effort needed to carry out an undertaking. And in doing so he tried to avoid any appearance that it was he who determined the goals sought.

The pattern of diffuse decision making is illustrated by one of the cases discussed in the preceding chapter, the case of the schoolboy who threw a rock through the window of the principal's house. The school board had the authority to exclude the boy from school activities without appealing to the community through a petition, but it chose to share responsibility as widely as it could for this controversial and severe policy.[2]

The composition of the school boards provides an even more telling example of the pattern of diffuse decision making. I have noted that the unified board was formally constituted in such a way that each member was elected from what had once been a different elementary-school district. The reasoning behind this was clear. By extending representation to all geographic areas, responsibility for decisions was diffused and both conflict and criticism were forestalled.

The high-school board that existed before unification had a similar pattern of geographic representation, although this was not expressed in a formal, written rule. Technically, the board members were elected at large, but in actuality an unwritten agreemet prevailed according to which each elementary-school district in the region served had a member on the board. To quote from an official school document, "The trustees of the high school are, by unspoken agreement, elected so that each elementary district is represented." For example, Charles Thomas of Lorraine represented the Lorraine and Bitter Valley districts before his death in the 1940s, and Jerold Whitman was the trustee representing the Gates district south of Starkey Flat.

Even the families living at the oil company facilities outside of town had a member elected to the board. According to one (establishment) person,

Before the [oil company facilities] were automated maybe a third or a quarter of the children in the school were from there. The board is pretty fair about these things, fairer than in the bigger towns. They always had a representative from the different areas, like Lorraine.

It is unclear how these unwritten rules were instituted. Bill Donelson, for example, could explain them only by saying that they just happened. But it is possible to guess why they came about. The case of the oil company facilities is especially suggestive. The people living there were predominantly outsiders and a potentially hostile segment of the community. By giving them a role in the decision-making process, the board members hoped to forestall criticism of their policies.

Why were people in Starkey proper willing to help vote into office a man from Lorraine, say, and another from the oil company facilities? Unfortunately, the data on school board elections are scanty. I witnessed only one, and in that case all the candidates were incumbents and were automatically reelected.

But the election process seems reasonably clear. The trusteeship was a time-consuming job, and it was not unusual for office seekers to run unopposed—as they did on the occasion I witnessed. What seems to have happened, typically, is that well before election time public opinion became focused on a likely candidate and he was prevailed upon. If, for example, the man serving from the oil company facilities was planning to leave office, a replacement from among his colleagues was sought and persuaded to run. Opposition candidates were quite unusual, so the election itself was normally a ritual procedure. It also seems likely that the community leaders were instrumental in focusing opinion on a candidate and ensuring geographic representation on the board. The leaders had an interest in forestalling criticism of the board, since typically they themselves were trustees serving the districts in which they lived.

The nature of the election process is illustrated by an incident I was told about. The Starkey elementary school drew students from an area that originally was made up of several distinct school districts. Before unification occurred, each of these was represented (by unwritten rule) on the Starkey Elementary School Board, which was composed of five members. In the 1950s one of the board members angered a handful of voters who were within the larger Starkey elementary school district but outside the smaller district that he represented. They threatened to vote against him at the next election, whereupon Bill Donelson went to them with the reminder that it was not their place to vote against a person representing another district.

The pattern of diffuse decision making is closely linked to another feature discussed earlier, the pattern of collaboration in community affairs according to which a variety of local organizations are invited to supply official representatives for an undertaking in order to give it the stamp of legitimacy as a genuine community effort. Both patterns take the same form—the active attempt to share responsibility—but they are directed toward different ends. The pattern of collaboration is motivated by the desire to convince the dubious that the affair in question is worth supporting after all. Responsibility is shared to avoid stigmatizing the affair as a private matter involving a few people. Diffuse decision making is the obverse, for here the goal is not to further some program of action but to protect its promoters, who seek to share responsibility so that they can dodge the criticism that may follow from taking charge. Both motivations—and patterns—may be manifest in the same affair. If the Women's Society decides to invite other organizations to nominate representatives to oversee some project, their purpose might be both to ensure the support of critics and to avoid the critics' criticisms.

Both of these patterns illustrate the importance of strategy in local affairs, for the person who was not skillful at employing the fundamentals of leadership was relatively ineffective in community life. The čase of the discontented families who threatened to vote against the school board member is illustrative. The dissidents could have arranged to have an opposition candidate on the ballot—a person from the apropriate neighborhood even—but they remained a small and ineffective minority, and as a result the incumbent ran unopposed. Matters might have been different if they had been able to convert Bill Donelson to their point of view, for he had a firm grasp of strategy and the capacity to crystallize opinion on issues.

The distinguishing feature of the political process in Starkey was the means by which the community—or some segment of it—was somehow moved to undertake, contribute to, and support specific goals. An account of the way local affairs were conducted does not lead to an analysis of the material bases of power or to some inner sanctum of decision making. Nor does it lead to a description of competing interest groups striving to alter the course of affairs in a way that would be more favorable to their personal interests or cultural beliefs. It leads, rather, to an investigation of the procedures and techniques (such as the patterns of collaboration and diffuse decision making) whereby collective goals are worked out, opinion is shaped, a degree of consensus is achieved, and action programs are set in motion.

It leads especially to a discussion of the leader. Changes were under way in the patterns of leadership in Starkey following World War II—fundamental changes inasmuch as the active and effective pusher whom community members would unhesitatingly name as a community leader virtually passed out of existence. In an earlier chapter I gave an account of the succession of leaders in Starkey's past; I need to continue that account here and then detail the decline that took place in the 1950s and 1960s.

I have noted that the two most effective community leaders during the 1930s were Brian Green, who ran his father's ranch just outside of Starkey, and Tony Giles, the gregarious principal. Two others were considered lesser lights: Jerold Whitman, who was too shy to fully develop into a leader and too committed to his ranch; and the articulate and affable Bill Donelson, whose role as an effective pusher was just getting under way when war broke out in Europe.

Donelson's effectiveness as a pusher grew considerably during the early 1940s, and he was the preeminent leader throughout most of that decade, easily surpassing Green, Giles, and Whitman. In addition, two new influentials joined this small cluster of local statesmen.

The first was Roland Peters, who had moved to Starkey during the Depression. He began working as an employee in one of the stores soon after he arrived, and before long he owned the business. After the United States declared war the local economy improved and the traffic passing through town increased. As a result, Peters' business thrived; by the mid-1960s he was quite well off by local standards, although he no longer ran the store. He leased it to a Donelson and took the full-time job of postmaster.

Peters had associations with both the establishment and the nonestablishment. Privately, in his interpretation of local affairs he was aligned with the establishment, and he was a close personal friend of Bill Donelson. But he was a discreet drinker and a leader in the slightly nonestablishment-oriented Lions Club, and his daughter married a local man whose family was decidedly nonestablishment.

It was not until the early 1940s that Peters began to assume a leadership role in the community. Around 1942 Green and Donelson went to Peters to ask whether he would serve as Starkey's air raid warden. He had one of the few telephones in town, and because he ran the store he would almost always be available in the event of an air alert. He was also considered a responsible, discerning, and tactful individual. At first he was unwilling, but Donelson and Green persevered and he finally gave in. I asked Peters why Donelson and Green had been the ones to ask him to fill the position. He said,

I'm not sure. I would imagine like now—if we had a defense system Saint Thomas wouldn't know who would be suited for warden. They would call me or Bill and ask who should be appointed. The people in the county get to know you and will call you if you get to leading. They find out that you know people. Perhaps they would still call up Bill and say, "We've got to appoint someone for warden, who can you suggest?"

Shortly after Peters had become warden he received a call from the county sheriff in Saint Thomas, who wanted to know whether he owned a gun. The sheriff remarked that he should have one and that he should be deputized; according to Peters, the sheriff said to him, "People put you in there, you have responsibility. You've got to have the authority to stop people if they drive through Starkey with their lights on." Peters concluded by saying, "That's the sort of way you get hooked into things and get going."

Peters' role in the community grew quickly. He was pressed by Bill Donelson into serving as a part-time fireman, became a leader in the local militia, and soon was a recognized pusher. He was in an ideal position to exert influence since, being the storekeeper, he occupied a central place in the community's informal communication system.

The second man to emerge as a community leader during the war years was Charles Thomas, the son of early settlers in the Lorraine region. He came from very humble beginnings but by 1940 had acquired holdings that, including both owned and leased land, amounted to over 100,000 acres; he had also acquired the reputation of a small-scale—but genuine—land baron. Thomas could be cunning and ruthless in acquiring land, but he could also be compassionate. There were instances in which it is reported that he compelled neighbors to sell him property he wanted, and others in which he gave large cash gifts to the destitute in his community.

Thomas' leadership in Starkey proper was limited primarily to school affairs, and he became an active pusher within the sphere of local education, serving as a high-school trustee from the 1930s until his death in 1949. But beyond the educational domain his leadership role was primarily that of the notable—at least this was true in Starkey proper, where his opinions were held in considerable esteem.

In the community of Lorraine it was another matter, for there Thomas was reputedly a man of power and not simply persuasion, and thus at home he became a leader of a very different sort from those found nearby in Starkey. In Lorraine hardly an issue arose that did not feel his influence, and when the occasion presented itself he could line up solid support (on matters concerning the high school, for example) even though some of his fellow community members would have wanted to oppose him. And he avoided neither partisan commitments nor controversial decisions. The scars of his dominance were still evident in the mid-1960s, in that his descendants and former support-ers still felt the hostility of some of their neighbors, who had once been Thomas' enemies.

Thomas' influence rested on three bases. First, he was an assertive person with a powerful personality. Second, because of his wealth he could obligate other people to himself by loaning tools and materials, offering gifts of land, pleading a neighbor's case to county officials, and so on. Third, he was believed to have used or threatened force in disputes with others. In one case it is claimed that his hired men— hooded and therefore unidentifiable—fired rifle shots over the heads of some of his opponents in an attempt to intimidate them.

Thomas' influence was related to Lorraine's isolation. It was not a simple matter to drive from Lorraine to Oak Flat to acquire such necessities as a broken tractor part or fence posts, so the people living in that remote area were more dependent on one another for loans and assistance than their counterparts in Starkey proper. A person like Thomas could more easily obligate his neighbors to himself in the smaller community. In addition, there were fewer restraints on the exercise of *ultra vires* power in Lorraine than in Starkey proper, where the sheriff was always much closer at hand.

The configuration of leadership in the 1940s had several aspects.

Bill Donelson was the most active and effective leader in Starkey, and little of note happened that he did not have a hand in. Peters, the storekeeper, also became an effective pusher, but he did not enjoy the prestige or influence of Donelson. He was sometimes described as the latter's front man or lieutenant, and he usually worked in conjunction with Donelson. Giles and Green were still quite active—Giles, for example, helped stimulate the community events honoring the local men who left for war service. And they worked closely with Donelson even though they were eclipsed by him—by now he was generally regarded as one of the local successes. Whitman was still too retiring to be an active leader, and Thomas limited his involvement in Starkey chiefly to school affairs.

The relations among these people were amicable with one striking exception: although Donelson and Thomas cooperated in such contexts as school board meetings—they were both high-school trustees—their relationship was marked by mutual distrust and antagonism. Though it was usually subdued, this festering animosity was widely known.

This is the only case in Starkey's history in which two leaders were not regarded as easy and friendly collaborators. Perhaps their bristly relationship is explained by personal idiosyncracies, perhaps by economic conflicts. There was something to this, for the two men had once been engaged in a bitter dispute over an economic transaction, and in the mid-1960s Donelson could still become quite angry while discussing it. But the singularity of their animosity seems remarkable. Perhaps it was due in part to the fact that the two men were the primary leaders of rival communities, and also in part to the fact that their leadership roles rested on different foundations. Thomas' position was one of power, whereas Donelson's was one of persuasion. Thomas was less inclined than other influentials to seek amity with his coleaders—he had nothing to lose from an argument with them. Consequently he could allow his relations with Donelson to become strained.

Starkey's leadership patterns as they existed in the 1940s are illustrated by the Starkey Fire Control, which was organized soon after the attack on Pearl Harbor. State officials were behind the undertaking, but the formation of the group was managed largely by Donelson through the Farm Bureau.

The community influentials played a dominant role in the organization. Green and Peters were two of the seven district leaders—who, as mentioned earlier, superintended the program of fire prevention in their districts. The organization's records indicate that Giles took an active part in the group, although he did not hold formal office (as might be expected, since he was not a property holder). And Donelson was elected to head the association.

Donelson was also selected to head the state-supported fire crew, which consisted of one full-time and four part-time firemen. A state fire-fighting official at the county seat initiated the small company. He went first to Peters and asked him to serve, but Peters declined. The next day he went to Donelson, who agreed to join. Together they went back to Peters and persuaded him to enlist. Two other community members were recruited. Neither was a leader in Starkey, but both worked in the community hub and were therefore available in emergencies. A fifth person was hired to fill the one full-time slot on the staff. His job was to care for the equipment and receive the call when a fire broke out. The person chosen was a comparative newcomer to the community and not someone whom many people knew about or whose reputation was established. Even though his full-time status made him the obvious choice to be fire chief, it was decided that he should not have the post since the one in charge would have to direct the efforts not only of the regular firemen but of volunteers as well, and he would have to do so on private property. A person of stature was clearly needed, and Donelson was selected. One person explained this with the remark that "During the [war] crisis it was felt that Bill would be the better fire chief since he knew people better than the full-time fireman."

The fire crew served Lorraine as well as Starkey, and this fact provides an illustration of the relationship between Donelson and Thomas. The traditional pattern throughout Starkey and Lorraine had been that farmers and farm hands alike dropped what they were doing to help whenever evidence of fire appeared in the sky. Fire fighting was a spontaneous, cooperative undertaking. If direction or coordination of the volunteer crew was needed, it was usually provided by the person whose crop or range land was burning. But in the Lorraine region during the decade or so before the Starkey fire company was formed a somewhat different pattern existed, for fire fighting, even on other people's property, was under Thomas' direction. As soon as he came onto the scene the volunteers—and the landholder—accepted his leadership. Once the official fire company had come into being, however, matters were technically under the direction of Donelson, the chief. This was a potential source of irritation, if not conflict, when the fire happened to be in the Lorraine region. Thomas and Donelson worked out a *modus vivendi* that was reasonably effective though not entirely amicable. One person described it for me:

Whenever there was a fire in the Lorraine country Donelson and Charles Thomas worked together. Charles wouldn't have someone from the outside coming in to lead a group in fire fighting in his own territory, but since Donelson was the official leader he had to accept it. The two worked together as coleaders, and they were both careful to get along.

By the early 1950s several changes had occurred in the list of people who occupied positions of influence in the community. In the late 1940s Thomas died, and at about the same time Giles moved away from Starkey for personal reasons. Early in the 1950s Green also moved away, and Whitman—who was now quite elderly—retired from community affairs. The only leaders remaining from the past were Donelson and Peters. In addition, two other men began to assume leadership roles during the 1950s.

The first was Harold Thomas, Charles' son. He was now (after his father's death) the most influential person in Lorraine. He was a far milder person than his father, and his position in his home locality was one of influence rather than power. His involvement in Starkey proper was limited almost entirely to school affairs. In particular, he was a prime mover behind unification, for he worked actively to sway local opinion in favor of the measure, and it was he who appeared before state officials and convinced them to accept unification of the Starkey schools in spite of the size of the proposed district. Throughout the 1950s he served on the high-school board, and he became noted for his judiciousness and dedication in that position. One nonestablishment person commented, "If they had four or five guys on the school board with as much brains as Harold Thomas they would be all right. He's outspoken but he's understanding."

John Bradford, one of Starkey's wealthy elite, was the second person to emerge as a leader during the 1940s. He had lived in Starkey only since his discharge after World War II, although his name was hardly new to the community, since it was his grandfather who owned the store in Saint Thomas and had acquired an enormous amount of seemingly worthless land in the Starkey region when many of the settlers left in the 1890s. Bradford was not a churchgoer, and he was a discreet but known drinker. Yet he was decidedly aligned with the establishment in his interpretation of local affairs.

Bradford's leadership, like Harold Thomas', was restricted primarily to school matters, and while his children were in school during the 1950s and early 1960s he served in turn on the Starkey Elementary and High School Boards. Owing to his membership in the Conservation Club and his wife's involvement in the Women's Society, he was also drawn into such community affairs as park improvements and the Starkey Barbecue, but he never served as a leader in any of these undertakings.

Even in school affairs Bradford did not exhibit the usual characteristics of the pusher. His leadership role was primarily that of the notable, and his influence was expressed indirectly through public support of issues and not through the active shaping of local opinion in face-to-face encounters. The following statements typify his local image as a leader:

You wouldn't see John Bradford wheeling a wheelbarrow, but if he thought you had a good project he'd send a crew down.

He came in for his share [of leadership] for a certain amount. He never got a hold strong, though. All the time his kids were in school he was in there pitching, in a pretty quiet way.

A typical example of his leadership role occurred when Bradford was on the elementary school board. He and the other trustees decided that a new elementary school had to be built—a costly project that would require a substantial increase in property taxes. A community meeting was called to discuss the issue, and Bradford apparently played a key role in winning its acceptance at the gathering. The meeting was described to me in the following way:

I was on the elementary school board at the time it was decided to build the new school. We anticipated that people would be against it, so we prepared the presentation very carefully. John Bradford is a good speaker, and he gave the argument in favor of the school at a special meeting. Nearly everyone raised their hands in agreement with the proposal, and this was something of a surprise.

One characteristic of the leadership patterns as they existed in the 1950s is striking. The only genuine pushers in that period were Donelson and Peters, whose leadership roles had emerged at an earlier time. The only new people to become leaders in the 1950s, Harold Thomas and John Bradford, limited their focus almost exclusively to school affairs.

This was perhaps a broad hint that fundamental changes were taking place in community life. No longer did a coterie of local influentials busily collaborate in the management of local affairs. No longer, apparently, was the whole spectrum of community issues capable of attracting the attention of young, ambitious men with the personal qualities needed for effective, all-around leadership as well as the desire to achieve the reputation of successful influential.

If these developments were hinted at in the 1950s, they were fully realized in the 1960s. By the mid-1960s—perhaps for the first time in the community's history—there were no recognized leaders in Starkey. Bradford withdrew from school affairs when his youngest child graduated from the high school in the early 1960s, and Thomas did so at nearly the same time; by now he had retired from farming and wanted to reduce the activities in which he had engaged as a younger man. Even Donelson and Peters had virtually relinquished their leadership roles by the early 1960s. The following statements express the state of affairs at mid-decade:

There are no leaders any more. Everyone looks out for themselves.

There are no longer leaders in Starkey like there used to be. Leadership today is a personal matter—if you want to be on the school board and you are concerned, then you can get on it.

There is no local leadership now. It's a state of chaos.

Donelson had retired from his farming operation, so he had the time to lead, and his health would have permitted him to do so. He also lived on the edge of the small town, so it was not inconvenient for him to play a greater role than he did in local affairs. Indeed, it was certainly not unusual to see him at one of the stores or at the post office during the day, talking with people as they came in to buy groceries or pick up their mail. But he was no longer the leader he had once been. A friend of his remarked,

Bill still gets things done in an easy way and no one knows what's going on. . . . But he's slowing off. You get to the point it's easier than fighting it all the time. Bill slowed off in the past five or six years. . . . If he sees something for the community he might have a friend or two in Saint Thomas, and he would say, "If you can help us with it that's fine." You see, guys don't want to stick their necks out—they would rather talk someone else into shoving it along.

Peters was now even less involved as a leader than Donelson.

But the decline of leadership patterns did not signify the demise of community affairs in Starkey—not by any means. Nor did they spell the end of the capacity to achieve collective goals. Rather, a new pattern emerged in community undertakings—or, more accurately, an old pattern received new and somewhat different emphasis. The major community organizations of the past, the Improvement Club and the Farm Bureau (and to some extent the Conservation Club), had always served as springboards for the promotion of local undertakings. They were vehicles used by the local influentials to accomplish community goals. As that coterie of leaders declined, the major community organization—now the Women's Society—continued to function as a means of carrying out local affairs, but it did so without benefit of genuine influentials.

In the mid-1960s leadership operated in an ad hoc fashion. The usual pattern was for a small group of people in the community to become interested in an undertaking and suggest it to the Women's Society. Even more commonly, the idea for the undertaking emerged within the Society itself. In either case, the issue was discussed within the organization and voted on, and if it was approved by a majority one or more members were appointed to lead the affair.

A result of the decline of the genuine community leader is that local affairs were carried out with much less success in the mid-1960s than before because action programs tended to lack the guidance and energy of the effective pusher. More often than in the past, undertakings tended to founder.

A number of events that occurred in the mid-1960s illustrate these principles, and in the following pages I present a detailed account of three undertakings that took place while I lived in Starkey.

The first case is the acquisition of the community public-address system. This illustrates not only how undertakings were carried out but also, since the action program involved real property, one way in which rights and responsibilities of collective ownership were handled.

Candidates for county, state, and occasionally national office attended the Starkey Barbecue in election years to campaign for votes. They were a major attraction and helped increase both attendance and receipts. A public-address system was needed for their political speeches, and the equipment that was rented for the purpose had at times proved to be either inadequate or defective.

Bill Donelson served as master of ceremonies at the barbecue, as at most other community gatherings. He felt the need (or desire) to have a satisfactory loudspeaker system more than most members of the community, and he was one of a small number of people who began discussing the idea that Starkey buy its own. His sister-in-law, Margaret Donelson, was the first person to raise the issue formally. She did so at a Women's Society meeting in 1965, but no action was taken. Several months later, early in 1966, she raised the matter again, adding that Bill Donelson had found out that suitable equipment would cost about $500. The women's group voted to allocate $300 of its own funds to the purchase, and a committee of Women's Society members was appointed to solicit the rest from other community organizations. Margaret Donelson was placed in charge of the committee. She was reluctant to take the job but finally relented.

A few days later Margaret and Bill Donelson discussed the matter at length in private, and they hit upon the idea of holding a box social at the Community Hall to raise money.[3] This was a form of entertainment that had been common in Starkey's past, and both Bill and his sister-in-law felt that the novelty of the affair would help attract a large crowd.

Margaret spoke informally with the other women on the committee that she headed. She suggested to them that, instead of soliciting contributions from the local organizations, each group should be asked to appoint one of its members to serve on a committee that would be in charge of the box social. The women agreed. The plan was discussed at the next meeting of the Women's Society, where it was agreed upon once more. The various organizations were contacted, and each agreed to provide a representative to serve on the box social committee.

The decision to seek a committee made up of representatives from the other organizations had a strategic purpose. The idea of purchasing a public-address sytem was meeting opposition. In general, those who were against it were members of the nonestablishment, and they viewed the plan as an extravagant whimsy that the establishment, and especially the Donelsons, were urging on the community. Since the Women's Society was associated in people's minds with the establishment, its sponsorship of the project merely increased the dissension. One purpose of establishing a box social committee was to spread responsibility for the event as broadly as possible.

Which of the two motivations, the desire to forestall criticism or the need to establish that this was a genuine community undertaking, was paramount in this instance? Was this a case of diffuse decision making or of the pattern of collaboration? To most members of the Women's Society it was the latter, for to them the main issue seems to have been to establish that this was truly a community event and thus to increase the base of support. But to Margaret Donelson it was a different matter. She was regarded as the instigator of the project and had become a primary focus of criticism. And she was the one, significantly, who originally urged that the other community organizations be invited to participate by providing representatives. Whatever reason others may have had for seeking a representative committee, Margaret Donelson's motivation was primarily to free herself from criticism.

Her attempts to avoid responsibility for the affair continued even after the box social committee was set up. She was the Women's Society representative on the committee, and it was tacitly assumed that she was in charge. But because of the criticism against her she left most of the responsibility for the affair to the other committee members, stressing to them that they should be the ones to make the decisions. At one point I commented to her that there were some people who opposed acquiring the public-address system, and she became exasperated and defensive. She said, "My heart isn't set on having a public-address system, and I hope people don't think it is. My children are grown, and I don't care so much. But I think it would be nice for the community."

The members of the box social committee were each assigned different tasks, such as arranging for entertainment for the evening, making posters, and decorating the hall. The latter turned out to be the most time-consuming job of all, and the woman who was assigned to it, Elizabeth Brink, quickly emerged as the pivotal figure in the undertaking.

Since Margaret Donelson had relinquished her authority over the committee, people began to regard Mrs. Brink as its de facto leader. For example, on the evening of the event, when a number of children sat at a table that had been reserved for adults people turned to Mrs. Brink to correct the matter. Both Margaret and Bill Donelson also channeled their ideas through her. Bill Donelson served as auctioneer at the gathering, and before he offered the dinners for sale he asked Brink what she thought the minimum bid should be. She hesitated, and Donelson suggested $2.00; she agreed. A square dance caller was hired for the evening, but his fee had not been decided in advance. After the receipts had been counted Margaret Donelson approached Elizabeth Brink and asked if she thought $25 would be enough to pay the man; again Brink agreed.

The profit from the box social, together with the contributions from the Women's Society and other organizations (including the Women's Chorus), made it possible to buy the equipment. It was purchased by Bill Donelson and Roland Peters—Peters because he could get the amplification system wholesale and Donelson because he would use it most often.

How were rights and responsibilities allocated once the system had been bought? The equipment was kept at Peters' home and he looked after its upkeep, whereas responsibility for its use was in both his and Donelson's hands. In one instance, for example, the adult leaders of the 4-H Club asked Donelson whether they could use the equipment at one of their meetings. Donelson tactfully suggested that it was not necessary for them to use the equipment and that it would be better if they did not do so, since the more it was used and moved about the sooner it would need repairs. The 4-H Club met without the system.

Donelson's and Peters' authority over the equipment was not formally granted to them, and no official discussion of these arrangements took place in Starkey. The two men simply assumed the responsibility. What is remarkable is that this stimulated very little comment in the community. In part this could have been because some community members regarded the issue as a matter involving only a few people and not a genuine community affair—to them the equipment was in effect private, not community, property. But it seems that too many people were involved in its purchase for this view to adequately explain the lack of criticism. Part of the reason people generally accepted these arrangements was that the two men still had the aura of community leaders; a certain legitimacy was attached to their taking charge of community property. Surely if virtually anyone else had assumed this responsibility he or she would have met opposition and the equipment would soon have been handed over to one of the community's formal organizations.

This case also illustrates both the general retirement of community leaders from their role as pushers and the tendency for leadership now to be ad hoc in nature. Although Bill Donelson played a part in the affair, he was not as actively involved as he would have been at one time. It was the Women's Society that formally initiated the undertaking, and it was largely the box social committee that conducted it. Active leadership was provided mostly by people like Margaret Donelson and Elizabeth Brink, who happened to belong to the community organizations and to have been assigned certain jobs in the affair.

The second case involved a visit to Starkey by the Pony Express. A college in Saint Thomas was planning a large anniversary celebration and for publicity it had arranged to have a stunt take place beforehand. A team of college students dressed as Pony Express riders would take turns riding horseback from the state capital, Sacramento, to the college campus, carrying a message of congratulations from the governor.

Fred Miller was a teacher at the Starkey high school and a graduate of the college. An official at the institution who knew him telephoned to say that the rider would pass through the community with a proclamation inviting the local people to the anniversary event. He asked to have a "mayor-type" person on hand to accept the proclamation. Fred commented to me that this "would just about have to be Bill Donelson."

Later that day the teacher went to Donelson with the news. Donelson was delighted and suggested that the affair be made a community event. Soon afterward Bill's daughter Barbara—who appeared in the controversy discussed in the preceding chapter—stopped by to see her father, who told her about the matter. They discussed it at length and came up with a plan to have local residents dress as Indians and stage a mock ambush as the rider came into town. Another group, representing a posse, would come to the rescue.

Bill asked his daughter to mention these plans to Fred Miller, since he had originally been the one contacted about the event. Barbara had only recently been involved in the dispute over Winthrop, the teacher of one of her children, and Miller, it happens, was one of Winthrop's main supporters. By her own account Barbara told her father, "I just can't call Fred up and do that because he already thinks I try to run everything, and it would just prove to him that I do." Bill went to the teacher instead, and the latter agreed to the plan. Bill then said that he thought the college officials should be told about the idea, and Miller volunteered to inform them by telephone. One person commented to me that "Bill didn't have to go to Fred; Bill knows the man at the college and could have called him directly himself." Donelson's action was described to me as an attempt "not to go over his [the teacher's] head." It was an instance of the pattern of diffuse decision making.

The rider was scheduled to reach the community shortly before noon, and the school principal decided to allow the students a long lunch period that day so they could witness the event. To accommodate the students a location in front of the high school (across from the park) was chosen as the place where the spectators would gather. The school was now implicated in the event, and this had an important result. The principal was suddenly transformed into a "leader" of the affair—at least in people's minds.

In discussing the Pony Express visit with some other women, Barbara Donelson suggested holding a community potluck at the park after the drama was over and the rider had passed through town. The women responded favorably. Barbara then went to the school to discuss her idea with Miller and the principal. She introduced her plan not as her own but as that of an informal group. By her account she said, "Some of us have been talking, and we thought we'd have a potluck. . ." Of course, neither the principal nor the teacher had any formal authority to decide wehether the community should hold a potluck, yet Barbara asked whether they thought it was all right and—predictably—they said they did.

Barbara and Bill Donelson were the principal managers behind the Pony Express event, and both exhibited the role of pushers in the affair. For example, Bill asked a leader of the 4-H Club to enlist a group of high-school students to serve as Indians and posse members, and he also asked several local cowboys to serve. A few days before the event took place he was chatting in front of the post office when a young girl rode by on horseback. Bill stepped into the road to stop her and asked her to serve as an Indian at the event. He also arranged to have these people gather at the appropriate time and place; he decided on the signals that would begin the ambush and rescue, and arranged to have Peters set up the public-address system beforehand. Bill served as master of ceremonies, providing a running account of the chase as it occurred and a formal welcome to the rider once it was over. He actively promoted the event by discussing it with community members. Barbara Donelson coordinated the potluck meal and on her own initiative placed notices advertising the affair on Starkey's two public bulletin boards.

Even this event—innocuous as it was—did not take place without friction. Miller was decidedly nonestablishment. Although he said nothing openly, privately he felt that the Donelsons were promoting the affair for their personal aggrandizement. They were doing it "for show," to "boost their own egos." Sensing Miller's attitude, Barbara Donelson commented, "He's really an 'agin'er,' that's a good word. If he had his way the rider would just change horses and leave, he [Miller] would just do the least possible."

The third case concerns the transferral of ownership of the Community Hall. In the mid-1960s the building was quite run-down, and since the Lions Club, which held title to the structure, could scarcely pay the taxes there was little hope that it could afford repairs. The Square Dance Club was the only group that used the hall regularly, so it felt a proprietory interest in it. During the spring and summer of 1966 discussion began among its members about renovating the structure—repairing the roof, putting right the disfigurement caused by removal of the stage, and the like—and at about the same time the club held several work days to make minor repairs and clear weeds from the grounds. But much remained to be done.

A rancher of the Howard region and a leader in the Square Dance Club, Peter Murray, chanced to speak informally with Starkey's representative on the county board of supervisors during the summer of 1966. Murray asked whether the county would consider assuming ownership of the building, repairing it, and removing it from the tax rolls. The supervisor thought the plan was feasible and promised to raise the idea at the next meeting of the board. Murray did not pursue the issue and the supervisors took no formal action.

By the end of summer the possibility that the county would improve and maintain the Community Hall had become a topic of general discussion in Starkey. As a result, in September 1966 the Women's Society appointed a committee to investigate the matter. The committee first contacted Roland Peters, a member of the Lions Club, hoping that he would take an active role in the affair. Their efforts proved fruitless. The committee also sent a formal note to the Lions Club stating that the Women's Society would propose to have the county assume ownership of the building. The men's organization was already acquainted with the issue, and most of the members were in favor since the Community Hall had become a heavy financial burden. Finally, the committee contacted Murray and told him of their role in the undertaking.

In October 1966 the Women's Society made plans to invite the supervisor to Starkey for a community meeting to discuss the matter.[4] A date was not set for the gathering, however, and the project came to a standstill. It would be four months before the meeting was held.

When the meeting was finally scheduled, the Women's Society sent postcards to each household in the community informing them of the assembly, and it contacted Starkey's organizations and asked them to send representatives. The meeting was held at midday at the Community Clubhouse, and the Women's Society provided a potluck lunch for the 50 or 60 people who came.

The gathering was chaired by Murray, who was asked to fill this role by the Women's Society on the ground that he had been a pivotal figure in the affair from the beginning. Murray opened the meeting by introducing first the supervisor and then the representative from each community organization. A discussion followed during which the supervisor again promised to present the matter to the entire board. He stated that he thought the proposal would pass but that it would probably take at least a year before the measure would be final. The issue rested at that stage when I left the community in the summer of 1967.[5]

A striking characteristic of this undertaking is that it foundered almost from the start. Little more was involved than contacting the county supervisor and calling a public meeting, yet over six months elapsed between the time the issue was first discussed and the time the gathering was finally held. The reason was simple: the project lacked effective leadership.

There were three possible sources of leadership. The first, the committee appointed by the Women's Society, lacked sufficient interest in the matter to bring it to a speedy conclusion. The second was Peter Murray. He had a direct interest in the project and regarded himself one of its principal leaders. But he lacked the time, the perseverence, and perhaps the talent necessary to conduct the program effectively. The third, Roland Peters, was called upon to manage the affair, but he had retired from community leadership and wanted to avoid becoming involved. He was also reluctant to steal authority from Murray, who he thought might resent it if he did. As Peters commented privately, "I don't want to jump in and take over for him." Peters' analysis of the difficulties of another community undertaking applied equally well to this one: "If I was [leading this project] I'd be out talking to guys with a little push and a little pull, I'd be working with it. You've got to fight it all the way. . . . You start talking about it, you get it discussed at meetings . . ." What was lacking was the skill and energy of an effective pusher.

But it is not true that the faltering pace of the affair signified a lack of interest either in the undertaking or in the Community Hall. The issue was widely discussed in Starkey, and most people expressed concern about the building's future, if only for the practical reason that they wanted a place large enough for community events. In addition, traditional sentiments were attached to the hall, for in people's minds it represented Starkey's past accomplishments as a community. One person, a relative newcomer, idly speculated about buying the building, tearing it down, and salvaging the lumber. He said, "But no one from the community could do this. His name would be mud, the community wouldn't like it at all."

Like most issues, the Community Hall project served to rekindle local animosities. For example, shortly before the Lions Club was formally told that the Women's Society was sponsoring a project to transfer legal ownership of the building, one nonestablishment member of the men's group said, "It makes me mad that there has been a lot of talk around Starkey lately about getting the Community Hall off the tax rolls, but no one has come to the Lions Club to talk to them about it." The context of the conversation made it clear that the Women's Society—which symbolized the establishment—was the object of his hostility. Once again, in his view, the "haves" were trying to run local affairs.

Animosities were heightened even further by the county's plan for investing authority over the hall. The county would own the building and pay for repairs, but it would lease the structure to a local group for a token fee of $1.00 a year and leave the day-to-day supervision to it. What had to be decided was which group should hold the lease.

The members of the Square Dance Club felt that the building should be leased to them since they used the hall more than anyone else and were the only ones to spend time caring for it in recent years. And they were strongly opposed to having some other group in charge. Three members of the Square Dance Club made the following comments:

I think the square dance group has as much right to get the Hall as the Lions Club if it's leased back to the community. The Lions Club hasn't done hardly anything for the Hall since they've had it, and they haven't kept the taxes up. The square dancers have used the Hall more than the Lions Club ever did. The Lions Club aren't strong [i.e., large] enough to take care of the Hall even if they did get the lease.

They [the Lions Club] let the Hall go so long, they don't seem to care about it. . . . The square dancers got interested in the Hall and started fixing it up. It's been there for years with no one interested in it, and now everyone wants to get in on it.

. . . the square dancers had better get the Hall. If the women's group gets it we'll be dancing out in the street half the time.

But most community members were strongly opposed to giving the lease to the square dancers. Most felt that the Square Dance Club would last only another year or two and that the leaseholder should be both more permanent and more community oriented.

Soon after it was apparent that the lease had become a controversial subject, a new element began to appear in discussions about the building. This was a compromise plan according to which a committee consisting of representatives from each major community organization would receive the lease and be responsible for the building. One person commented,

There would be fewer hard feelings if the Hall was run by a board of directors rather than by a single organization like the Lions Club. If the Lions Club runs it, it will be like the Women's Society running the Clubhouse. There have been a lot of hard feelings over that . . .

Another said,

If anybody takes over the Hall . . . it should be a small group of representatives of all the organizations in Starkey. That would include the Lions Club, Women's Society, and square dancers. Maybe the church would have a representative, but they wouldn't use the hall, so probably not. . . . It would be better to stick to the three civic organizations—square dancers are kind of like a civic organization [the speaker was a member of the Square Dance Club]. If you had representatives from the organizations, there would be less conflict. If any one group takes it over, like the Lions Club or square dancers, it will make some people mad. The best thing would be to have two representatives chosen from each of the groups, to make up a six-man board.

It is difficult to be certain who began circulating this compromise plan, but it seems to have been Peter Murray.

This case stimulates comparison with that of the public-address system. Why did the question of authority over collective property provoke dissension in one instance but not in the other? Phrased somewhat differently, would controversy concerning authority over the Community Hall have ceased if Donelson and Peters had volunteered to serve as stewards over the community structure as they did over the public-address system? Almost certainly not. The status of community leader was not—and never had been—sufficient to fully elevate a person above suspicion and jealousy. To a large portion of the community, Donelson's and Peters' authority over the building would have been almost as objectionable as supervision by the Women's Society.

The reason controversy did not arise over the public-address system is probably that few people felt that they would fail to receive its benefits with Donelson and Peters in charge. The master of ceremonies at almost all gatherings large enough to call for a loudspeaker was Bill Donelson.

But the Community Hall was a different matter. Donelson was not a member of the Square Dance Club, for example, and he could not be counted on to protect its interests if the need arose. His and Peters' status as community leaders was a necessary but not sufficient basis for legitimizing their authority over collective property like the loud-speaker system. These were reputable men with a history of public service and responsibility, and hence they could be entrusted with community possessions. But this trust stopped where potentially seri-ous disagreement began, and at that point the property was transferred to the hands of a representative body of some kind.

Chapter 11 Conclusion

ONE OF THE most distinctive interpretations of the small town in America is what can be called the commercialist interpretation. According to this interpretation, the affairs of the local community are chiefly a result of profiteering interests, the desire for economic gain. This was Thorstein Veblen's idea (1923a, 1923b:129–65), which we encountered earlier. In this view the town leaders—and the town itself—were oriented by and large toward bringing about greater financial reward for both merchant and landowner. This was also, to a degree, Page Smith's interpretation. The emphasis in Smith's account was on the covenanted community, in which individual interests are constrained for the collective good; and yet the antithesis of the covenanted community, in his view, was the cumulative town, which comes very close to Veblen's idea of the country trade center with its focus on private interests and personal economic advancement.

Richard Hofstadter offers an especially persuasive version of the commercialist interpretation. According to him, America has never really had vigorous small towns with strong feelings of community identity and active social lives—except perhaps during and shortly after the colonial period. This was due largely to the farmers' exploitation of "the great American land bubble." The farmer, like the town dweller, has been engaged in buying property in order to sell again at a profit; thus he has been highly mobile and has developed little community sentiment, little interest in communal action. Hofstadter (1955:42–43) writes,

There was among [American farmers] little attachment to land or locality; instead there developed the false euphoria of local "boosting," encouraged by railroads, land companies, and farmers themselves; in place of village contacts and communal spirit based upon ancestral attachments, there was professional optimism based upon hopes for a quick rise in values.

The community activity that did appear was oriented toward economic or commercial ends; local affairs—summed up by the term *booster-ism*—were at bottom commercial matters (for other discussions of boosterism see Atherton 1954:3–32; Boorstin 1965:113–70; Davies 1958; Doyle 1977, 1978; Moline 1971:40–49, 73–93, 103–7, 127–58; Smith 1966:97–106; Still 1941:187, 197–206; Veblen 1923b:142–65; Wade 1959).

The evidence from Starkey suggests another component of boost-erism in addition to the commercial component, for it is difficult—I think impossible—to detect any important economic motives behind the booster or improvement activities that occurred there. It is hard to see what commercial advantage would have come, say, from the construc-tion of the swimming pool. On purely economic grounds it is even more difficult to explain why it was the school principal and one of the teachers who spearheaded the undertaking. The reputation that the principal had in Starkey was not that of a devoted booster of land values or of loal trade, but one of civic pride. Even the man's most outspoken critics never alluded to economic motivations behind his actions, and if personal motives were ever singled out to explain his booster spirit they were always the motives of personal aggrandize-ment—the desire to stand out, to be important. This was true of every other leader in Starkey's past as well.

Similarly, such community events as the Ladies Aid Bazaar, the Community Christmas Program, and the Starkey Barbecue simply did not have a significant commercial aspect. The Starkey Barbecue is an especially suggestive case, for even though its purpose was to raise money, the money was spent for projects like town beautification and park improvements, which in turn offered no detectable commercial advantages to anyone. The booster groups themselves, like the Improvement Club, the Farm Bureau, and the Women's Society, gave no evidence of economic incentives.

This is why Starkey is a crucial case study of the small town in America. The tendency among historians to focus on commercial incentives behind boosterism may be due not only to the actual impor-tance of economic interests in local affairs but also to the fact that

noncommercial motives tend to become blurred or even indistinguisha-
ble when combined with commercial ones. This is because once
economic interests have been identified, it is easy to conclude that they
tell the whole story, even if they do not. Starkey had almost no aspira-
tions—or opportunity—for economic growth, nor was it an arena for
political decisions with significant economic implications. There was
very little scope in the community for the pursuit of commercial benefits
through local affairs. As a result, the noncommercial component of
boosterism can be isolated and viewed with unusual clarity.

Rural sociologists as a whole have been more inclined than writers
like Hofstadter to emphasize the noncommercial component of the
small town in America. Usually two criteria are employed in doing so.
The first is a sense of community consciousness, whereby the local
people express a feeling of belonging to the town. The second is social
participation, whereby the existence of community is manifest from
community members' attendance at local churches, schools, social
clubs, and the like (for example, see Alexander and Kraenzel 1953:18,
Sanderson 1939:3–7, and Slocum 1962:374–82). In this interpretation,
what distinguishes the community from a mere aggregate of households is a sense of community identity together with a body of local
affairs.

There is little to object to in this as far as it goes. The difficulty is
that it does not give attention to an essential feature of the small town in
America, which is that local events can be subsumed by and large
under the rubric of boosterism, for the goals that are sought in collective
undertakings are generally those of community betterment, and participation in activities of all kinds is construed locally as giving support to
the home town. In this connection it is significant that rural sociologists
(and anthropologists, for that matter) almost never refer to boosterism in
their work. It is usually historians like Hofstadter and Boorstin who do
so. By focusing on the noncommercial element in small-town life the
rural sociologists have identified something important that the historians tend to miss, but in doing so the same sociologists have missed
something important—the local focus on improvement—that the historians have identified.

It is a central thesis of this book that the quality of improvement—
boosterism—is necessary for understanding the small community in

America, and that this has a noncommercial component in addition to the commercial one. The noncommercial component consists of the aspiration to make the home community a self-respecting town—to make it better than before and better than its neighbors. This aspiration in turn needs to be seen in the context of what I have called the ideological dimension of community, that is, the ideas and beliefs by which the community members represent the community to themselves, by which they evaluate its features, and on which they act when engaging in local affairs. The ideological dimension of community contains an ideal that defines what the good community is and, therefore, what the local group should strive to achieve. In Starkey, for example, the good community was thought to exhibit an active social life and to have the capacity to undertake such projects as building a community hall, a park, and a swimming pool. Even attendance at a high-school basketball game was an expression of boosterism, for it amounted to supporting the home team and, thus, the town. This may be expressed somewhat differently by saying that community activities were symbolic. They demonstrated that the locality lived up to the community ideal, that it could rise above both discord and lethargy.

One reason for asserting that boosterism is an essential for understanding the small town in America is that community improvement is a basis for collective effort and local leadership. This is obviously true for the commercial component of boosterism. Community members are willing to improve roads, build parks, and entice factories to locate in their community because the individual stands to gain as local population and land values rise. Yet the noncommercial component plays a similar role, and the ideological dimension of community may even be conceived of as the cumulative town's equivalent of the covenant, for it helps define a body of common interests for the locality to pursue.

The establishment–nonestablishment division in Starkey is a further illustration of the importance of the noncommercial component of boosterism in local affairs. Just as some people acquired considerable local prestige as active and effective contributors, others were criticized for failing to contribute, or for the quality of their contributions, and they became bitter. The establishment–nonestablishment division grew out of this friction. What is more, linked to the idea of community improvement (in Starkey at least) was the notion of moral respectability.

Part of the community ideal was that Starkey should be a morally upstanding locality, and in particular that it should be a sober one. Consensus was hardly total, however, and some people were disapproved of on moral grounds. This too helped stimulate the establishment–nonestablishment division, and the nonestablishment noncontributors became associated with the drinkers in people's minds.

Boosterism was also implicated in intercommunity relations in the Starkey region. Of course boosterism is rooted in rivalry, since it implies an attempt to surpass neighboring towns in trade and growth, together with a desire to measure the hometown favorably in relation to other towns in noncommercial terms. Yet some nearby localities are almost inevitably superordinate to one's own—in trade relations, for example—and a hierarchy of communities results. The self-respecting community wants to avoid being absorbed by the larger one, and it asserts its identity in a variety of ways. It is in this context that we understand such issues and events in the Starkey region as the disagreements that developed over school unification, the assignment of school buses to specific routes, and the proposed location of a junior college in the county. These issues generated opposition not simply because they involved conflicts of interest among people living in different regions but because they represented symbolically the subordination of one community to another within the hierarchy.

Ideas do not provide their own motivation, so we need to ask why at least some people in Starkey were willing to divert so much of their time, energy, and enthusiasm toward the community ideal. I have suggested that the motivation was the desire to achieve a good personal reputation. Notions about community improvement provided not only an ideal for the locality to pursue collectively but also a criterion for defining what counted as meritorious behavior for those who wanted to win their neighbors' approval.

With this we shift to a different level of analysis, and also to another major thesis of this book. It is that Starkey was a community in a specific sense, for it was a significant arena for the achievement of social rank: Starkey was a reference group with its own criteria of personal merit. Although the individual might identify with others outside the community, that person still cared about his or her standing within the local social system and engaged in actions that would advance him or her within it. What is more, the community as a whole (or some portion of it) was an interested audience that devoted part of its attention in private conversations to assessing one another's personal qualities and social position. The reference group character of the community is signified by the existence of a system of social categories of strictly local application—these include the distinctions between "insiders" and "outsiders" (or periphery and core), old family and new family, establishment and nonestablishment, community leader and nonleader. These social classifications imply an active process of social evaluation among community members and the allocation of social recognition according to strictly local criteria.

This constitutes a distinct approach to community, one that does two things. First, it identifies an essential feature of community—the feature that enables us to say whether a community exists in a locality or whether that locality is (to use Max Gluckman's phrase, in Frankenberg 1957:6) a mere "collocation of houses." A community exists to the extent that the locality is organized according to its own criteria of social merit, that its members seek to promote themselves within the social system, and that they use local criteria to assess one another's standing. When interest in measuring oneself and others in relation to this social system is gone, so is the community.

Second, this approach leads to the identification of patterns of community organization and, thus, to the definition of similarities and differences among localities. Certain criteria of social evaluation tend to become focal points of inerest and achievement within the local social system and to give that system its form. In Starkey before World War II, for example, two such focal points were the principles of individual economic achievement on the one hand and cooperation and cohesion on the other. The ambitious person who wanted to establish a good name could set out to accomplish this primarily by climbing the agricultural ladder, contributing to the community, or both, and the members of Starkey were differentiated from one another largely on the basis of these two factors. What is more, it is likely that this pattern of social differentiation was very common throughout rural America. The agricultural ladder was certainly widespread, and so was the focus on local improvement.

By the mid-1960s this pattern of orgnization had changed in Starkey. On the one hand, the principle of contributing had lost some of its earlier importance, as had the community ideal behind it and the

improvement activities that it stimulated. These features had not completely disappeared, of course. A number of community activities—
such as the maneuvers involved in acquiring a public-address system—suggest that people still had some feeling about community-
mindedness, and their disapproval of the Lions Club for its ineffective-
ness reflected an ideal image of what a community organization should
accomplish. The notion that a newcomer could become part of the
community within a short time by becoming active in community life
suggested the continuation of the principle of contributing—as did the
persistence of the establishment–nonestablishment division.

But other evidence indicates that the community ideal was losing
its punch. In particular, the community's earlier self-confidence had
faded, and in its place there was a general sense of malaise. Admit-
tedly, this is difficult to be certain about, but World War II seems to have
been a turning point, for shortly after it was over Starkey's self-image
apparently was far less positive than before.

World War II seems to have been the turning point for another
development that leads to a similar conclusion. Not long after the war
was over it was being said that the church was no longer the center of
the community, that it no longer enjoyed a sort of hegemony over local
affairs that were wholesome and family oriented. The church had once
stood as a symbol of the community not so much because its role in
local affairs was truly great but because it epitomized the sober and
upstanding character of the events that occurred there. The nondrinkers
and the church goers were believed to have the upper hand, and their
moral presence was felt even at such secular events as the meetings of
the Farm Bureau. In this sense the statement that the church had
declined can be read as implying that the community itself had
declined, for local affairs no longer seemed to be firmly in the grasp of
an effective, upstanding, and community-minded group of people.

The church's decline is linked in people's minds with another
matter: the growing importance of the schools, especially the high
school. Local affairs had increasingly less to do with community
improvement, with upholding the community ideal, and relatively more
to do with school policy. Expressed somewhat differently, Starkey
seems to have been moving slowly in the direction of becoming at
bottom a school district. Questions about the school were looming

quite large in people's conversations, and the schools even supplied the key to community boundaries. And a striking tendency since World War II was for leaders to limit their influence and active community involvement to school affairs.

This represents a shift in the focus of community affairs away from local improvement and toward the school system. The community ideal, once at the core of the community, was losing ground, and the prestige that attached to the active contributor was losing its luster. What is more, the school affairs that were becoming the center of attention were of a fundamentally different character from the activities springing from the booster spirit, for people's involvement in school affairs was rooted not in a collective ideal or in the desire to achieve a good reputation among neighbors, but in the individual's desire to see his or her children receive a suitable education. The community was coming more and more to resemble a form of special-interest group.

The principle of economic achievement had also become modified by the mid-1960s. First, it had changed in the sense that there was now a two-tiered pattern of stratification, with little opportunity for those in the lower tier to move to the higher tier. For example, a young man whose family was not among the major landholders now had little hope of advancing beyond the level of ranch foreman unless he left town altogether and found a job outside of farming. Second, the stratification system became relatively more important as a principle of local organization, which is suggested in the fact that by the mid-1960s the distinction between the "haves" and the "have-nots" had become a significant component of the establishment–nonestablishment division. The social–economic hierarchy had penetrated into a new area of local life. It follows that the relationship between the two principles of local organization had changed: as the principle of contributing declined, that of economic achievement advanced.

I remarked that the earlier pattern of social differentiation in Starkey was probably not unique, and it seems likely that the pattern that existed in the mid-1960s was also representative of a wide number of small American communities. This is because the changes that had taken place in Starkey's pattern of organization reflected processes that were being felt in almost every part of rural America. For example, the development of the two-tiered stratification system was a manifestation of changes in agricultural economics that have been felt throughout the country (see Hatch 1973), and the gradual transformation of the farming community into little more than a school district seems equally widespread.

The changes that had occurred in the local organization of Starkey (and in rural America generally)—in particular, the deemphasis of the principle of contributing and the growing emphasis on economic achievement—need to be seen in a wider context of changes taking place in the larger society. This context has been discussed by the historian Robert H. Wiebe (1967). Nineteenth-century American society, he writes, lacked an efficient, centralized system of organization. This was "a society without a core," for it had no real "national centers of authority and information" (p. 12). The basic feature of the society, rather, was the "island-community"—the relatively autonomous and independent town, together with its hinterland, that had the capacity more or less to supply the needs and manage the affairs of its members on its own. And the community "moved by the rhythms of agriculture," inasmuch as this was still largely an agrarian country. As Wiebe writes,

Relatively few families lived so far from town that they did not gravitate to some degree into its circle, and these people at least thought they knew all about each other after crossing and recrossing paths over the years. Usually homogeneous, usually Protestant, they enjoyed an inner stability that the coming and going of members seldom shook. (p. 2)

It was in the context of the town that the individual sought to achieve a decent living, a meaningful existence—and a good name. People were judged according to strictly local criteria: "Distinctions that would have eluded an outsider—the precise location of a house, the amount of hired help, the quality of a buggy or a dress—held great import in an otherwise [seemingly] undifferentiated society" (p. 3).

But changes were under way in the last decades of the nineteenth century. For example, people were moving to the cities, which were becoming both huge and heterogeneous. And the cities were producing their own special values:

The individualism and casual cooperation of the towns still had their place in a city. But new virtues—regularity, system, continuity—clashed increasingly with the old. The city dweller could never protect his home from fire or rid his street of garbage by the spontaneous voluntarism that had raised cabins along the frontier. (p. 14)

Power was also becoming increasingly centralized in the cities, a result (among other things) of changing patterns of capital and finance; and the consolidation of business was taking place across the country (pp. 111–43).

These changes were accompanied by a wide variety of others in such spheres of life as politics and values. One crucial development was the emergence of a new middle class (pp. 111–32) made up of businessmen, teachers, doctors, lawyers, social workers, journalists, and the like—men and women with special training and skills who exhibited a proud identification with what they did more than with where they lived. Their prestige came from their occupations and not from the special social categories of the small town. What is more, professions like medicine and teaching were becoming nationally integrated through professional organizations, and formal requirements were being instituted for those who wanted to enter the profession.

The rural population was also touched by these changes: a new class of businessman-farmer had already appeared by the turn of the century (pp. 125–27), but by and large the gradual breakdown of the island commuities and the emergence of an occupation-oriented middle class took place more rapidly in the cities than in the country, and indeed, Wiebe suggests, these very changes, progressing farther and faster in urban than in rural portions of the country, "widened the gap between the major cities and rural–small town America" (p. 130).

It seems that the growing emphasis on economic achievement in Starkey after World War II can be viewed as the spread of a middle-class orientation to the community. Surely the process had been under way much earlier, but by the time the locality emerged from the war the effects of the changes were wholly apparent—the population was visibly and self-consciously different.

The storekeeper illustrates this process to an extent, for his equipment, methods of financing, and merchandise had become more complicated and required more technical competence than before. The occupational specialization of the storekeeper had increased. The same was true of the garage owner. Tractors, cars, and trucks were no longer simple contraptions that most local people had the know-how and tools to fix. A substantial investment in capital and experience was needed if one wanted to be a successful garage owner and mechanic, and the occupational identity was now unmistakable. The professionalization of the rural schoolteacher was even more striking after World War II, in part perhaps because the great influx of students into the universities and colleges due to the GI Bill served to upgrade the average level of training. It seems indisputable that in the mid-1960s the Starkey teachers identified more with their profession and with their colleagues elsewhere than before World War II began.

But Starkey was primarily a farm community, and it is to the agricultural sphere that we must look to fully appreciate the infusion of a middle-class perspective into the community and its effects on the principle of economic achievement. By the end of World War II it was no longer appropriate to say that the rancher was simply making a living from his land. He was now the proprietor of a large-scale operation that represented a sizable capital investment and involved modern, complicated methods of management and bookkeeping.

It is true that the prosperity accompanying World War I also pushed agriculture toward big business by stimulating the consolidation of farms and the purchase of increasingly modern and expensive equipment. But World War I was followed by about twenty years of depression, which curtailed the full flowering of these developments. The farmer was simply in a better position after World War II—if only because the value of land, the farmer's chief form of collateral, continued to rise, making it possible to borrow more each year for the purchase of equipment and other improvements. The farmer's situation was completely different before and after World War II. The farmer went into this war poor and beggarly—a country rube—and came out of it a respectable member of the American middle class.[1] Indeed, by the mid-1960s the grain and cattle ranchers had come to dominate the regional middle class throughout the inland portion of the county. There were now few businessmen, even in Oak Flat, who could rival the well-established agriculturalists in socioeconomic status.[2]

The assimilation of the local agriculturalists into the American middle class must have been accompanied by a fundamental shift in cultural orientation. One aspect of this shift has already been mentioned: the tendency for farmers to identify with management instead of with labor, a development that is all the more striking when seen in historical perspective. There was a time when the American farmer automatically referred to himself as a laborer, not a business owner (see Hofstadter 1955:64–65, 121–23; Johnstone 1940:121–23). What is more, at one time the farmer's suspiciousness of the city tended to focus on the wealthy and aristocratic, but increasingly it was "the idleness of the unemployed and the tactics of industrial unions" that stood as symbols of urban corruption (Johnstone 1940:152). Similarly, in Starkey as late as the 1920s and 1930s the hired man often lived in the farmer's home and ate at the farmers' table, but in the mid-1960s he lived away from the farm, often in town, and went to work with a lunch pail.

Yet another aspect of the cultural shift, of course, was the tendency for the rancher to identify with his occupation as much as or more than with his community, a development that can be summarized by saying that there developed in agriculture a new image of success (Johnstone 1940:138, 152). Increasingly, it was what a person did for a living—the principle of economic achievement—that counted in his self-evaluation.

This leads directly to the deemphasis of the principle of contributing. The regression of this principle was part of the overall process of deterioration characteristic of small rural communities all over America. I noted earlier that our understanding of this process is still limited, but one critical factor surely must be the fact that modern transportation and communication make it possible for local people to look increasingly outward; the people living in Starkey could be as much a part of Oak Flat or Saint Thomas as of Starkey itself, if indeed they were part of any community at all.

This in turn was but one part of a larger and more subtle process: the loss of local autonomy to agencies and institutions outside the locality. This process has received systematic treatment in the literature (see especially Vidich and Bensman 1958 and Martindale and Hanson 1969), and it includes the growing abdication of decision making to county, state, and other centers of power; a growing dependence on economic factors, like farm prices, that are national and even international in character; the introduction into the community of local branches of nonlocal commercial enterprises such as banks and supermarket chain stores; and the diffusion into the small town of ideas and styles via mass communications. Increasingly, the community is losing its autonomy, its own distinctive institutions, and is more and more dependent on the institutions, dynamics, and forces of urban mass society.

A growing loss of autonomy in this sense may have contributed to the decline of the principle of contributing in Starkey, for as the larger society grows in importance in people's lives the strictly local affairs will attract less attention. For example, one can easily imagine the effect of juxtaposing high-school basketball games with the professional basketball that can be seen on television. Concurrently, as the local community lost prominence, interest in the local social system did so as well, and the community ideal became less important as a criterion for assessing oneself and others.

A difficulty with this analysis of community deterioration is that the notion of mass society can easily become a catchall. It needs to be separated into its component parts, and each needs to be evaluated individually. And one of its most important parts has received little systematic treatment in the literature on rural America. This is the matter mentioned earlier, the infusion of a middle-class perspective into the community. The occupational categories of the rural community may have a strictly local aspect—categories like farmer, rancher, and schoolteacher often have very distinctive connotations in the context of the local social system. Yet these categories also have a general aspect, and in this sense they are a part of mass society. They constitute a common denominator by which locals are classified with nonlocals and by which the individual articulates with a larger system of social differentiation. As the size and capitalization of farms (and the business-like character of farming) increased throughout this century, and especially during and after World War II, the nonlocal aspect of the social categories became increasingly pronounced, as did the middle-class focus on occupation as a criterion of social identity.

This development affected the way in which prestige was allocated in the small town. Active involvement in local life has lost much of its importance as a measure of social standing because local affairs have come to seem somewhat petty in relation to the affairs of business.

Occupation has always been important in towns like Starkey, but at one time there were some pople who were willing to sacrifice in the sphere of individual economic achievement in order to acquire eminence in that of community participation. But no longer. Now the men who at one time would have stood out as effective leaders chose to leave local affairs mostly to women, who had not—at least not yet—entered significantly into the occupational arena. By the mid-1960s the man who devoted his time to conducting local affairs instead of to business would have been known not for his sense of civic responsibility but for his misplaced sense of importance. There was no longer any question that business came first. The community leader is a very sensitive index of this change, yet clearly he was not the only person affected by it.

In short, a culprit in the gradual death of the rural community in America is the industrialization of farming; this has turned the family farm into a big business, hastened the middle-class focus on occupation in the countryside, and reduced the importance of town affairs.

Notes

Introduction

1. This process will be discussed at greater length in later sections. For a general and comprehensive account see Warren 1972. See also Kinton 1970, Sanders and Lewis 1976, and Sharma 1974.

2. See Hofstadter 1955, Johnstone 1940, Shideler 1973, and Wiebe 1967.

3. Most of the Starkey region consists of low, rolling hills that as a rule do not rise more than 600 feet from the floors of the narrow valleys and canyons. The majority of the hills are comparatively bare, supporting only wild grasses unless planted to wheat or barley, and they appear dry and brown much of the·year. Patches of oak and occasionally pine occur in some sections.

Starkey is far enough inland to have greater temperature extremes than the regions nearer the coast, where the weather is moderated by the ocean. The temperature in Starkey often falls a few degrees below freezing on winter nights, but temperatures of 50° or 60° Fahrenheit are normal in the daytime during the cold season. Snow is quite rare. Summers are warm, and temperatures between 100° and 110° are common at midday.

Nearly all precipitation falls during the winter, from December to March. The mean annual precipitation is about 10 inches at the town of Starkey itself and decreases to the east. The mean rainfall on the eastern border of the community is less than 8 inches per year. Precipitation increases to the north, reaching as much as 18 inches (mean) per year in some parts.

4. Like *Starkey*, the name *Oak Flat* is a pseudonym, as are the place names of all nearby localities. I have also changed all personal names.

5. Material for this book was drawn from a variety of sources, chiefly my own presence in Starkey. I visited the cafe and the post office daily to engage in informal conversations, and I conducted a regular program of private interviews in people's homes. My wife and I attended local affairs and were generally active in community life.

Several people took a particular interest in the research and were unusual in their ability to see what was significant from the standpoint of my work. Two ranchers taught me a great deal about local farming and ranching and kept me informed about current economic matters in the vicinity. Another individual was especially useful and insightful in discussing local social affairs and in interpreting them. Little that took place in Starkey escaped this person's notice, and much of what follows has been improved and deepened by this individual's perceptiveness.

The sources of my historical information are diverse. Two elderly men were especially important in supplying material, and both were remarkable sources of information.

This was due not only to their grasp of what I was after but to their high standards of empirical evidence as well. They seldom merely asserted what they believed to be true, but as often as possible cited evidence that corroborated their accounts. The first of these men had moved to Starkey with his family in 1888, when he was 12 years old. The second, the son of a homesteader who had lived in Starkey since 1885, was born in the community in 1890. Additional historical information was acquired from four other people whose memories extended back to the 1880s or 1890s, and from about twenty people whose personal knowledge of Starkey extended to the early years of this century.

Use was made of historical records, such as old maps and the early issues of the Oak Flat newspaper, which contained occasional items pertaining to Starkey. Data on early landholdings were acquired from a title insurance company in Saint Thomas that was kind enough to open its records to me. Such documents as the minutes books and membership lists of community organizations were also acquired. Two published county histories also contained biographical sketches of many of the early residents of Starkey. These written documents were discussed at length with community members in order to augment the information they contained.

Chapter 1. Economic Development

1. For an account of the northern limits of the Southern California boom of the 1880s, see Dumke 1944:157–68.

2. To acquire a homestead the settler had to file a claim on the property, live on it for at least a portion of each year for five years, make specified improvements, and pay a modest fee. To acquire a preemption the settler filed a homestead claim on a parcel of land, and after six months he or she commuted the claim and bought the property outright. In order to fulfill the requirements for a timber culture claim the settler had to plant and maintain trees on forty acres of the property (see Hibbard 1939).

3. Many farmers raised a few cattle, since the hilly portions of their properties were used as pasture. But cattle played a minor role in the livelihood of these people; most of their pasture land was needed to feed draft animals.

4. To my knowledge, none of the Starkey farmers expanded his operation to such an extent that he needed more than one full-time hired man.

5. These facilities had nothing to do directly with the drilling of oil, and there were no oil wells in the vicinity of Starkey or in any of the communities associated with the locality.

Chapter 2. The Crystallization of Community

1. I did not use central-place theory as a model for the account that follows, although the similarities between that approach and mine are obvious; see Berry 1967, and Berry et al. 1976:126–33, 226–42. For a historical account of the relations among small communities in a different part of California, see Broek 1932:72–75, 92–100, 129–35, 149–55.

2. The reliability of this and another map of Starkey drawn from memory (see the following two paragraphs) is reasonably high. Each has been checked against old photographs and existing structures in town, and each has been discussed by several longstanding members of the community.

3. These cooperative enterprises will be discussed at length later.

4. The community of Howard dissolved altogether when its school closed after World War II. This process is described later in the book.

3. Starkey's Social Life   275

5. This figure is a rough approximation. It represents the population of the census district that included both Oak Flat and Starkey (among other communities). Although the boundaries of the census district corresponded roughly with the limits of the hinterland of Oak Flat, they did not do so exactly.

Chapter 3. Starkey's Social Life

1. It seems that a vigorous local social life and local forms of entertainment were thought to be morally uplifting. The viewpoint that probably prevailed in Starkey was expressed by Edward Alsworth Ross, a sociologist at the University of Wisconsin, in his *Principles of Sociology*. According to Ross (1920:466–67), amusement and recreation were worthwhile if they were "self-made, home-made, church-made, or school-made." For example, he wrote that "entertainments held in the school house ordinarily were supervised by the teacher and, in any case, the school trustees were in the background as board of censors." But Ross noted that "amateur amusement" was losing ground to commercial recreation, including the pool hall and the movie theater, which were far less wholesome since "more money can be extracted from young people by offering them the high-flavored, the *risqué*, the sensational, than by offering them the pure and elevating. The conscience of the individual amusement-caterer is well-nigh a negligible factor, for if he is restrained by scruples he will be forced out of business by a less scrupulous rival." What is needed, Ross suggests, is *"the communal provision of recreation."*

2. These quotations are from the oral accounts of two women who helped found the organization.

3. Dances rotated from town to town on an informal basis, and on almost any Saturday night it was possible to find entertainment of this kind within driving distance.

4. Refreshments were sold at one meeting in 1927, the cost being $.20 for adults and $.10 for children. A total of $14.00 was collected. Assuming that an equal number of children and adults were at the meetings—the entire family usually went—about 46 children and 47 adults were present.

5. The Starkey Farm Bureau continued to function until the late 1940s or early 1950s.

6. The number of people at each meeting was reported in the minutes. About 10 members usually attended, although the number sometimes went as high as 25.

7. The preceding discussion of community organizations is not exhaustive. For example, during World War I a group of women established a Red Cross Auxiliary to assist in the war effort, and a rather small and ineffective chapter of the Grange existed for a number of years.

8. The line separating the two sides of the division was somewhat amorphous, and it was not always possible to place a person unequivocally in one camp or the other. The question of amorphousness is an essential one, and it will be dealt with in a later chapter when I discuss the modern manifestation of the split.

Perhaps because of this amorphousness, the community members themselves did not always have a clear picture of the division in their own minds. They often conceived of the community as a collection of individuals, and they did not always consciously employ the idiom of factional divisions. Nevertheless, the establishment–nonestablishment division was implicit both in their evaluation of individuals and in their conception of the community, and it was an important factor in the dynamics of community life, as the following data show. The question of the local image of the division will be dealt with in a later chapter.

It is not altogether clear how far back in time this division extends. Evidence for it is to be found in people's discussions of the Improvement Club, so it goes back at least to the early 1920s, and it seems likely that it existed well before then.

9. Frances Green was the wife of Brian Green, a community leader discussed in the next chapter.

10. Mr. Smith apparently allayed the woman's fears about him, for she allowed him to drive her to the home of a Starkey resident who was a part-time deputy sheriff. But the deputy refused to become involved in what he considered a family argument, so Smith drove the woman home again, told her to go inside, and waited in his car in case she needed his help, which she did not.

11. It is not clear whether any of the other farm towns in the hinterland of Oak Flat were divided on the issue of drinking the way Starkey was. It appears that at least one other community was not, perhaps because a large portion of the settlers in that area were Irish Catholics. The latter did not share the strong feelings against alcohol that characterized the Presbyterians and Methodists who prevailed among the Starkey settlers.

12. The minister at this time lived outside the community, and the parsonage was rented.

Chapter 4. Patterns of Leadership

1. It is unlikely that Donelson or Turner would have reacted publicly to the breach of a moral norm if they thought they lacked the backing of the community, since the principal sanction behind their influence was public opinion.

2. Fred Turner did not play an active role in the Farm Bureau and was not elected to office. I cannot say why this was so.

3. This was the Bradford ranch, which had been acquired by the Saint Thomas storekeeper when many of his customers in the Starkey area defaulted on their debts. The ranch was devoted chiefly to cattle, but some portions were suitable for farming.

4. The project evidently did receive WPA support, although I am not certain how much.

5. The county assumed responsibility for the park once it had been completed, although community projects for its improvement did not cease by any means. A full-time employee was hired by the county to superintend and care for the park, and his wages, and the general financial support for the park's upkeep, were provided by county taxes.

6. When the pool had been completed, it fell under the supervision of the park caretaker. Once each week it was drained and the high-school boys scrubbed the sides.

Chapter 5. Principles of Local Organization

1. Some years ago Raymond Firth wrote that the term *value* is both hard-worked and vague in its meaning (1953:146). Perhaps it is less hard-worked in the 1970s than it was when Firth made the remark, but the vagueness is still there. I will use the term *principle* instead of *value* as much as possible, not because it is any more precise but because I want my own meaning to emerge from the discussion without being colored by association with past usage.

2. Smith argues that the cumulative town was less common and important in American history than is usually supposed (1966:36), in that a substantial portion of the communities that sprang up as settlement took place were not truly cumulative at all but were colonized towns. The latter were modified versions of covenanted communities (pp.

17–30), formed by populations that were relatively homogeneous in belief and purpose. According to Smith, since the cumulative town was not as common as has been supposed, it can hardly have been as significant in fostering the values of competition and individualism in America as is often suggested. For the most part, these values came from the city rather than from the country (pp. 208–9).

3. The pattern of social fragmentation or exclusiveness of local organizations is well reported in the literature on twentieth-century communities. For example, in the late 1920s Albert Blumenthal studied a small mining town in the Rockies, and he found that the Masons ranked highest in prestige among the community organizations. Membership in the Masons was highly restrictive, and applicants who did not measure up to their standards were "black-balled" and excluded (Blumenthal 1932:266). Walter Goldschmidt (1947:124–47), in his study of a rural California town during the 1940s, noted a very close connection between class structure and local church membership.

Starkey's pattern of inclusiveness may have been less unque than it appoaro, however. Starkey was a mere village compared to the towns studied by Blumenthal and Goldschmidt; it was small enough for the value of cohesion to prevail.

4. For a discussion of reference group theory, see Hyman 1968.

Chapter 6. Starkey After World War II
1. The stimulating effects of the war on the community life of country towns was almost certainly not uncommon; see Neely 1944:333–34.

2. The Starkey Fire Control, like the local militia and air watch, was not a strictly local creation. Similar units were begun in other localities nearby, and the entire system apparently was fostered by government officials outside the community.

3. See Warren (1972) for an extensive and original treatment, as well as a bibliographical introduction, to the general problem.

4. Another strictly local social distinction will be discussed at length in chapter 9. This is the division between the establishment and the nonestablishment, which was closely linked to the one between the periphery and the core.

5. These changes in the relationship between farmer and farm worker and in their respective identities have roots going back even before the turn of the century (see Johnstone 1940:145–52 and Hofstadter 1955:121–23). I do not mean to suggest that it was after World War II that these developments came about. My point, rather, is that the changes were stimulated enormously by the war and that the gap between landholder and nonlandholder had increased markedly by the time it was over.

6. Two Mexican-American men lived in the community year round. Both were single, had been in Starkey for several years (one since 1953), and had regular jobs on irrigation farms. Their names and faces were not altogether unfamiliar to others in the community, even though few ever had occasion to speak to them. I have included them in the periphery.

Chapter 7. The Hierarchy of Communities
1. Haga and Folse 1971, Slocum 1962:374–82, and Taylor 1945:427–29, 432, discuss the literature on this topic.

2. Several months after I left Starkey the bond issue was defeated at the polls by a margin of nearly two to one. Even in the city of Saint Thomas the vote was less than the needed two-thirds majority. The inland section voted overwhelmingly against the mea-

sure; in Starkey the vote was nearly five to one against: 21 voted in favor, 97 were opposed.

According to accounts in the Saint Thomas newspaper, a principal reason for the defeat was oppostion to a raise in taxes. But the matter of location was clearly important among inland residents. At one public meeting in Oak Flat a few days before the election, a college official is reported to have emphasized that the question of location had already been settled and was not now at issue, but at least half the discussion focused on that topic. One of the two leading opponents of the measure—a man who actively campaigned against it through public talks and debates and written statements to the press— was from the inland section, and the matter of location was clearly a central issue in his mind.

3. The one that did not close was owned by a man from the Central Valley who had recently retired from the grocery business, bought the store in Starkey, and moved into the community to take charge of his investment. He was almost totally uninvolved in community life and unaffected by local norms. The other store was run by a man who had lived in Starkey all his life and was very sensitive to local patterns.

Saint Thomas also held a yearly festival analogous to the Homestead Celebration, but the event at the county seat was hardly noticed in Starkey and the stores in the smaller community did not close for the occasion. By all accounts they never had.

4. As mentioned earlier, the minimum size of agricultural holdings was growing increasingly larger, with the result that there were fewer and fewer landholders and, therefore, fewer and fewer people living outside of town. The correlate of this is that an increasing number of people were living at the community hub. Under state law a school with an average daily attendance of less than five and a half pupils was required to close and to consolidate with another district. As the schools closed, the small communities that had coalesced around them gradually disappeared.

5. The controversy was deeply rooted in the structure of the small community. Charles Thomas, the man who for several decades had been the foremost individual in the Lorraine–Bitter Valley area and whose death in the early 1940s I noted earlier, amassed a good deal of wealth and land during his lifetime. He was also a very forceful person and did not shrink from asserting his will over others, and consequently the Lorraine–Bitter Valley community was sharply divided between his supporters and opponents. His presence was still felt in the mid-1960s, over twenty years after his death. By now his holdings had been allocated to his heirs (his widow and several children and grandchildren), and the division in the community was between them and their friends and allies on the one hand and their arch-rivals on the other.

The proximate cause of the controversy that led to the withdrawal of the children of the two families from the Bitter Valley school was the construction of a new teacherage. The school was built on land originally owned by Thomas and donated by him to the school district, and the new teacherage was to be located on the school grounds. According to the deed, the land reverts to the Thomas estate if the school closes, so in the view of the Thomas' antagonists the new teacherage would eventually benefit the Thomas family, for sooner or later it would come into their hands.

6. This type of change is widely reported in the literature on rural America. Neighborhood communities in the open countryside are progressively losing their identity and are becoming absorbed by the trade centers with which they are attached. See Kolb 1959:42–67, 107–8 and Slocum and Case 1953.

7. Throughout rural America the relationship between town and country has steadily improved (Kolb 1959:109–10), in part perhaps because of the automobile. The farmer is

no longer set apart from the town to the extent that he was earlier in the century. It is also possible that the declining animosity toward the town is due to a declining sense of community. As the sense of community identity in the country neighborhood diminishes, the members of the small locality no longer experienc as intense a reaction to the threat of absorption by a higher-order community.

Chapter 8. The Pattern of Community Affairs

1. The principal horizontal division on the woman's chart was drawn between what I am calling the major landholders and the "have-nots." Those in the upper category were, in her words, "characterized by wealth or land, and there is competition among them over having a large, new tractor, or a fancy seeder," whereas "the people in the category below this don't have the means for expressing their competiton." The "main concern" of the people in the lower category, she suggested, was "such things as PTO and 4-H Club," that is, local organizations. (The woman herself belonged to a major landholder household.)

She subdivided the major landholders into three groups. One line set apart what I am calling the wealthy elite from the other well-to-do members of the community; the other divided the wealthy elite into an upper group and a lower group.

The woman did not elaborate on the horizontal divisions within the category of "have-nots," although the way she conceived of this category was hinted at in several comments. For example, I asked her where one family fit into the scheme, and she replicd, "They're pretty low. None of them ever do much work; that is, they don't work hard like the people in the [major landholder] category." They were not as industrious and therefore not as respectable. At another point she stated that the people "at the bottom" were ones "who work a short time and then quit and draw unemployment. ... They change jobs frequently."

2. The practice of grave digging had also changed significantly. Shortly before World War II a funeral home in Oak Flat began providing a mechanical digger for the excavation of graves, and by about 1950 it had become quite unusual for graves to be hand dug. During the two years I lived in Starkey just one grave was dug by hand, and this only because the mechanical equipment was not available when needed. The reason given for this change was that community members were increasingly disinclined to do the back-breaking work. One person lamented, "There's been no one to replace the older ones who dug." Another said, "I think they got away from [hand digging graves] because there got to be so many people in Starkey who you didn't know, and people wouldn't want to dig graves for them."

I suspect that the local opinion was wrong. It seems likely that the cooperation that originally came about in grave digging was due to the fact that without it the bereaved family would have to do the work itself. And it would have been thought quite inappropriate for it to do so. When the mechanical digger became available the family no longer needed assistance, so the pattern of cooperation was dropped. But surely it would reappear if somehow the mechanical digger were no longer at hand, for sentiments about the bereaved family were probably still quite vigorous.

3. It is impossible to fully re-create all that was invoved in the split, but clearly the minister was not without supprt for his actions from within the congregation, although their support was quite guarded.

About eight or ten families made up the core of the church before the split took place. Most of the adult members of these families occupied lay offices in rotation, and all took active part in policy decisions and in the routine affairs of the parish. Several were Sunday School teachers, and three of the families had charge of the Community Christmas Program. Although there were differences in religious views among the members of the core, most were fundamentalists. Probably a majority of the people who were outside the core but regularly attended services were more "modern" in their views.

Even a few of those in the core seem to have shared the minister's concern about the conservatism of some of the parishioners. For example, one of them commented to me, "A small group, primarily [two families], ran the church. . . . For example, a big issue was the content in Sunday School class—they were presenting Pentecostal material. It might be better with the ones gone that left the church."

Ronald Frankenberg's discussion of the "stranger" in Glyceiriog (1966:96–98) may provide a clue to the way the split took place. In Glynceiriog, a small Welsh border town, leadership in local affairs was commonly thrust upon relative newcomers and outsiders, or "strangers." As a consequence, the "stranger" took the blame whenever a crisis arose, and the villagers were able to avoid open conflict among themselves (Frankenberg 1957: ch. 3; 1966: ch. 4). It seems possible that the minister in this case was cast in the role of "stranger."

4. High-school baccalaureate services were withdrawn from the Methodist church in similar fashion. At one time they were held in the meetinghouse and were presided over by the minister, but in the mid-1960s they were school affairs held in the gym, and both the Pentecostal and Methodist ministers were invited to participate as guests.

5. The Methodist minister now lived in Oak Flat and served the churches of both communities. His duties with the Oak Flat church occupied most of his time, and he devoted but a few hours a week to the Starkey congregation.

6. The Society's relinquishment of these two affairs to the PTO signified a shift in focus. On the one hand, the members of the Women's Society were aging. Originally this had been a group for young married women, and their emphasis on children was perhaps inevitable given the traditional ideas about the female role. By the mid-1960s, however, the leading members of the Society no longer had youngsters of their own, and the PTO was now the logical group to assume the responsibilities that were dropped. On the other hand, the relinquishment of these affairs probably corresponded with a broadening of the Society's local orientation. The emphasis was shifting away from children specifically and toward the community generally.

7. In the mid-1960s approximately 22 people attended the monthly meetings; it is unlikely that the average attendance ever exceeded 30.

8. Elsewhere (Hatch 1973:250) I have referred to this as the Starkey Men's Club, piling one pseudonym on another. At this point it seems justifiable to acknowledge that it was a chapter of Lions International.

9. Later in the book I suggest that the pattern of collaboration should be seen in the context of another feature of community life to which it is very closely related: the pattern of diffuse decision making.

Chapter 9. Public Amiability, Private Disharmony

1. This finding is at variance with Max Gluckman's (1963) analysis, according to which gossip is limited to the members of a group and both marks and maintains the group's boundaries. See also Gluckman 1968 and Paine 1967, 1968.

2. The idea that divisions of opinion at the private level tend to be random and not systematic appears to underlie Boissevain's analysis of factionalism (Boissevain 1964:1285–86).

3. It is axiomatic that the establishment–nonestablishment division pertained only to the people in Starkey who were involved to some extent in the community life, and not to those who were truly members of the periphery. What is more, the division pertained only to Starkey proper, and not to Bitter Valley or Pinefield.

4. Technically, his offense was not trespassing but shooting a firearm from the side of a public road.

5. The woman's maiden name was Donelson; it was not her married name. For convenience I use the name she was born with.

6. By contrast, see Steiner (1928:32–41, 172–73), who is quick to recognize the importance of conflict in the American farm town. For discussions of the anthropological literature on factionalism see Bujra 1973 and Truoba 1073.

Chapter 10. Conducting Local Affairs

1. There were some situations in which hierarchical patterns of authority did appear, of course. For example, the school board had clear authority over the principal, the principal over the teachers and other school employees, the ranch owner over his hired help. All of these cases fall within the economic or occupational sphere and not that of community affairs. They do not contradict the basic principle that nonhierarchical patterns typified the way in which the community itself was run.

2. The pattern of diffuse decision making must surely be very common in rural communities in America. During World War II, for example, a local defense council in Arkansas attempted to institute a civilian defense program in one rural county. The council's first plan was to contact "the accepted county leaders such as bankers, teachers, civic leaders, etc." and to ask them to undertake the program. This procedure failed, not because the leaders were unwilling to work in the program's behalf but because they were "afraid of the consequences of personally assuming the initiative." A second procedure was now tried. A number of local organizations were contacted and asked to sponsor the programs. "Response was entirely satisfactory in the latter case because the leader was given an opportunity to operate within and through existing organizations, which in so doing made a group rather than an individual problem of it" (Longmore and Standing 1944:45).

3. A box social is an event to which each woman brings a meal for two packed in a box; the men bid for the meals as they are auctioned and eat with the woman whose dinner they have purchased.

4. The supervisor had specifically requested such a meeting to ensure that the proposal enjoyed general support in Starkey (and perhaps also to achieve some exposure among his constituents). It does not seem likely that the Women's Society would have called the meeting if he had not requested it, for the issue of transferring legal ownership of the Community Hall was probably not sufficiently controversial locally to warrant such a tactic.

5. The Community Hall was subsequently transferred to county ownership and the improvements made.

Chapter 11. Conclusion

1. See Davis 1956, Davis and Goldberg 1957, Davis and Hinshaw 1957, Hatch 1975, and Shideler 1973.

2. I cannot say what the position of the major landholders was vis-à-vis such professional people as doctors and lawyers, because there were none of the latter in Starkey. A few lived and worked in Oak Flat, but I was not sufficiently close to that town to see this particular feature of its social life.

References

Alexander, Frank and Carl F. Kraenzel
1953 *Rural Social Organization of Sweet Grass County, Montana.* Bozeman: Montana Agricultural Experiment Station, Bulletin 490.
Atherton, Lewis
1954 *Main Street on the Middle Border.* Bloomington: Indiana University Press.
Barnes, J. A. 1954 "Class and Committees in a Norwegian Island Parish." *Human Relations* 7:39–58.
Bennett, John W.
1969 *Northern Plainsmen: Adaptive Strategy and Agrarian Life.* Chicago: Aldine.
Berry, Brian J. L.
1967 *Geography of Market Centers and Retail Distribution.* Englewood Cliffs, N.J.: Prentice-Hall.
Berry, Brian J. L., Edgar C. Conkling, and D. Michael Ray
1976 *The Geography of Economic Systems.* Englewood Cliffs, N.J.: Prentice-Hall.
Blumenthal, Albert
1932 *A Sociological Study of a Small Town.* Chicago: University of Chicago Press.
Boissevain, Jeremy
1964 "Factions, Parties, and Politics in a Maltese Village." *American Anthropologist* 66:1275–87.
1965 *Saints and Fireworks: Religion and Politics in Rural Malta.* New York: Humanities Press.
Boorstin, Daniel J.
1965 *The Americans: The National Experience.* New York: Random House.
Broek, Jan Otto Marius
1932 *The Santa Clara Valley, California: A Study in Landscape Changes.* Utrecht: N. V. A. Ossthoek.
Brunner, Edmund de S., Gwendolyn S. Hughes, and Marjorie Patten
1927 *American Agricultural Villages.* New York: George H. Doran.

Bujra, Janet M.
    1973 "The Dynamics of Political Action: A New Look at Factionalism"
    American Anthropologist 75:132–52.
Caughey, John W.
    1970 *California: A Remarkable State's Life History.* 3d ed. Englewood
    Cliffs, N.J.: Prentice-Hall.
Curti, Merle
    1959 *The Making of an American Community.* Stanford, Calif.: Stanford
    University Press.
Davies, Pearl J.
    1958 *Real Estate in American History.* Washington, D.C.: Public Affairs
    Press.
Davis, John H.
    1956 "From Agriculture to Agribusiness." *Harvard Business Review* (Janu-
    ary–February), 34(1):107–15.
Davis, John H. and Ray A. Goldberg
    1957 *A Concept of Agribusiness.* Boston: Harvard University, Graduate
    School of Business Administration, Division of Research.
Davis, John H and Kenneth Hinshaw
    1957 *Farmer in a Business Suit.* New York: Simon and Schuster.
Doyle, Don Harrison
    1977 "Social Theory and New Communities in Nineteenth-Century Amer-
    ica." *Western Historical Quarterly* 8:151–76.
    1978 *The Social Order of a Frontier Community: Jacksonville, Illinois,
    1825–70.* Urbana: University of Illinois Press.
Dumke, Glenn S.
    1944 *The Boom of the Eighties in Southern California.* San Marino, Calif.:
    Huntington Library.
Firth, Raymond
    1953 "The Study of Values by Social Anthropologists." *Man* 53:146–53.
Frankenberg, Ronald
    1957 *Village on the Border.* London: Cohen and West.
    1966 *Communities in Britain: Social Life in Town and Country.* Harmonds-
    worth, Middlesex: Penguin Books.
Galpin, Charles J.
    1911 "The Social Agencies in a Rural Community." In *First Wisconsin
    Country Life Conference,* pp. 12–18. Madison: University of Wisconsin,
    College of Agriculture.
    1915 *The Social Anatomy of an Agricultural Community.* Madison: Univer-
    sity of Wisconsin Agricultural Experiment Station, Research Bulletin 34.
Gluckman, Max
    1963 "Gossip and Scandal." *Current Anthropology* 4:307–16.
    1968 "Psychological, Sociological and Anthropological Explanations of
    Witchcraft and Gossip: A Clarification." *Man* 3:20–34.

Goldschmidt, Walter
1946 *Small Business and the Community: A Study in the Central Valley of California on Effect of Scale of Farm Operations.* U.S. Senate. Special Committee to Study Problems of American Small Business.
1947 *As You Sow.* Glencoe, Ill.: Free Press.
Haga, William J and Clinton L. Folse
1971 "Trade Patterns and Community Identity." *Rural Sociology* 36:42–51.
Hatch, Elvin
1973 "Social Drinking and Factional Alignment in a Rural California Community." *Anthropological Quarterly* 46:243–60.
1975 "Stratification in a Rural California Community." *Agricultural History* 49:21–38.
Hibbard, Benjamin H.
1939 *A History of Public Land Policies.* New York: P. Smith.
Hofstadter, Richard
1955 *The Age of Reform: From Bryan to F.D.R.* New York: Vintage Books.
Hyman, Herbert H.
1968 "Reference Groups." In *International Encyclopaedia of the Social Sciences* 13:353–61. New York: Crowell, Collier, and Macmillan.
Johnstone, Paul H.
1940 "Old Ideals Versus New Ideas in Farm Life." In U.S. Department of Agriculture, *Farmers in a Changing World,* pp. 111–70. Washington, D.C.: GPO.
Kenny, Michael
1966 *A Spanish Tapestry: Town and Country in Castile.* New York: Harper & Row.
Kinton, Jack F.
1970 *The American Community: A Multidisciplinary Bibliography.* Monticello, Ill.: Council of Planning Librarians, Exchange Bibliography no. 151.
Kolb, John H.
1959 *Emerging Rural Communities.* Madison: University of Wisconsin Press.
Kolb, John H. and Edmund de S. Brunner
1933 *Rural Social Trends.* New York and London: McGraw-Hill.
Kroeber, Alfred L.
1953 *Handbook of the Indians of California.* Berkeley: California Book Company.
Landis, Benson Y.
1922 *Rural Church Life in the Middle West.* New York: George H. Doran.
Longmore, T. Wilson and T. G. Standing
1944 "Developing Local Leadership in Agriculture's War Effort." *Rural Sociology* 9:44–49.

Martindale, Don and R. Galen Hanson
    1969 *Small Town and the Nation: The Conflict of Local and Translocal Forces*. Westport, Conn.: Greenwood.
Moline, Norman T.
    1971 *Mobility and the Small Town: 1900–1930*. Chicago: University of Chicago Department of Geography Research Paper no. 132.
Neely, Wayne C.
    1944 "The Impact of the War on a Mid-West Rurban Community." Rural *Sociology* 9:327–40
Paine, Robert
    1967 "What Is Gossip About? An Anternative Hypothesis." *Man* 2:278–85.
    1968 "Gossip and Transaction." *Man* 3:305–8.
Ross, Edward Alsworth
    1920 *The Principles of Sociology*. New York: Century.
Sanders, Irwin T. and Gordon F. Lewis
    1976 "Rural Community Studies in the United States: A Decade in Review." *Annual Review of Sociology* 2:35–53.
Sanderson, Dwight
    1939 *Locating the Rural Community*. Ithaca, New York State College of Agriculture at Cornell University, Cornell Extension Bulletin 413.
Sanderson, Ezra Dwight and Robert A. Polson
    1939 *Rural Community Organization*. New York: Wiley.
Sharma, Prakash C.
    1974 *A Selected Bibliography on Small Town Research*. Monticello, Ill., Council of Planning Librarians, Exchange Bibliography no. 713.
Shideler, James
    1973 "Flappers and Philosophers, and Farmers: Rural-Urban Tensions of the Twenties." *Agricultural History* 47:283–99.
Sims, Newell L.
    1912 *A Hoosier Village*. New York: Columbia University Press.
Slocum, Walter L.
    1962 *Agricultural Sociology: A Study of Sociological Aspects of American Farm Life*. New York: Harper.
Slocum, Walter L. and Herman M. Case
    1953 "Are Neighborhoods Meaningful Social Groups Throughout Rural America?" *Rural Sociology* 18:52–59.
Smith, Page
    1966 *As a City upon a Hill: The Town in American History*. New York: Knopf.
Spillman, W. J.
    1919 "The Agricultural Ladder." *American Economic Review*. Supp. 9, pp. 170–79.
Steiner, Jesse Frederick
    1928 *The American Community in Action: Case Studies of American Communities*. New York: Henry Holt.

Still, Bayrd
    1941 "Patterns of Mid-Nineteenth Century Urbanization in the Middle West." *The Mississippi Valley Historical Review* 28:187–206.
Taylor, Carl C.
    1945 "Techniques of Community Study and Analysis as Applied to Modern Civilized Societies." In Ralph Linton, ed., *The Science of Man in the World Crisis,* pp. 416–41. New York: Columbia University Press.
Taylor, Carl C. et al.
    1955 *Rural Life in the United States.* New York: Knopf.
Trueba, Henry Torres
    1973 "Nahuat Factionalism." *Ethnology* 12:463–74.
Turner, Frederick Jackson
    1958 *The Frontier in American History.* New York: Henry Holt and Company.
Veblen, Thorstein
    1923a "The Country Town." *Freeman* 7:417–20, 440–43.
    1923b *Absentee Ownership and Business Enterprise in Recent Times: The Case of America.* New York: B. W. Huebsch.
Vidich, Arthur J. and Joseph Bensman
    1958 *Small Town in Mass Society: Class, Power, and Religion in a Rural Community.* Garden City, N.Y.: Anchor Books.
Wade, Richard C.
    1959 *The Urban Frontier: The Rise of Western Cities, 1790–1830.* Cambridge, Mass.: Harvard University Press.
Warren, Roland L.
    1972 *The Community in America.* 2d ed. Chicago: Rand McNally.
West, James
    1945 *Plainville, U.S.A.* New York: Columbia University Press.
Wiebe, Robert H.
    1967 *The Search for Order: 1877–1920.* New York: Hill and Wang.
Williams, James M.
    1906 *An American Town.* New York, J. Kempster.
Wright, Louis B.
    1955 *Culture on a Moving Frontier.* Bloomington: Indiana University Press.

Index